IMAGES
of America

TEXAS SESQUICENTENNIAL WAGON TRAIN

TEXAS WAGON TRAIN ASSOCIATION

JAN. 2 — JULY 3, 1986

"CIRCLE TEXAS FOR THE PAST AND FUTURE"

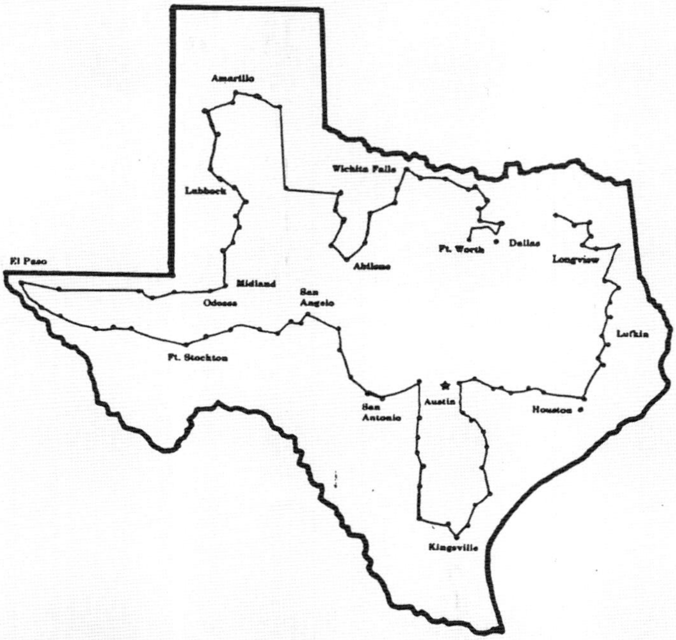

This zigzag, oddly shaped circuitous route around Texas began in Sulphur Springs, a small town of 15,000 located an hour's drive east of Dallas. After traveling 3,228 miles for six months in a clockwise route around the state, the train completed the journey in the Fort Worth Stockyards. Thirteen wagons and their drivers decided to travel full circle and continued back to the starting point.

ON THE COVER: Wagons of several styles, pulled by either horses or mules, traveled along at four miles per hour in a scene that could have been viewed 150 years ago, rather than in 1986, when the Texas Sesquicentennial Wagon Train rolled. (Photograph by Dominick J. Cirincione.)

IMAGES
of America

TEXAS SESQUICENTENNIAL WAGON TRAIN

Dominick J. Cirincione
and J'Nell L. Pate

ARCADIA
PUBLISHING

ISBN 978-0-7385-8488-1

Published by Arcadia Publishing
Charleston, South Carolina

Printed in the United States of America

Library of Congress Control Number: 2011923574

For all general information, please contact Arcadia Publishing:
Telephone 843-853-2070
Fax 843-853-0044
E-mail sales@arcadiapublishing.com
For customer service and orders:
Toll-Free 1-888-313-2665

Visit us on the Internet at www.arcadiapublishing.com

The authors dedicate this book to the 10,000 people who chose to ride with the Texas Sesquicentennial Wagon Train and to the thousands more pioneers who, in the 19th century, traveled to the West in covered wagons.

Contents

Acknowledgments

First of all, the authors would like to thank Jan France for having the idea for the train and pursuing it so vigorously that it came to fruition. Her early efforts guaranteed that the Texas Sesquicentennial Wagon Train journey would take place. Her help with factual data also was greatly appreciated.

We also would like to thank John Paul Davidson, former Tarrant County College (TCC) public service librarian, and Nigel Parker, present director of archives/record management for TCC, for their support in copying the photographs from the Heritage Room Collection that Dominick J. "Nick" Cirincione donated to them 25 years ago. Eddie Sandoval, recently retired director of counseling at TCC, assisted us in identifying persons in the photographs.

Quentin McGown, a Fort Worth lawyer who served as the business manager for the train, provided pictures and was a valuable source for checking facts. He also helped plan, with Red Steagall, a big reunion event for the train's 25th anniversary year. Thanks also go to Joan Wells, former director of the North Fort Worth Historical Society Museum, and Teresa Burleson, current museum director, for their assistance in allowing the photographing of the artifacts of the Texas wagon train in the museum's possession and for helping in many other ways.

Rita Adams, genealogical librarian for the Sulphur Springs Library, provided assistance with Sulphur Springs photographs and information. We called her our key contact in Sulphur Springs. Thanks also to *Sulphur Springs News-Telegram* editor Bruce Alsobrook and Butch Burney for permission to use photographs from their newspaper and to Jerome Sims for a *Dallas Morning News* photograph.

Unless otherwise noted, all images were taken by coauthor Dominick J. Cirincione as a class project for a Tarrant County Junior College (now Tarrant County College) photography course in 1986.

INTRODUCTION

The year 2011 represents the 25th anniversary of the Texas Sesquicentennial Wagon Train that took six months in 1986 to travel around the Lone Star State to commemorate its 150th birthday. As numerous celebrations occurred throughout the sesquicentennial year, the very visible and well-publicized wagon train wove its way slowly around its route during the first half of that year, beginning January 2 in Sulphur Springs and concluding July 3 in the Fort Worth Stockyards.

One of the authors of this book, Dominick J. Cirincione, took the majority of the photographs in 1986, when he traveled on weekends to catch up with the wagons on their planned route. At the time, he was a student in a photography class at Tarrant County Junior College (TCJC). At the conclusion of his project, he donated 130 photographs of the train to the Heritage Room of the Northeast Campus of TCJC and was honored with a reception. It was one of the official sesquicentennial projects of Fort Worth. Copies of a letter and certificate honoring Cirincione are included.

As the wagon train made stops in various towns and cities around the state, dignitaries from each community presented the train with plaques, keys to the cities, and other acknowledgments of the visit. These artifacts and memorabilia have been donated to the North Fort Worth Historical Society Museum in the Fort Worth Stockyards. They became a permanent exhibit in the museum and are seen by thousands of visitors each year.

Any citizen of Texas over the age of eight or 10 in 1986 most likely will remember the wagon train, because its route was planned to come within approximately 100 miles of each community in Texas. Folks from many of the towns chose to ride their horses or join with the train to ride a day's journey or more. Rules of the train said that any person who chose to ride could not travel just through his or her own town but must stay for an entire day's ride. This assured that each participant got a brief feel of what the pioneers really experienced. Following its successful circle around Texas, the wagon train was named to the *Guinness Book of Records* as the "longest consecutive wagon train in never having left any one state."

The schedule of the wagon train was as follows:

January: 2, Sulphur Springs Civic Center and Como/Pickton; 3, Winnsboro; 4, Quitman; 5, Hawkins; 6, Gladewater; 7–8, Longview; 9–10, Marshall; 11, Carthage; 12, Clayton; 13, Mount Enterprise; 14–15, Nacogdoches; 16–17, Lufkin; 18, Corrigan; 19, Livingston; 20, Camilia; 21, Sam Houston National Forest (open camp*); 22–23, Conroe; 24, Montgomery; 25, Tomball; 26, Hockley; 27–28, Hempstead; 29, Brenham; 30, Carmine; 31, Giddings.

February: 1, Elgin; 2, Austin N/E 290; 3–4, Austin South 183; 5, Mendoza (Archie Roberts Ranch); 6, Luling; 7, Gonzales; 8, Cheapside; 9–10, Cuero; 11, open camp; 12, Goliad; 13, Refugio; 14, Sinton; 15, Robstown; 16–18, Kingsville; 19, Alice; 20–21, San Diego; 22, Freer; 23, open camp; 24, Tilden; 25, Christine (Duncan Hirsch Ranch); 26, Poteet; 27, San Antonio; 28, San Antonio (Freeman Coliseum).

March: 1, San Antonio (Freeman Coliseum); 2, San Antonio; 3, Spring Branch; 4, Johnson City; 5, Lyndon B. Johnson State Park; 6, Fredericksburg; 7, Kerrville; 8, Hunt; 9, Felix Kline Ranch (open camp); 10–11, YO Ranch (open camp); 12, Junction; 13, Tillman Ranch (open camp); 14, Menard; 15, Eden; 16, Eola; 17–18, San Angelo; 19, San Angelo (Twin Buttes open camp); 20, Mertzon; 21, Bernhart (open camp); 22–23, Big Lake; 24, Rankin; 25, McCamey; 26, open camp; 27–28, Fort Stockton; 29, open camp; 30, Balmorhea; 31, open camp.

April: 1, Kent; 2, Plateau (open camp) ; 3–4, Van Horn; 5, Allamore (open camp); 6, Sierra Blanca; 7, Fort Quitman (open camp); 8–9, Fort Hancock; 10, Tornillo; 11, San Elizario; 12–14, El Paso; 15, open camp; 16, Smith Ranch; 17, Cornudas (open camp); 18, Salt Flat (open camp); 19, open camp; 20–22, Guadalupe National Park; 23, Old Polly Holobeke Ranch; 24, Bob Farmer Ranch (open camp); 25, Orla; 26, Mentone; 27–28, Kermit; 29, Notrees; 30, Odessa.

May: 1, Odessa; 2, Midland; 3, open camp; 4, Patricia; 5–6, Lamesa; 7, O'Donnell; 8, Tahoka; 9, Lubbock; 10, Levelland; 11, Littlefield; 12–13, Spring Lake; 14, Dimmitt; 15, Hereford; 16, Canyon; 17–19, Amarillo; 20, Claude; 21, Ashtola (open camp); 22, Clarendon; 23, Brice (open camp); 24–25, Turkey; 26, Matador; 27, Glenn; 28, Dickens; 29–30, Pitchfork Ranch (open camp); 31, 6666 Ranch (open camp).

June: 1–2, Benjamin; 3, Rochester; 4, Haskell; 5, Stamford; 6, Hawley; 7–8, Abilene; 9, Albany (open camp); 10, Fort Griffin (open camp); 11, Throckmorton; 12, Olney; 13, Archer City; 14, Windthorst; 15–16, Wichita Falls; 17, Henrietta; 18, Nocona; 19, Muenster; 20–21, Gainesville; 22, Whitesboro; 23, Pilot Point; 24, Denton; 25, Ponder; 26, Argyle; 27, Lewisville; 28, Irving; 29, Grapevine/Colleyville; 30, North Richland Hills.

July: 1, North Richland Hills; 2, Gateway Park (Fort Worth); 3, Fort Worth Stockyards/Saginaw.

*Open camp meant a campsite was not near a town and was without facilities other than what the train brought along.

One

Planning the Wagon Train

Texans are a proud bunch. They believe that they are distinctive and unique because Texas existed as a separate republic for 10 years after winning its independence in 1836. Most citizens looked forward to the important milestone as the year of 1986 approached, because it represented 150 years since that independence was won. The Texas Legislature created a Texas Sesquicentennial Commission to plan the celebrations.

Jan France, a resident of Sulphur Springs, a small town east of Dallas, conceived the idea for a wagon train in June 1983. She planned the route to have 150 overnight stops in 150 communities to represent the 150 years since Texas's independence. She picked the towns and drove the entire route three times, conferring with officials and setting up committees. Jan sent letters to the other 49 states to invite them to send a representative wagon or rider to participate. She created a logo and determined that the purpose of the train was to commemorate the pioneer spirit of Texas. Her idea attracted great attention.

Those who became involved after May 1985 joined the Texas Wagon Train Association, of which Charles Oliver became president and chairman of the board. Others were vice president Bill Ketchum, Gwen Brown, Ed Phelps, treasurer and founding director Bob McCombs, and communications coordinator Ann Scamahorn. On the advisory board were directors Donald Stringer and Lonnie Day, retail committee chairman Glen Courson (who provided an office for the association), and administrative assistant John Hunter. On the administrative staff were business manager Quentin McGown, administrative director Nancy J. Boren, executive director of promotions Jan France, head camp jack West Pearce, wagon master Garry France, and administrative assistant Lou Mallory.

Those who participated in the wagon train needed to become a member of the association. Individuals could join for $15; families paid $25. The train would be limited to 150 horse-drawn vehicles with official outriders. A limit of 300 horseback riders at any one time was set. Selected to be honorary officials of the wagon train were wagon master Walt Garrison and four honorary assistant wagon masters—Billy Bob Barnett, Tom Landry, Gib Lewis, and Glen Courson.

Official business sponsors became the only ones who could advertise on the wagons. They were Copenhagen/Skoal/Skoal Bandits, Billy Bob's Texas, Glen's Sporting Goods, Winchester Repeating Arms Company, WBAP 820 Dallas/Fort Worth, Morrison Milling Company, Wrangler, Valley Ranch Cowboys Center, Grandy's, Inc., Cook County College, Cody Marketing, Inc., Adkins Seasoning, Marmon Motor Company, Coca-Cola, Smith & Wesson, Dairy Queen, National Trailer Sales, Hobbs Division of Fruehauf Corporation, Belco Manufacturing, Ford Motor Company, Texas National Bank Dallas, Coachman Industries, Inc., Contel and Texas Telephone Association, Purina Mills Incorporated, John Deere, American Honda Motor Co., Inc. Power Equipment Division, Southwestern Bell Telephone, and Specialty Processing Corp.

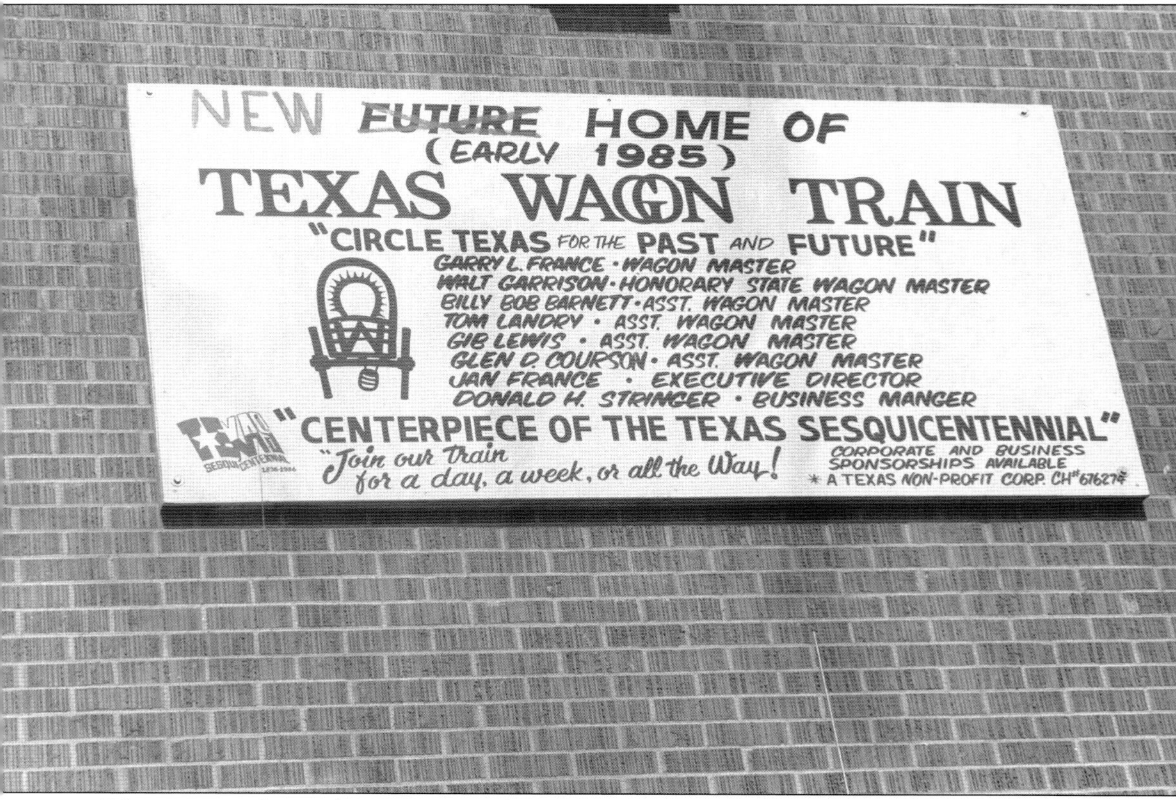

This sign explains the transition that occurred as the newly formed Texas Wagon Train Association developed. The committee selected extremely recognizable big-name personalities as honorary dignitaries for the train. Then the association found office space in Irving for a central headquarters during the planning stage. A Pioneer Farm in Fort Worth inspired Jan France to create the logo.

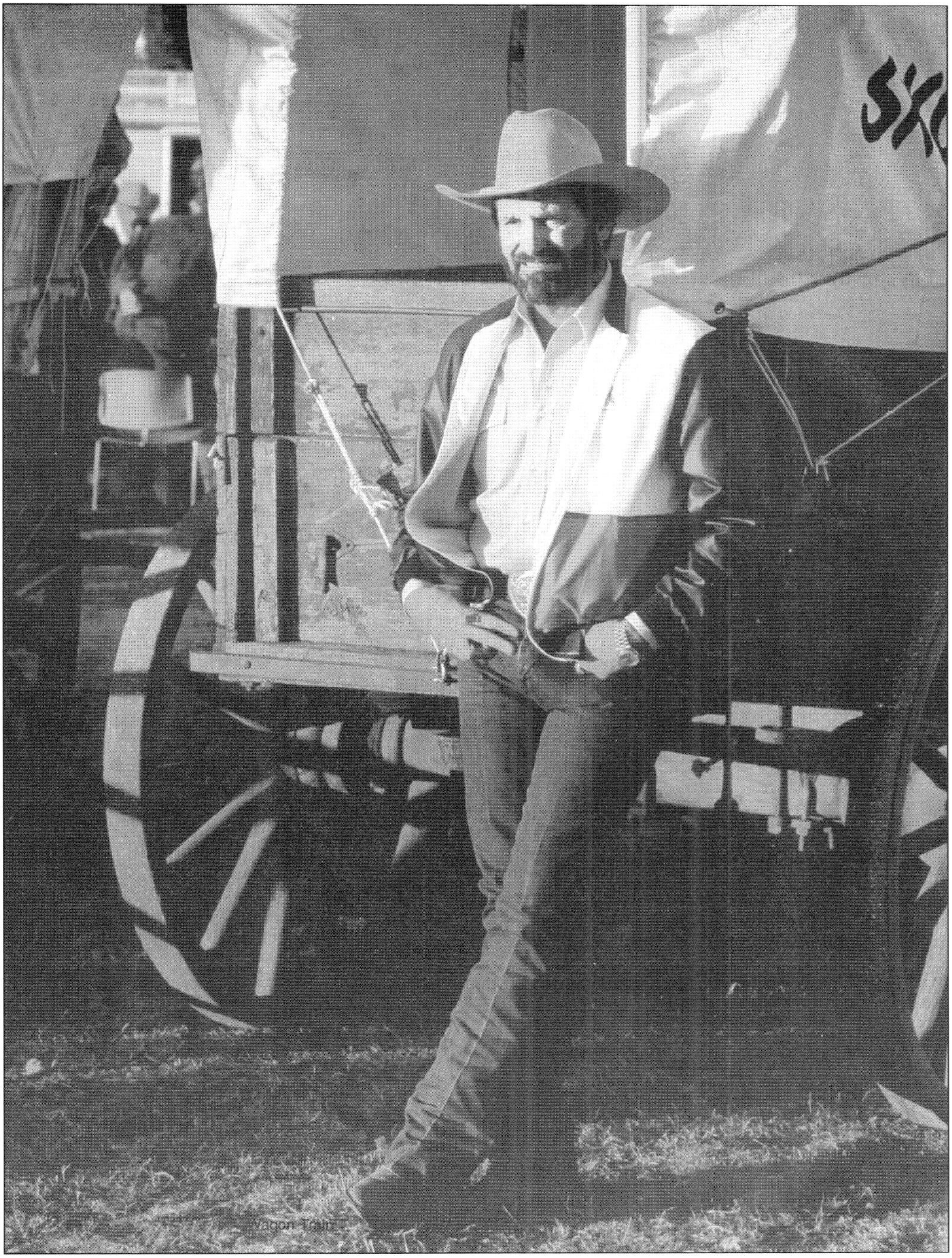

Walt Garrison, best known as a fullback for the Dallas Cowboys National Football League home team, helped them win Super Bowl VI in 1972. He was a true cowboy in the Western sense as well, having entered rodeos when he was 15 and worked on ranches in the summers as a teenager. The Texas Wagon Train Association asked him to be its honorary wagon master. (Courtesy Quentin McGown Collection, Tarrant County Archives.)

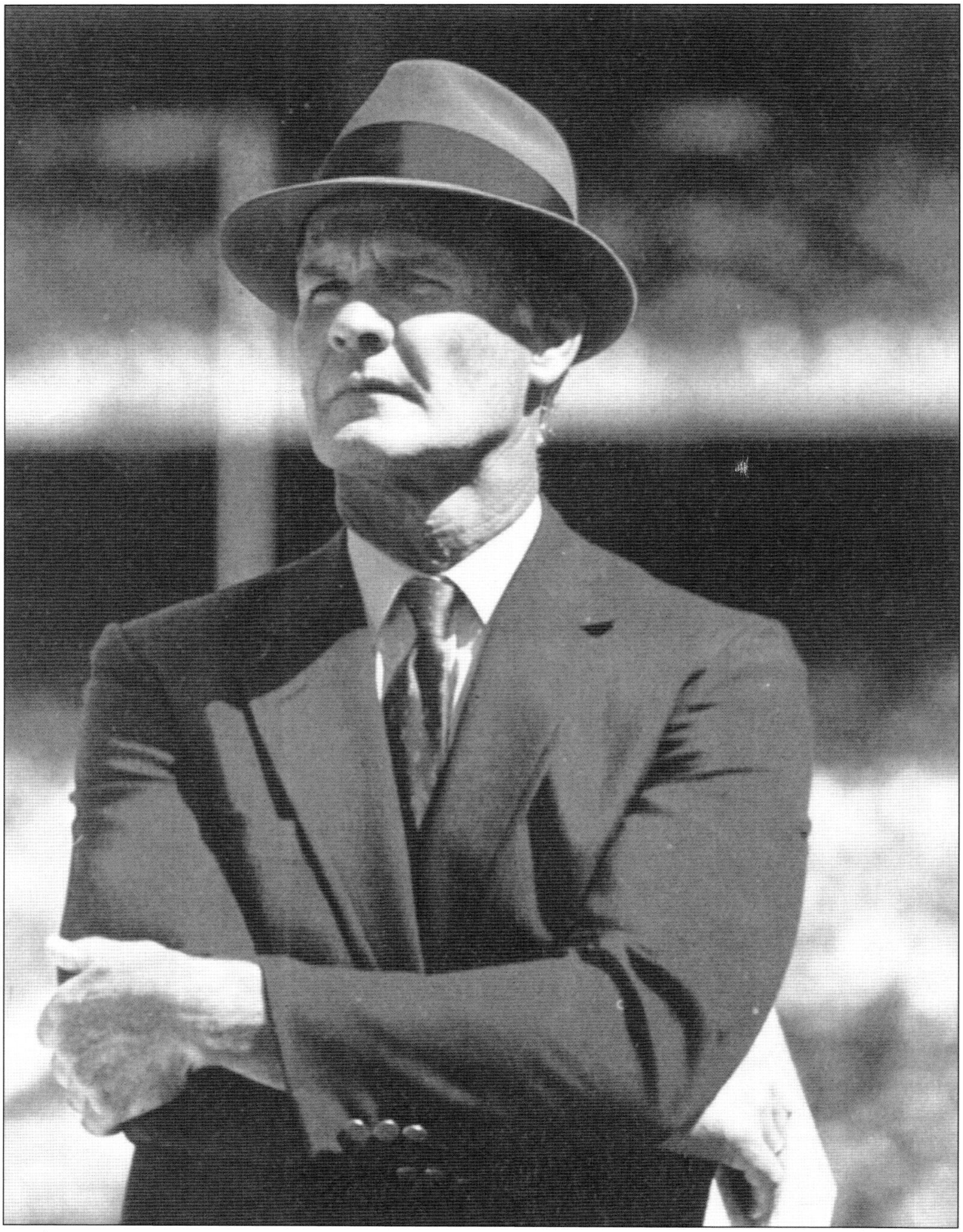

An honorary assistant wagon master for the wagon train, Tom Landry served as head coach of the Dallas Cowboys from the beginning of the franchise. He put together 20 consecutive winning seasons, five Super Bowl appearances, and two Super Bowl wins. Landry's last season as coach of the Cowboys was 1988. (Courtesy Quentin McGown Collection, Tarrant County Archives.)

Also an honorary assistant wagon master was Billy Bob Barnett, who grew up on a ranch where his father was foreman. He also became a professional rodeo calf roper. When Barnett came with his father to the Fort Worth Stockyards to sell cattle, he did not know that he would, with some investors, later open Billy Bob's Texas, the largest honky-tonk in the state, at the stockyards. (Courtesy Quentin McGown Collection, Tarrant County Archives.)

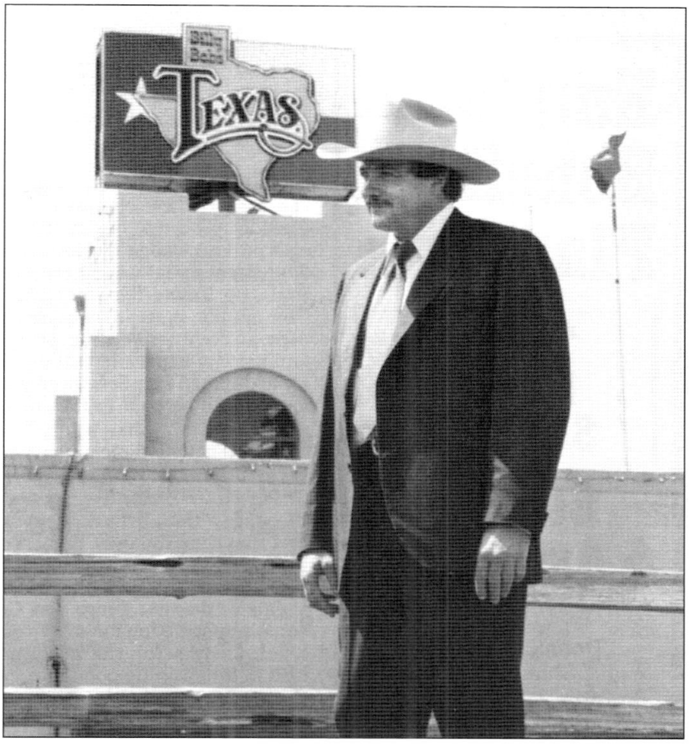

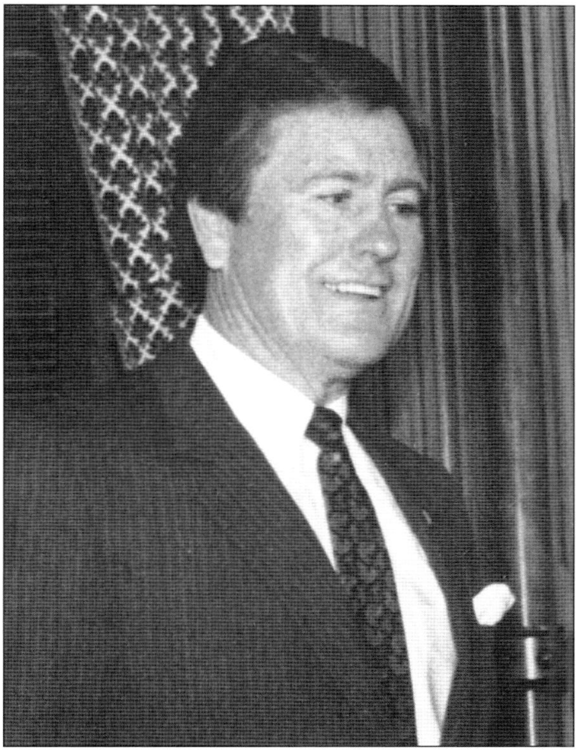

Gib Lewis was serving as speaker of the Texas House of Representatives in 1986, when he was also asked to be an honorary assistant wagon master. He originally came from rural Limestone County in Texas and loved the outdoors and to hunt. Lewis lived in Fort Worth and represented a Tarrant County district in the Texas Legislature. (Courtesy Quentin McGown Collection, Tarrant County Archives.)

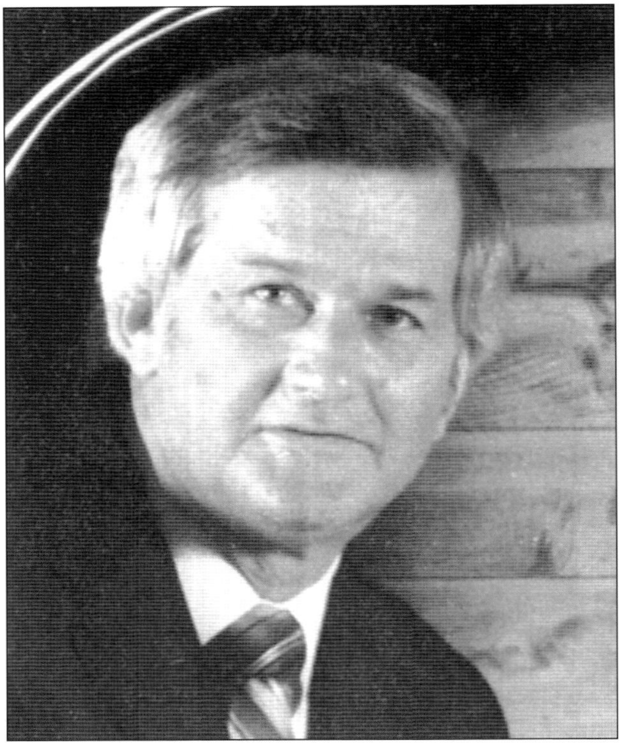

As owner of a sporting goods store, Glen Courson, the final honorary assistant wagon master, thought of the idea of a Winchester Repeating Arms Company commemorative rifle and carbine and their auction as a part of the Texas Sesquicentennial Wagon Train finale. The Winchester Repeating Arms Company agreed with the commemorative idea and even became an official sponsor of the wagon train. Two Smith & Wesson pistols made for the sesquicentennial later sold for $18,000 at auction. (Courtesy Quentin McGown Collection, Tarrant County Archives.)

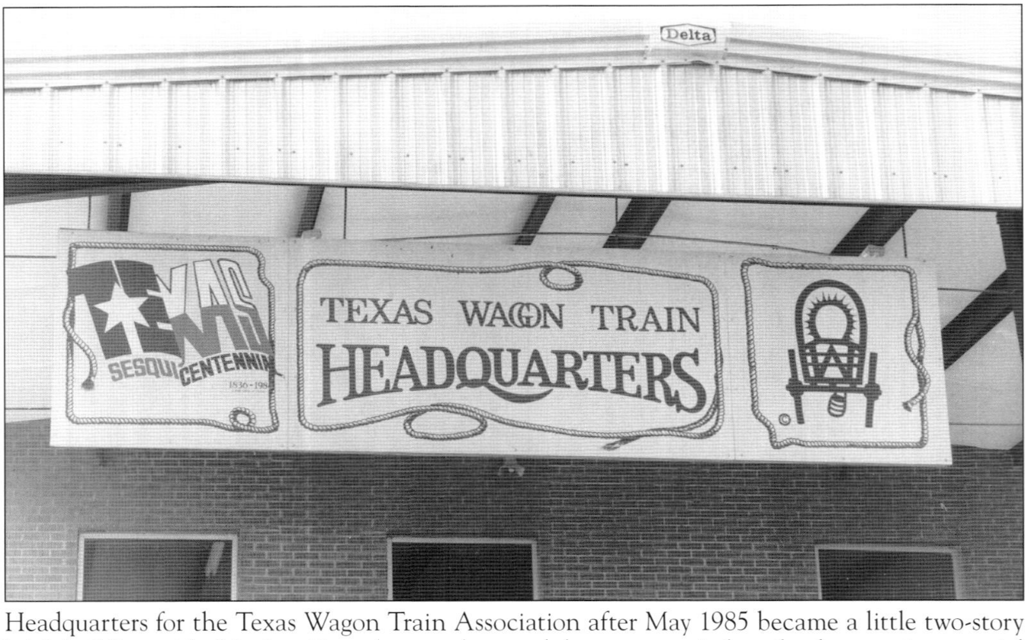

Headquarters for the Texas Wagon Train Association after May 1985 became a little two-story brick building with this sign. Note the state logo and the wagon train logo for the sesquicentennial on each side of the sign. Jan France of Sulphur Springs had the idea for the train and became executive director of the association. Her husband, Garry France, whose family had lived in Sulphur Springs for five generations, became wagon master.

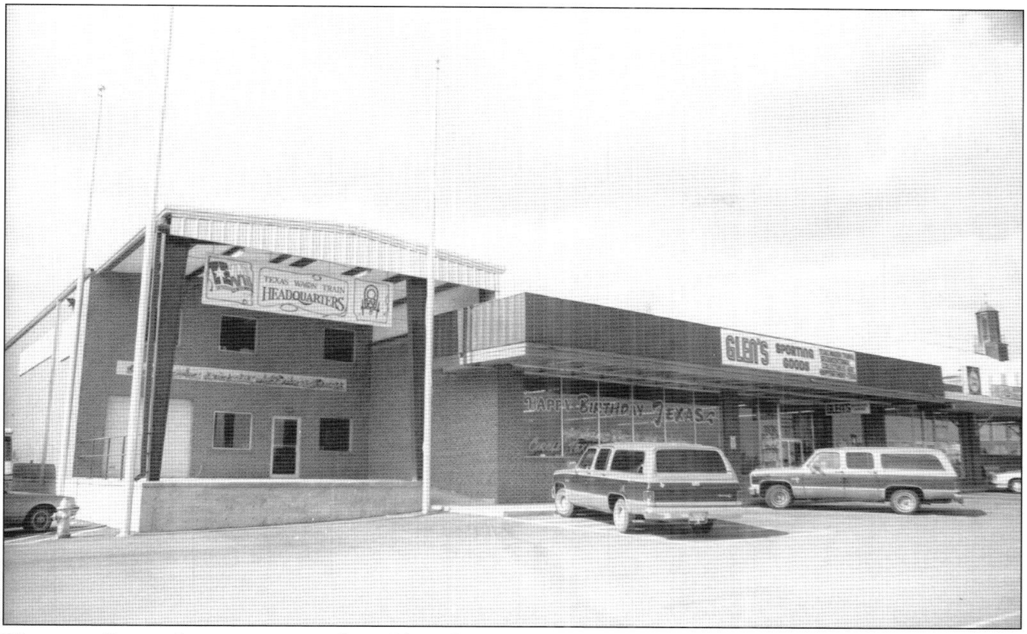

This small storefront connected to Glen Courson's sporting goods store in Irving served as the headquarters for the wagon train project. Courson, a sponsor, served as one of the honorary assistant wagon masters as well as offering the office space. Twenty-eight official sponsors provided in-kind types of donations, such as equipment and vehicles.

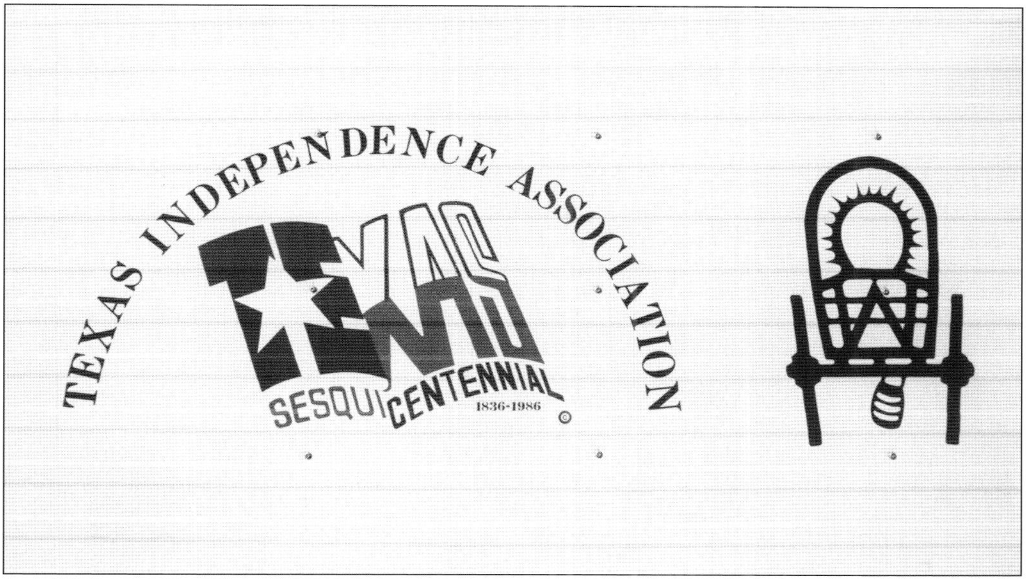

The wagon insignia, which officially represented the wagon train, was made into a branding iron for marking wagons that completed each 1,000 miles of travel during the six-month trip. After each 1,000 miles they traveled, participants could get chaps, and other items as well, branded with the logo. The drawing of the wagon became a familiar symbol throughout Texas during the 3,000-mile route of the wagon train. The branding iron was made in Hunt, Texas, and destroyed after the journey was completed so that it could not be reused.

TEXAS WAGON TRAIN
ASSOCIATION

The Texas Wagon Train Association, identified by this logo, gained membership from 10,000 people who participated in the train over the course of the six months. Moving along on any one day were 150 people—counting drivers, riders, and support personnel. Business manager Quentin McGown said it was like moving a town down the road. He felt like the mayor.

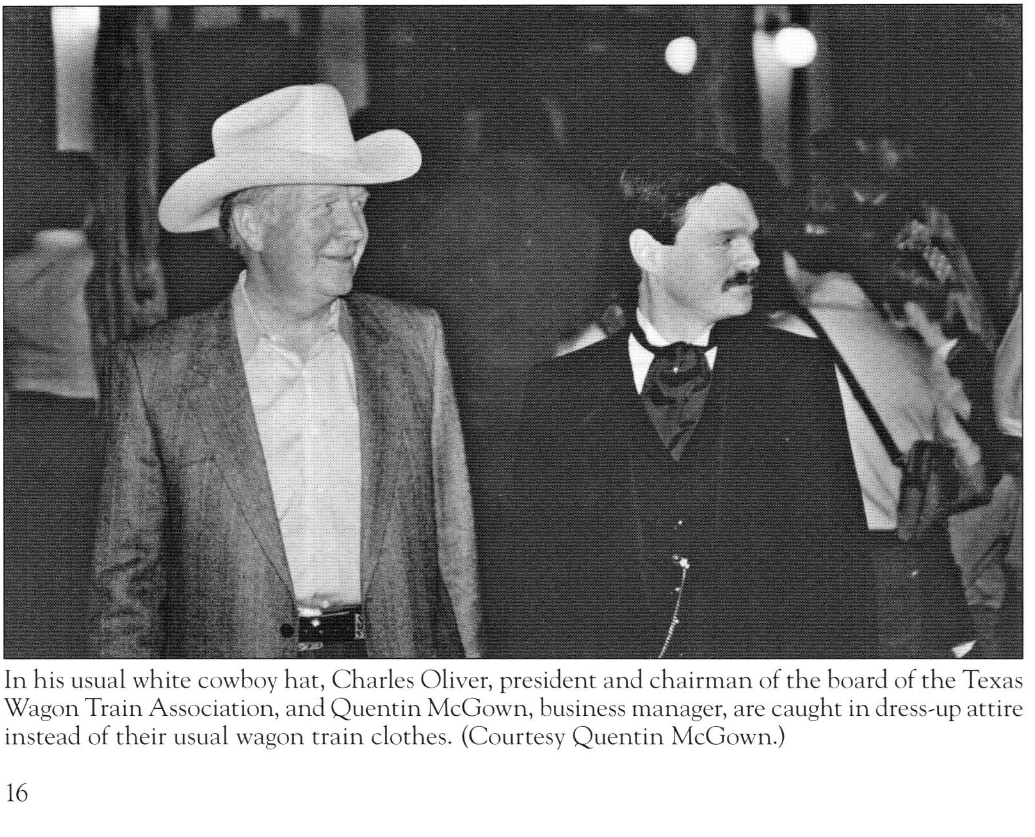

In his usual white cowboy hat, Charles Oliver, president and chairman of the board of the Texas Wagon Train Association, and Quentin McGown, business manager, are caught in dress-up attire instead of their usual wagon train clothes. (Courtesy Quentin McGown.)

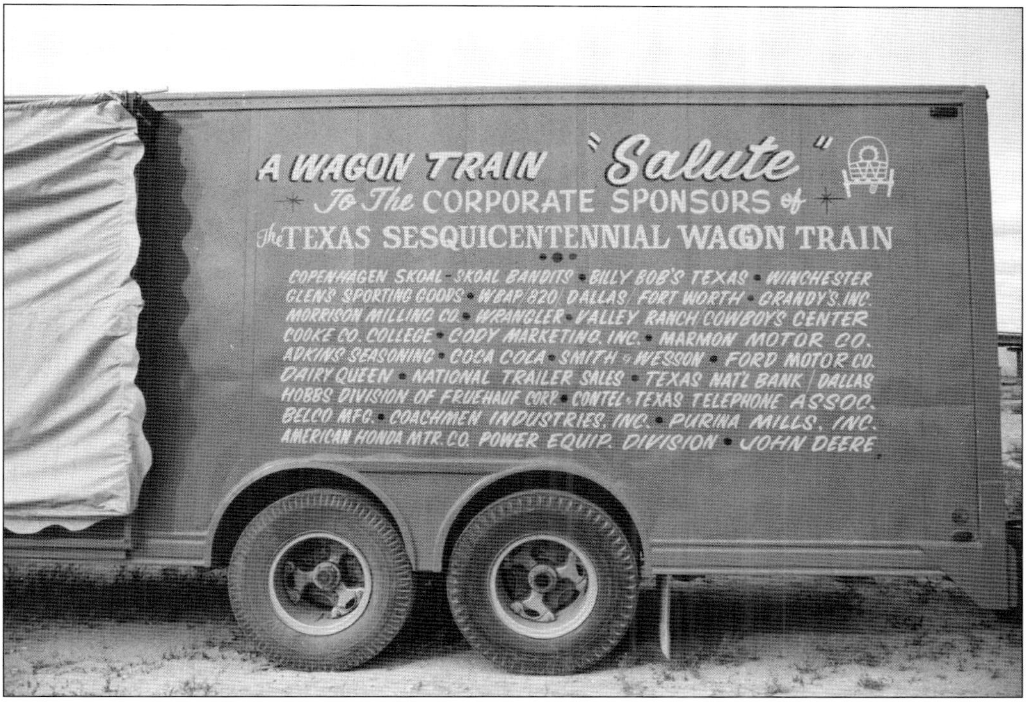

Only the official sponsors of the Texas Wagon Train Association could advertise on the wagons. It took many sponsors to make it all happen, and they deserved the salute. Others could place a small plaque on their wagon identifying who they were. Wagons lined up and drove each day in a planned order. The sponsored wagons came first, then the most authentic ones. Lastly, rubber-tired wagons could follow. Horseback riders accompanied at the end.

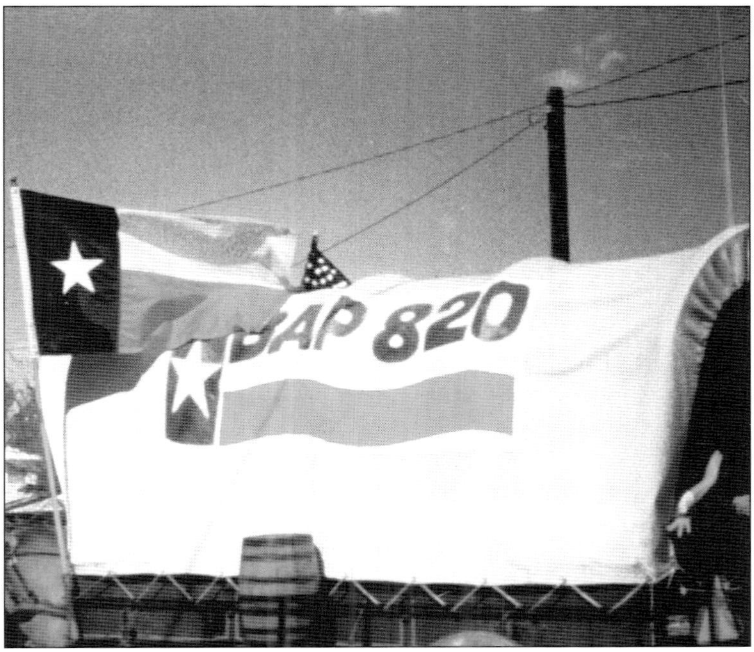

One of the official sponsors was the Dallas–Fort Worth metroplex radio station WBAP 820. Amon Carter, publisher of the *Fort Worth Star-Telegram* for many years, began the first radio station in Fort Worth. Its sign-in sound was a cowbell, and its call letters stand for "We Bring A Program." Glenn Pearce, brother of the head camp jack West Pearce, drove the WBAP wagon. (Courtesy Azle Historical Museum.)

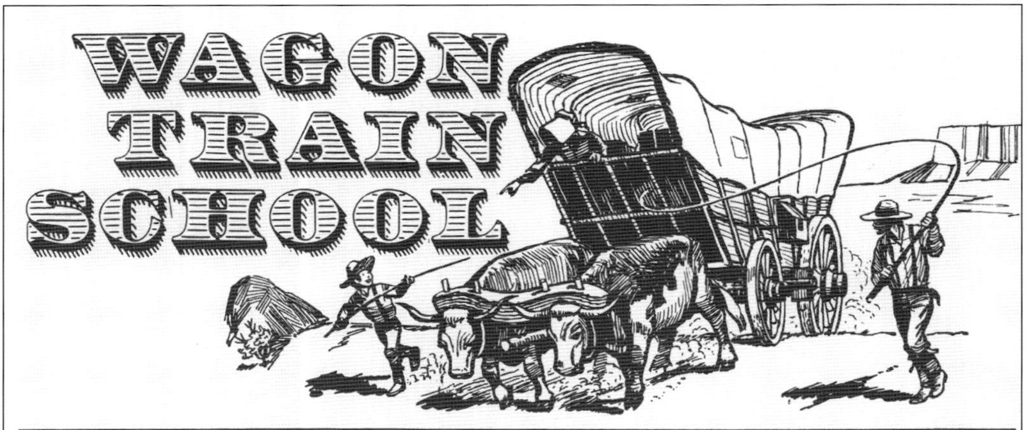

A Special Texas Sesquicentennial Project Of

COOKE COUNTY COLLEGE

Gainesville, Texas

Under Sponsorship Of The Texas Wagon Train Association

When it became necessary for parents to take school-age children along on the train, Jan France appealed through her state representative to the Texas Legislature. She met with the Texas Education Agency, and they proposed the Texas Sesquicentennial Independent School District. House Bill 8 in the 1985 biennial session created it. Cook County College in Gainesville agreed to provide the facilities, equipment, educational materials, and teachers for the classes.

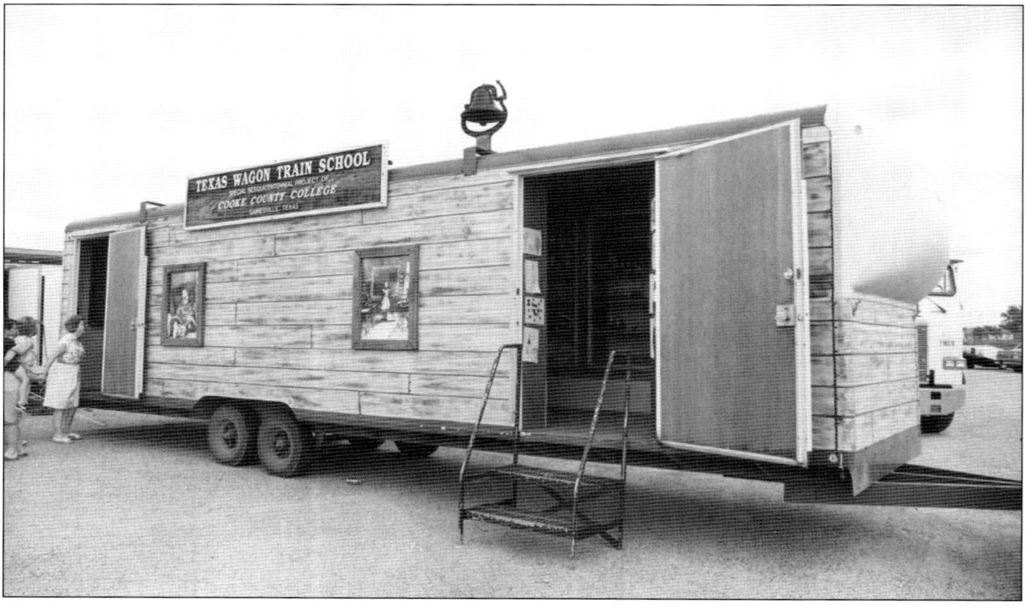

Cook County College provided the 8-foot-by-36-foot trailer, redesigned as a one-room school. Head teacher Anita Pitchford took a semester's leave of absence to work variously with Debi Garner, Susan Venus, and Randy Russell to provide state-sanctioned classes for the 27 students. Flexible hours and field trips enlivened the children's day. Replicas of McGuffey Readers, donated Encyclopedia Britannica volumes, and state-of-the art computers assisted in their learning.

Principal at J.M. Lindsay Elementary School in Gainesville, Anita Pitchford (pictured) chose to become head teacher for the portable school. She decided that students would have shorter class hours than a usual school, but they would be able to gain a broader education because of all the towns and ranches they would be visiting. Fifteen-year-old Reka France, daughter of the wagon master, was a freshman in the school. (Courtesy Quentin McGown Collection, Tarrant County Archives.)

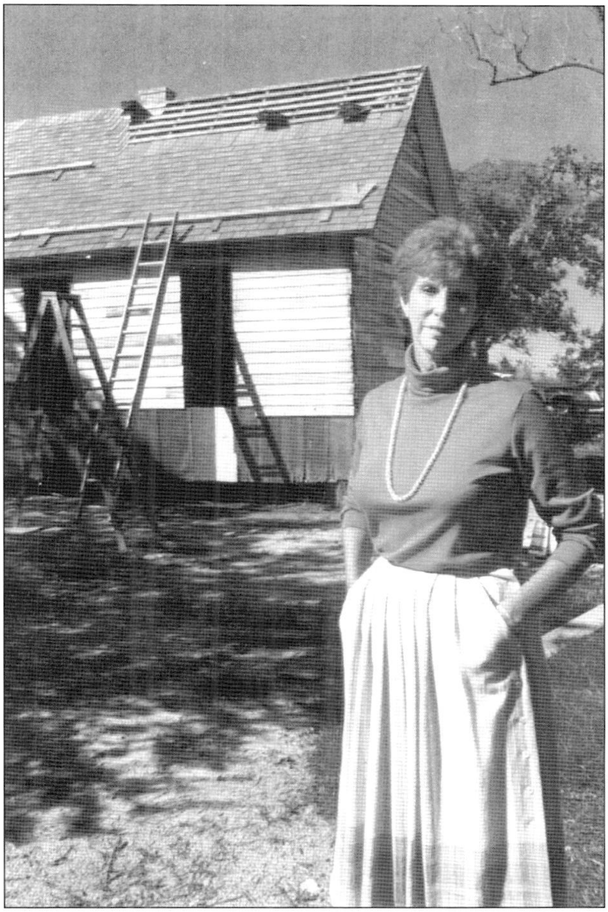

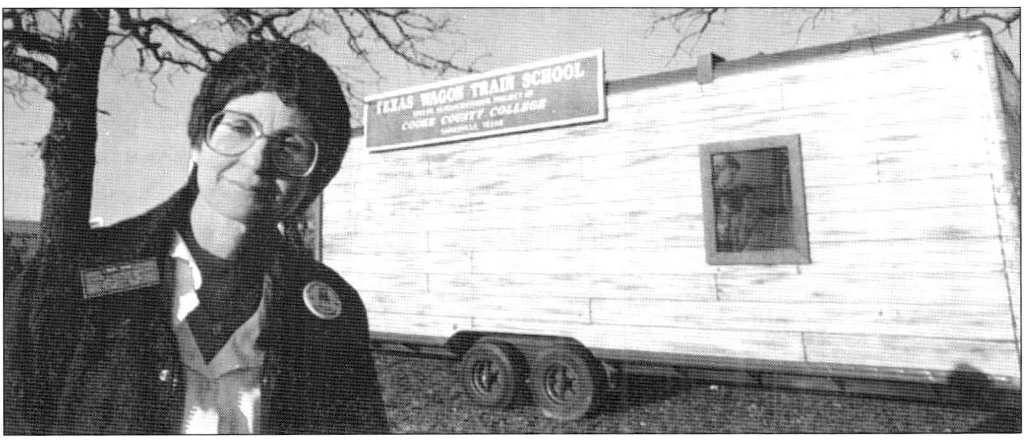

Linda Mast of Cook County College became the school coordinator, even though she did not travel with the train. The school's course of study matched the normal public school curriculum for each child's grade level as much as possible. Over the six-month period, more than 200,000 schoolchildren from all over Texas visited the wagon train. (Courtesy Quentin McGown Collection, Tarrant County Archives.)

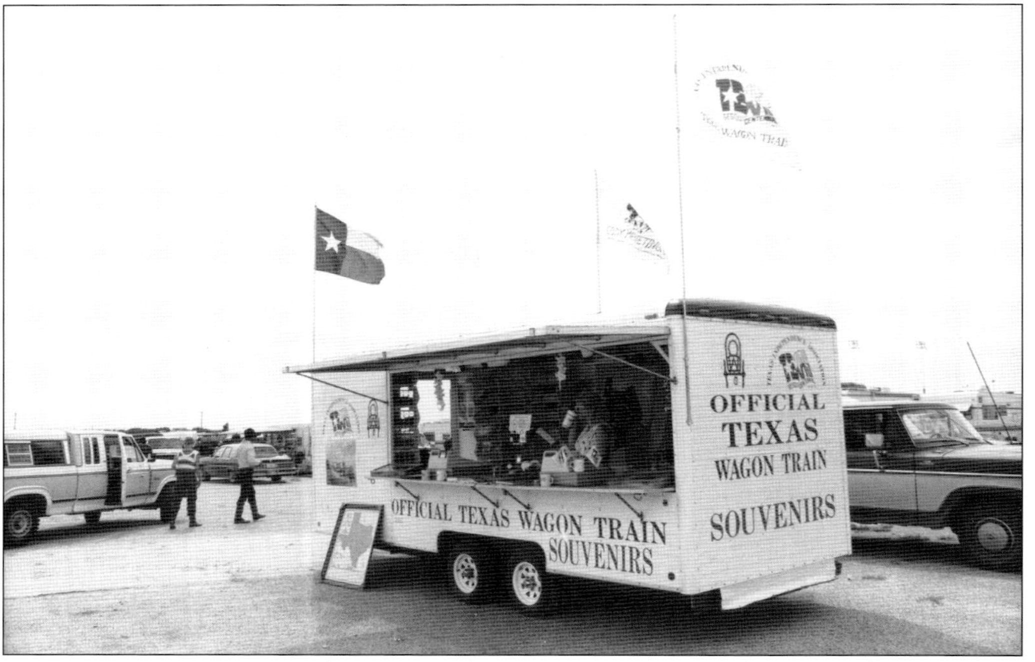

A souvenir wagon set up at each campsite. The wagon train served as the most visible celebratory institution of the Texas Sesquicentennial Commission, pledged to help the state celebrate 150 years since winning its freedom from Mexico in 1836. As it circled around Texas during its journey, the wagon train honored the state's two most important holidays: Independence Day on March 2 and San Jacinto Day on April 21. Visitors to the train loved having souvenirs to buy.

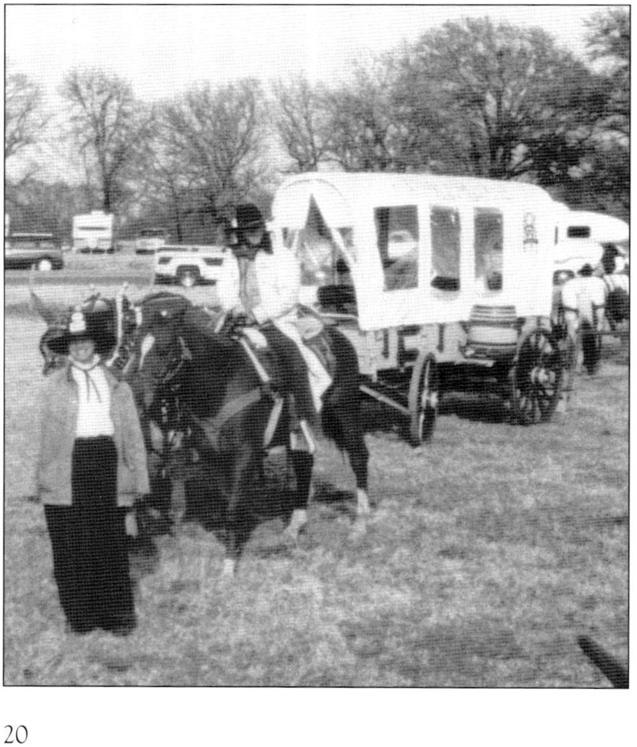

Jan France, who first had the idea for the wagon train, stands in front of her wagon, which was the official wagon of the Texas Sesquicentennial Wagon Train, and Bonnie and Beth, her team. Beth had been part of the LBJ Ranch tour for many years, so banners reading "Welcome Home Beth" abounded at the ranch stop. Ranch personnel gave Beth a bouquet of carrots and apples and Jan a bouquet of yellow, long-stemmed roses. Jan's stepson Rowdy France, on the horse, was a student at the wagon train school. Jan's costume is what she wore each day, her skirt copied from one she saw at the Annie Riggs Museum in Fort Stockton and her hat a gift from Bob Moorhouse of Pitchfork Ranch. (Courtesy Jo Anne Thielemann.)

Two

The Six-Month Journey around Texas

The taming of the American West has universal appeal, with visions of wagon trains moving across the plains remaining in the minds of people indefinitely. It is an easily understood and identifiable symbol of man reaching out for the next frontier that touches the human spirit. A wooden wagon with iron-rimmed wooden wheels being pulled by a team of work animals, exposed to nature and the elements, presents a challenge to overcome and endure. For its citizens, the Texas Sesquicentennial Wagon Train provided the opportunity to experience a sense of what it was like when wooden wagons were kings of the road. Those who experienced a daylong run of the wagon train, unhitching the animals and hitching them up for the start of another long day, learned an appreciation of a lifestyle that was difficult physically. This photographic documentary attempts to capture the essence of the moment with wagon train images frozen in time.

Nearly three years of planning would be put to the test, as 104 wagons set out on the cold morning of January 2, 1986. Would bad weather slow down the train? Would all the campsites be available and ready? Could the train keep to its schedule without getting behind and throwing all the celebrations off by a day or two in those small towns and cities?

The mantra became, "Rain, sleet, or sun, the wagon train rolls on," as *Dallas Morning News* reporter Leslie Pound described. J.D. Paul, age 70, was the only participant who had ridden in a wagon train for the Texas centennial in 1936. Those in that train saw a more rustic trip, as they hunted rabbits and deer for food. One family in the 1986 train used a wooden bow in its wagon that was used during early pioneer days by its ancestors.

Weddings, numerous horse and wagon accidents, unruly horses, and even a death occurred during the course of the journey of the wagon train. Pam Burchell, a young wife and mother from Newark, let someone else drive her wagon one day while she drove his support truck. She died in a traffic accident early in the trip near Tomball.

The train made all of its scheduled stops on time as it visited cities and towns and camped in 150 of them as a living exhibit of the Western and independent heritage of Texas. Many thousands of persons witnessed this historic event. Those who drove the wagons and rode the horses for the entire trip felt like special, close-knit family by the time the adventure concluded on July 3 and 4 in the Fort Worth Stockyards.

The Texas Sesquicentennial Wagon Train was voted the number one event by the Texas Press Association and one of the top 10 events of the year by the Associated Press. Photography crews came from Japan, England, Germany, South Korea, Australia, and many other countries just to film the wagon train.

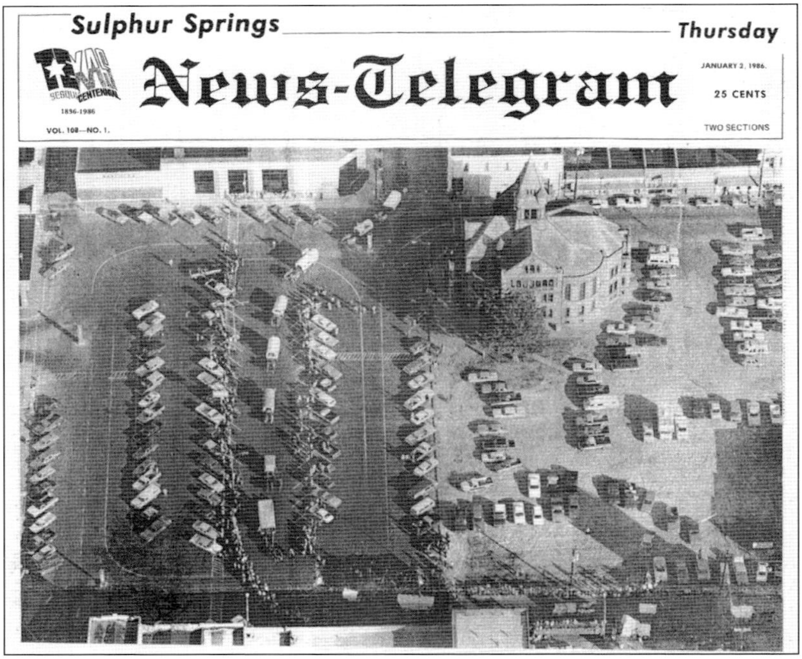
Sulphur Springs Thursday
News-Telegram
VOL. 108—NO. 1.
JANUARY 2, 1986.
25 CENTS
TWO SECTIONS

An aerial view of downtown Sulphur Springs on the morning of January 2, 1986, reveals the intense interest in the start of the wagon train and the single-file movement between two lines of onlookers. Nearly an hour was needed for the entire lineup of 104 wagons to pass through the lines. (Courtesy *Sulphur Springs News-Telegram.*)

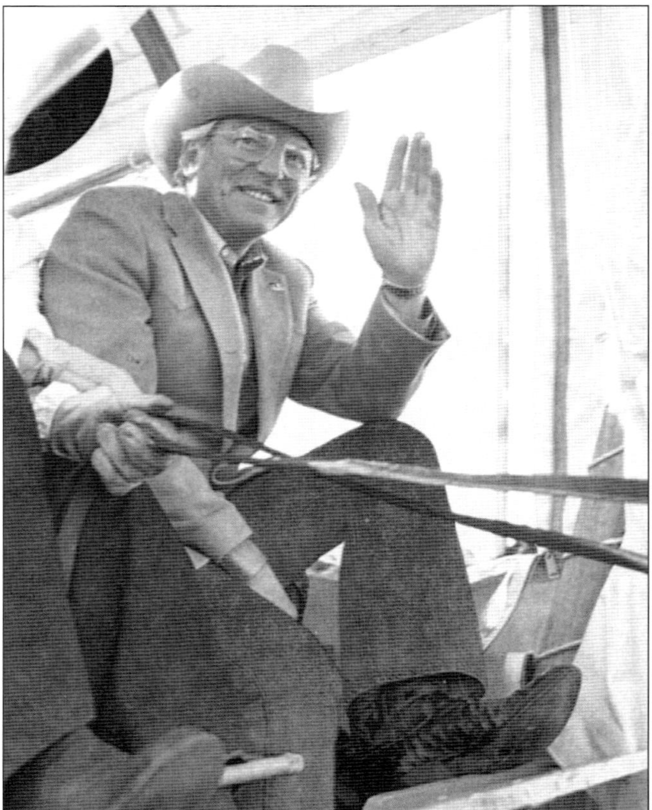

As the train left Sulphur Springs, Gov. Mark White of Texas rode in the first wagon driven by Jan France, executive director of the Texas Wagon Train Association and wife of the wagon master, Garry France. Also in the lead wagon that first day was David Baucom, mayor of Sulphur Springs. Serving as assistant wagon masters for the trip were Perry Joe Frost, Mike Lowrey, Vicky Hazard, Vern Renz, and Doug Medlin. They spread out and rode by the wagons as they stretched a mile or so long. (Courtesy Quentin McGown Collection, Tarrant County Archives.)

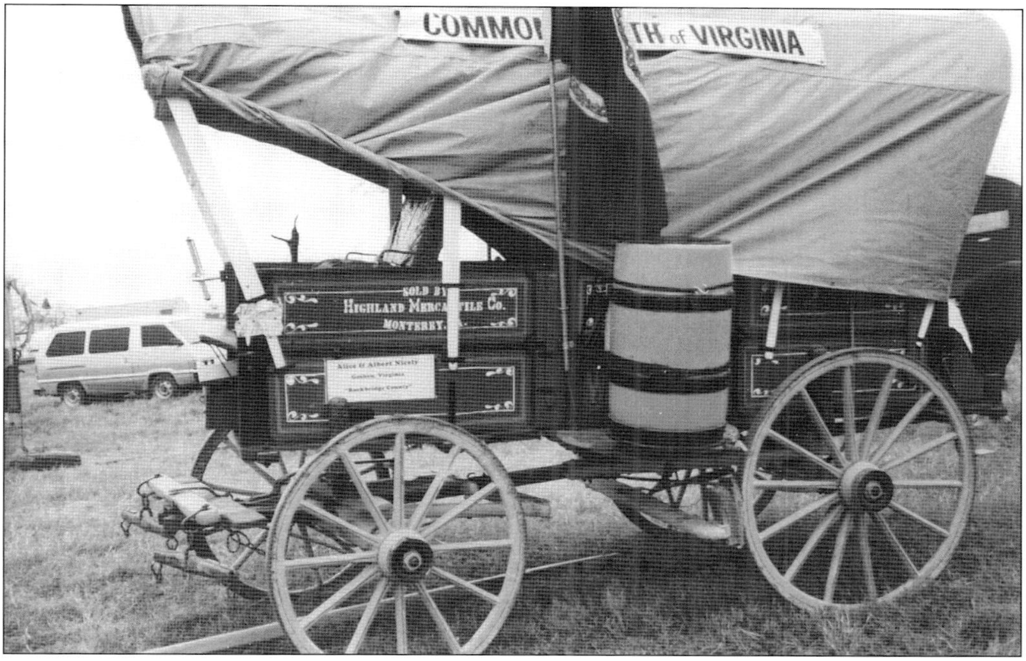

Wagons came from all over the United States to participate in the historic Texas Sesquicentennial Wagon Train. On its canvas, this one proclaims "Commonwealth of Virginia." Other states represented by wagons or riders were Arizona, Arkansas, California, Colorado, Florida, Georgia, Illinois, Indiana, Iowa, Kansas, Louisiana, Maine, Maryland, Mississippi, Missouri, New Mexico, Ohio, Oklahoma, Pennsylvania, Tennessee, and Wisconsin. Some wagons had been the official wagons of their states 10 years earlier in the United States bicentennial train. (Courtesy Victoria and Phillip Williams.)

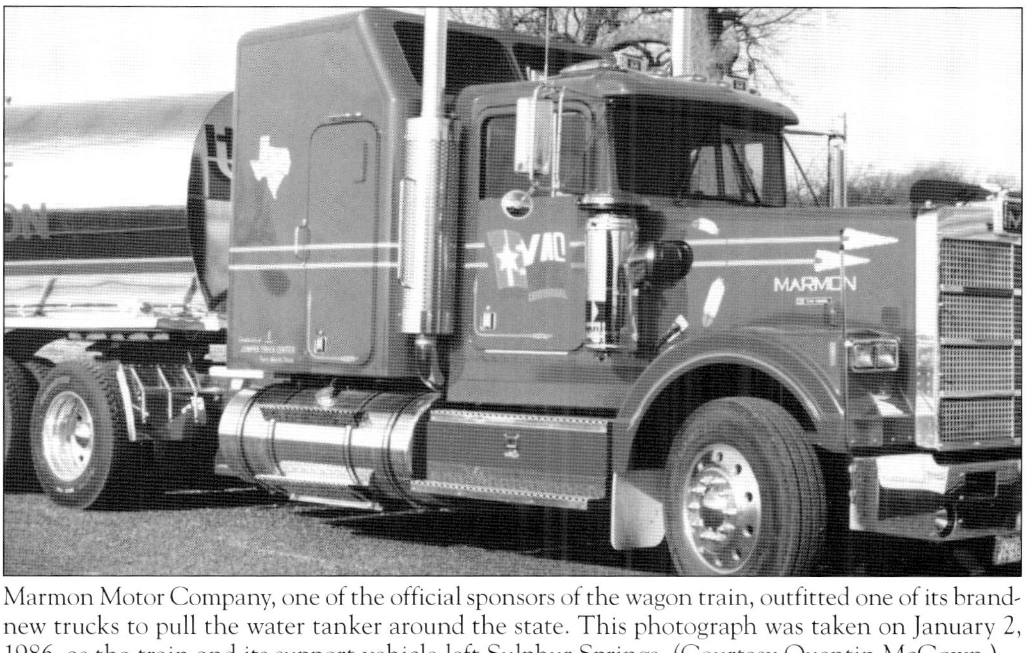

Marmon Motor Company, one of the official sponsors of the wagon train, outfitted one of its brand-new trucks to pull the water tanker around the state. This photograph was taken on January 2, 1986, as the train and its support vehicle left Sulphur Springs. (Courtesy Quentin McGown.)

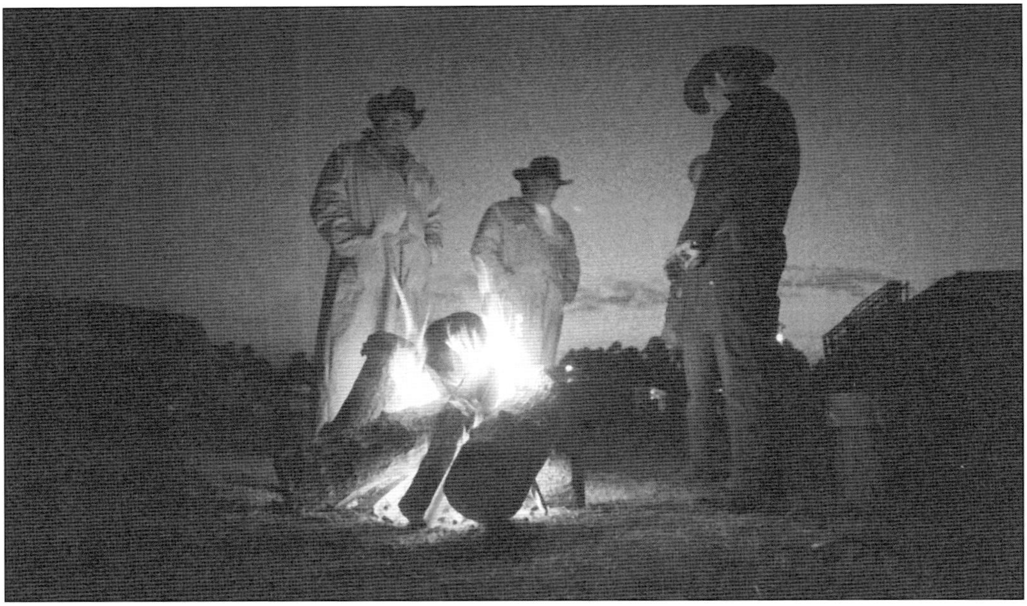

By the third day after leaving Sulphur Springs, the temperature was down to 22 degrees. Large campfires brought cheer to the camp. This trip was as realistic as possible, barring a few changes in the wagons for the sake of safety. "Wagons, ho!" was the headline over this photograph when it appeared on February 2, 1986, in the *Dallas Morning News* after a reporter visited the train. (Courtesy *Dallas Morning News*.)

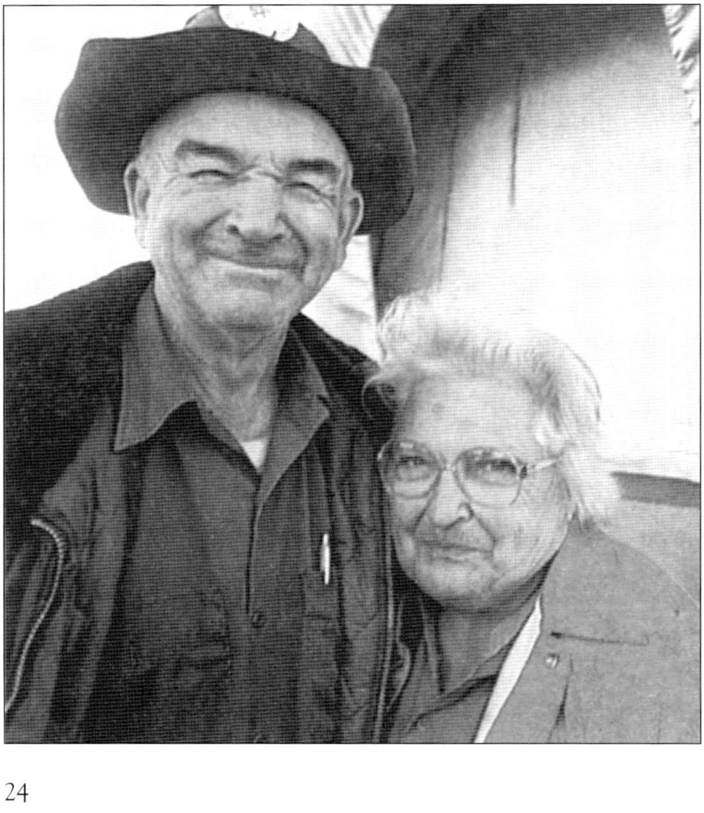

Driving all the way from Galesville, Wisconsin, in their wagon were Elmo and Helen Luns. They were on the road for 12 months total and covered 6,000 miles before they got back home. The Lunses left Wisconsin in September 1985 and arrived back home in September 1986. (Courtesy Tarrant County Archives, Quentin McGown Collection, Fort Worth, Texas.)

Hazel Bowen, age 78, from Antelope, Texas, was assigned the Texas wagon from the US bicentennial and rode second in line. Her wagon, restored by Charles Oliver, came from a museum near the Alamo. She had driven the same wagon 10 years earlier, in 1976. The Texas wagon's route that time stretched from Houston, Texas, to Valley Forge, Pennsylvania. Four other trains began in as many states and later merged. She called the trips "a piece of cake" compared to what pioneers in the 19th century endured. (Courtesy Quentin McGown Collection, Tarrant County Archives.)

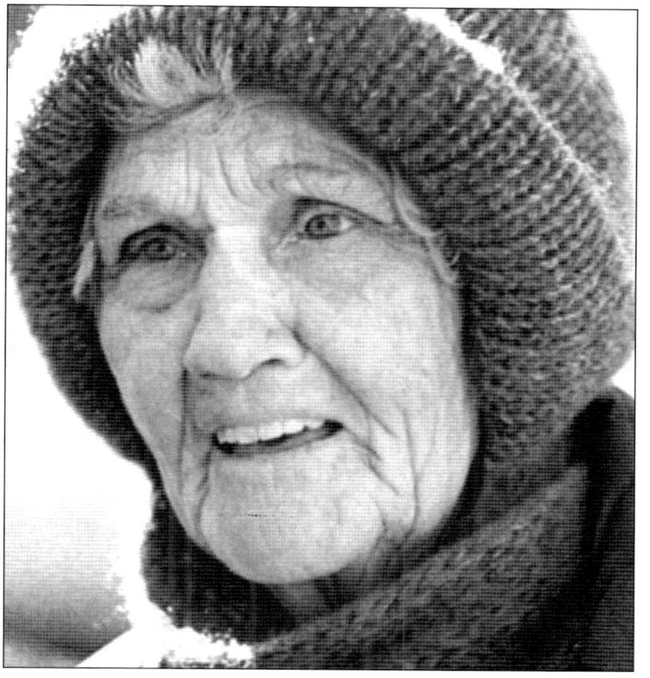

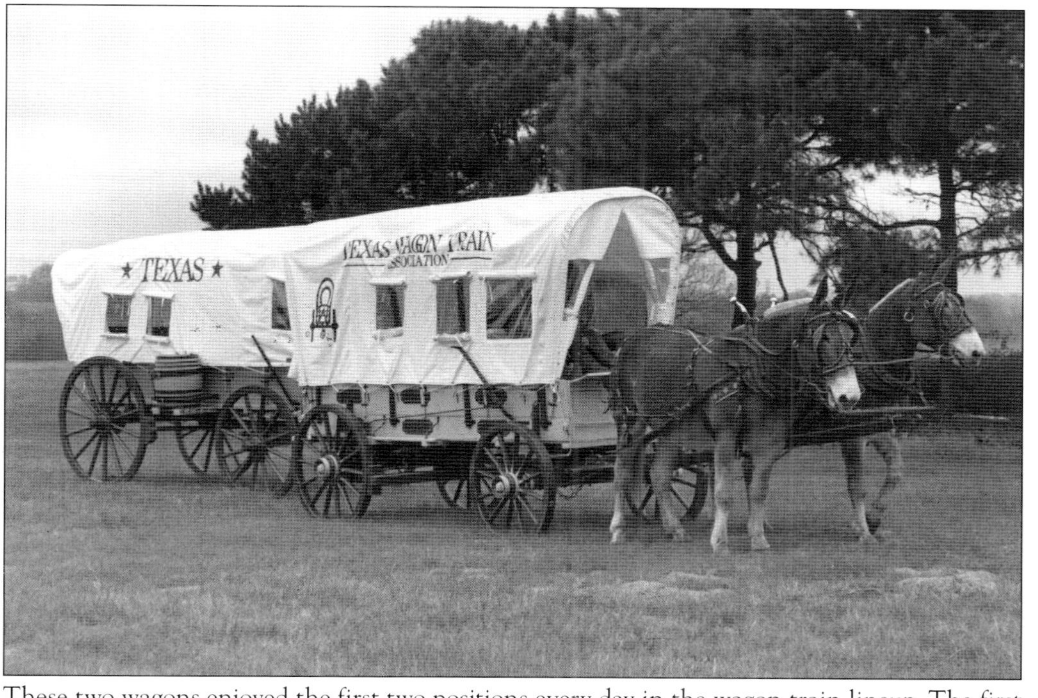

These two wagons enjoyed the first two positions every day in the wagon train lineup. The first was the official wagon of the Texas Wagon Train Association, which Jan France, executive director and official meeter and greeter of dignitaries, drove each day. Hazel Bowen drove the official Texas wagon, which she had also driven 10 years earlier during the bicentennial of the United States. (Courtesy Texas Wagon Train Association Collection, North Fort Worth Historical Society.)

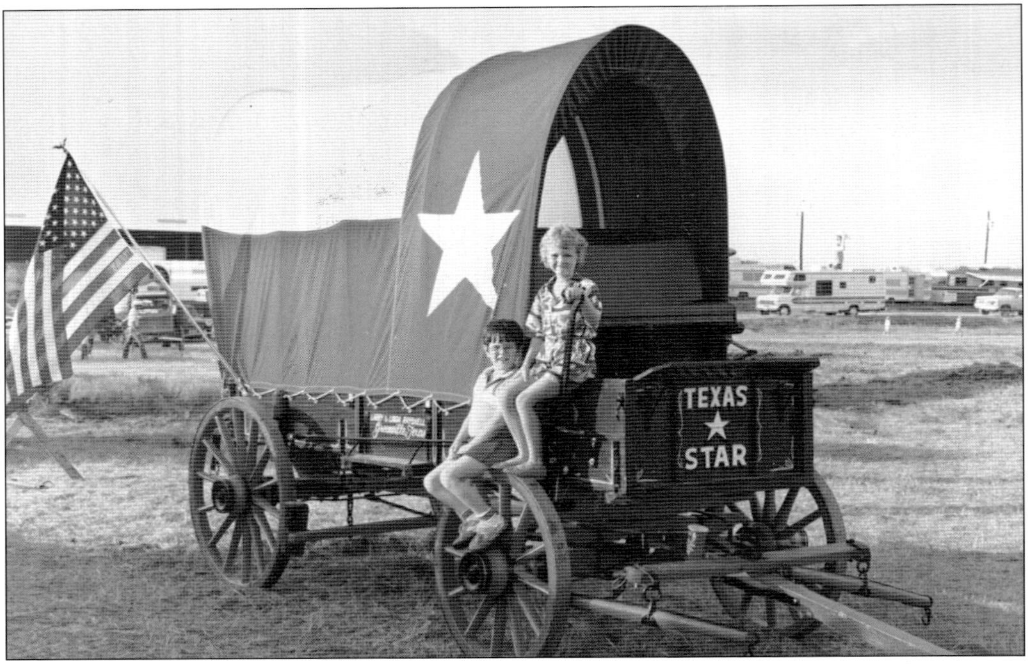

The white stripe in the Texas flag pattern blends into the background here, but it is there. Many of the drivers provided patriotic images, like flags on their wagons. This one is just a bit larger than most. (Courtesy Quentin McGown.)

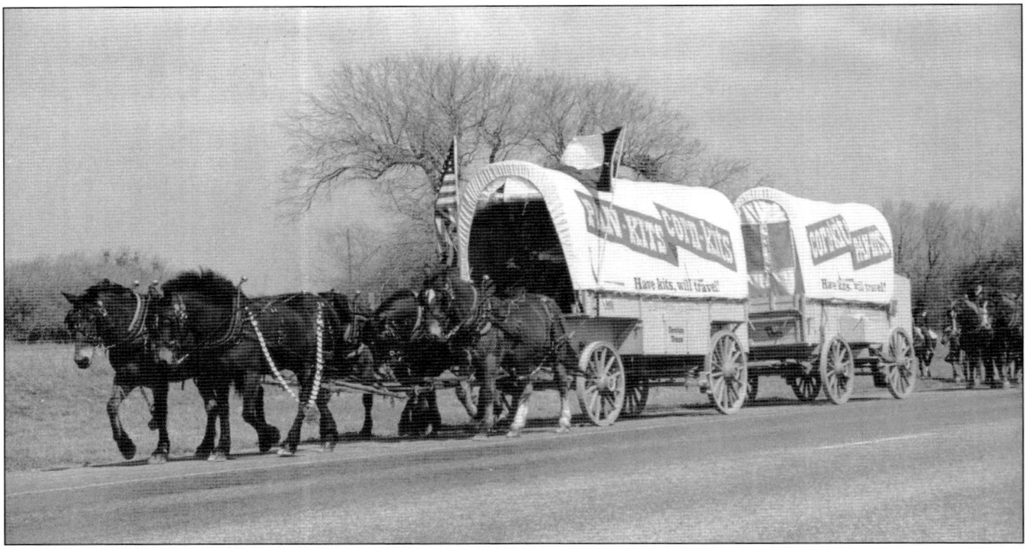

This unusual configuration of double wagons was supported on the train by one of the official sponsors. Morrison Milling Company of Denton was advertising its Corn-Kits. Morrison hired two Shivers brothers from Oklahoma to drive the two wagons. Fred and his wife, Deb, had spent their honeymoon on the bicentennial train in 1976. David and Teresa Shivers joined them this time. Between the two couples, there were four children, the youngest a girl of 16 months named Kristie. The Shivers brothers leased out their saddle and harness business building in Oklahoma for the six months that they participated in the wagon train.

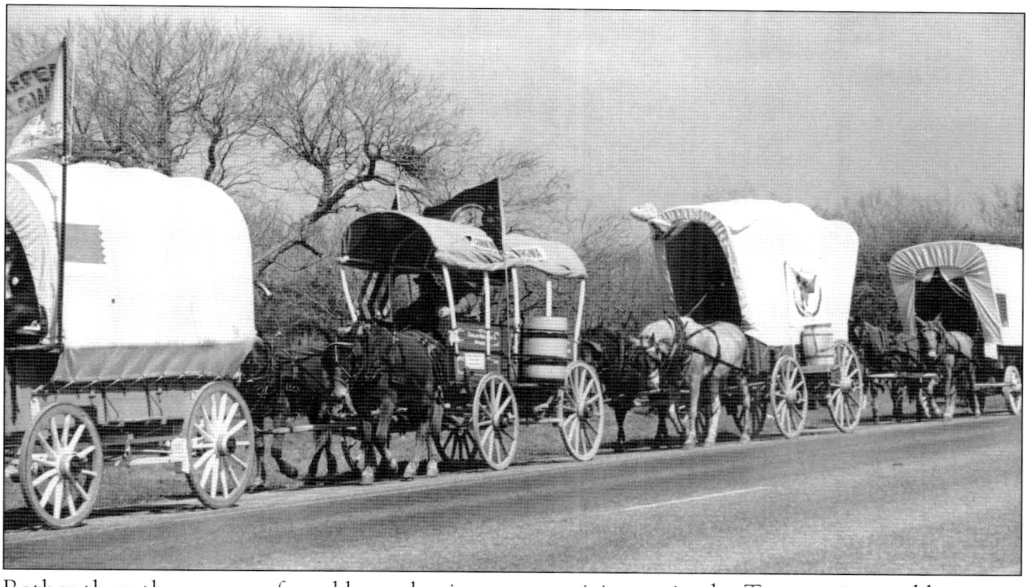

Rather than the oxen preferred by early pioneers, participants in the Texas train used horses or mules for pulling their canvas-covered wagons. Some of the wagons boasted rubber tires to make for a smoother ride, but other riders preferred to rough it with the authentic wooden wheels with iron rims. Authentic or not, each had to have a hydraulic brake for safety on the trip. The wagon train circled the capitol while in Austin early in February, and the legislature and governor issued proclamations about the train.

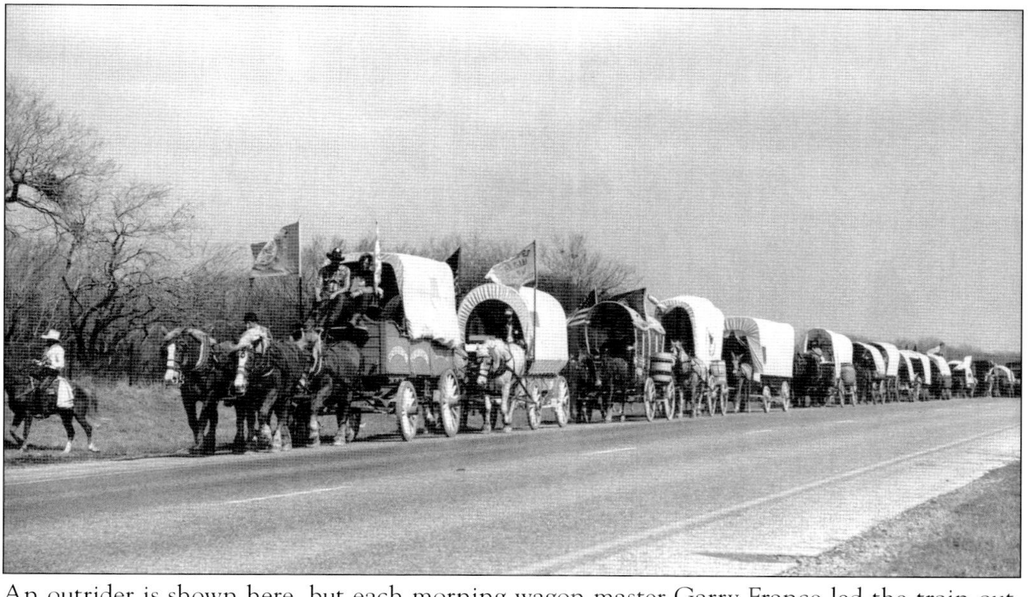

An outrider is shown here, but each morning wagon master Garry France led the train out, calling "Wagons, ho!" His wife, Jan, usually drove the first wagon, but this day of February 15 on the way to Robstown, someone else was driving. Ina Nell Wood from Fort Worth became her codriver for all but the first three weeks. This photograph captures the size of the event and why crowds of people along the route always got excited. In February, a bout of flu spread through the participants of the train.

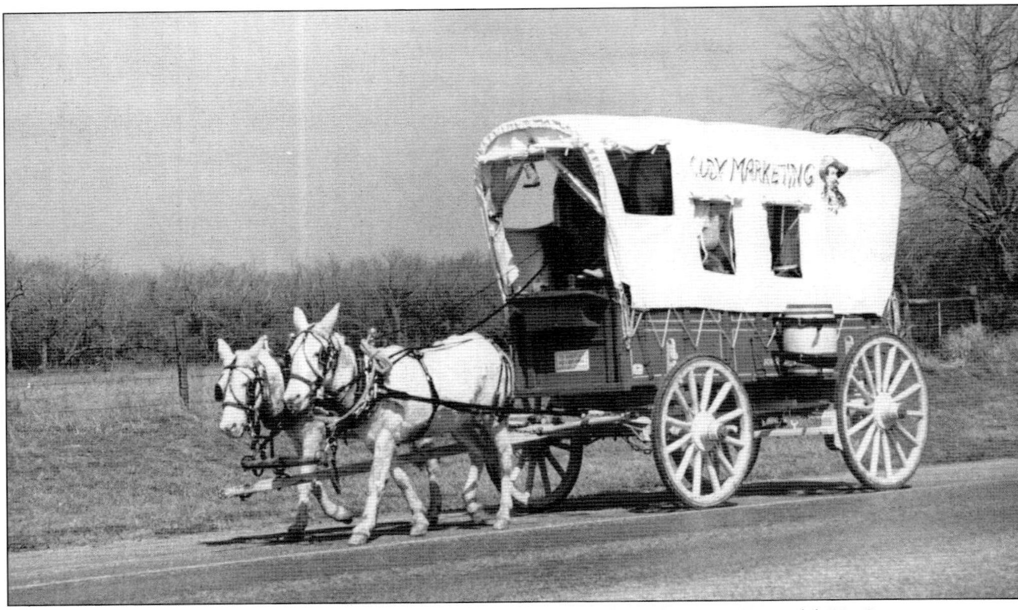

Cody Marketing, Inc. sponsored this wagon with two white horses. Donald H. Stringer owned Cody Marketing and was the first business manager of the Texas Wagon Train Association. At the conclusion of the wagon train's six-month trek, Stringer's company produced a one-time, full-color magazine about it. Now a collector's item, the magazine is housed in museums, perhaps, or stacked in boxes in attics across the state.

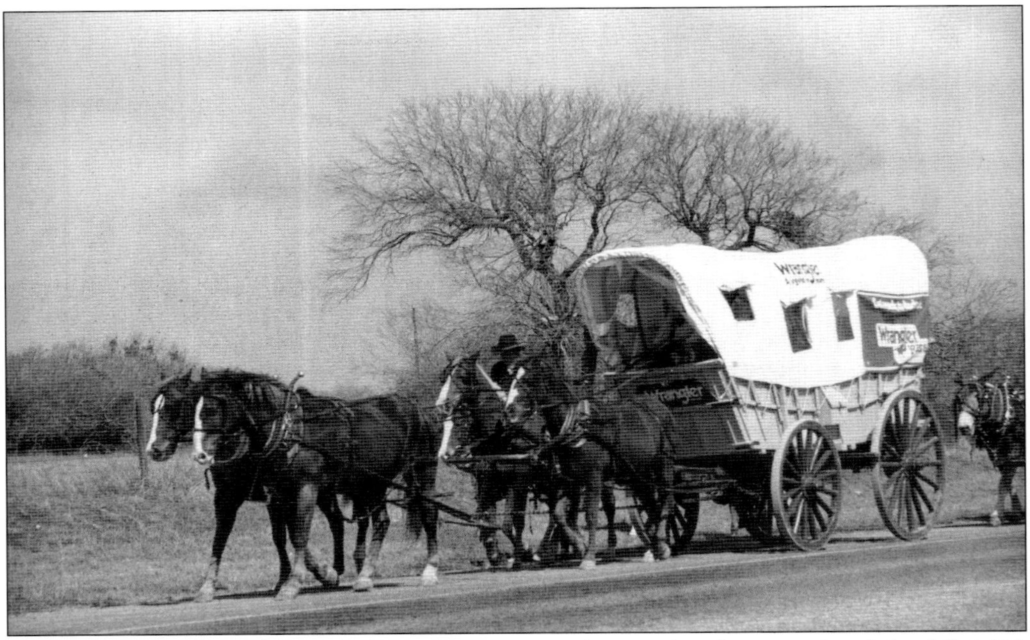

This wagon, sponsored by Wrangler Jeans, was one of a very few that completed the full 3,000 miles. For each 1,000 miles traveled, a wagon received the official wagon train logo branded on its back or side. Following the conclusion of the trip, this wagon was placed on display near the historic railroad station in Grapevine and remains there today.

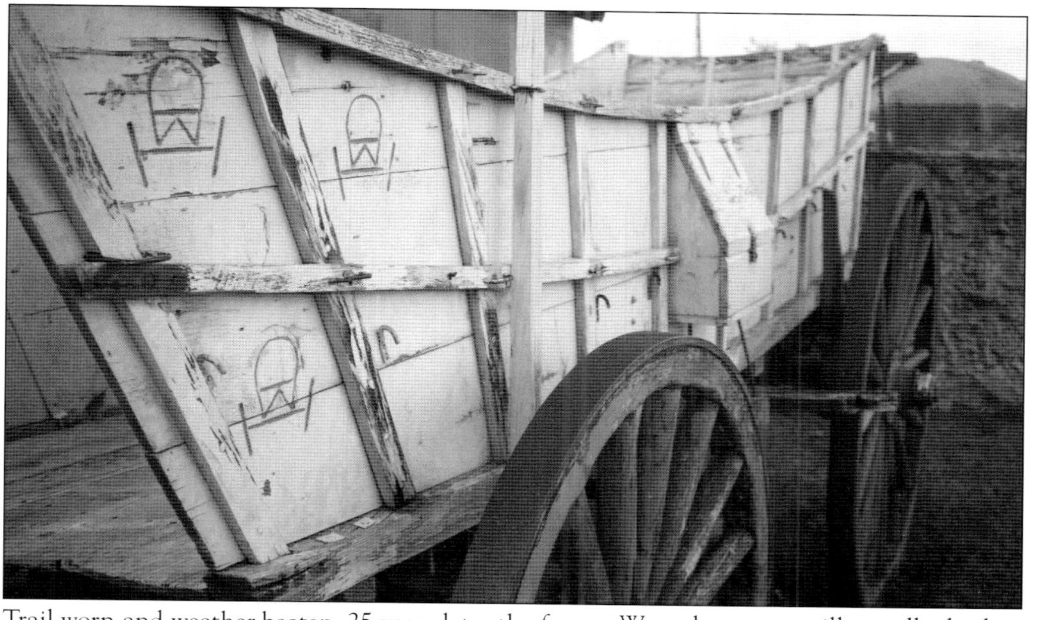

Trail-worn and weather-beaten, 25 years later the former Wrangler wagon still proudly displays its official Texas Sesquicentennial Wagon Train logo brands, proclaiming its feat of completing the entire 3,000-mile, six-month journey. Visitors in Grapevine who view the wagon perhaps do not realize the monumental accomplishment the little wagon and its drivers made.

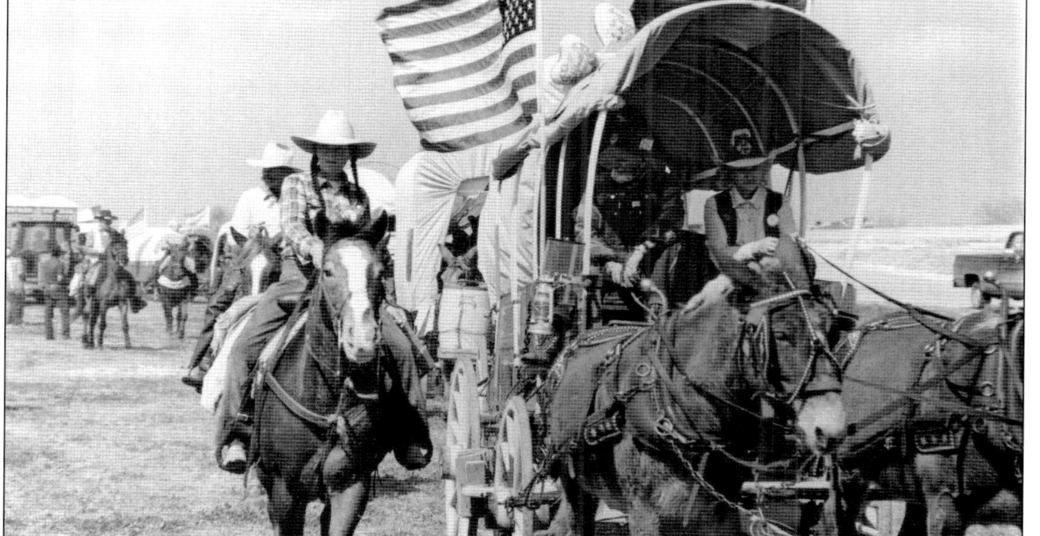

Pictured here on horseback are husband and wife Margaret and Vern Renz, outrider and assistant wagon master, respectively. The average rate of travel with horses and mules in the Old West was 4 to 4.5 miles per hour. By oxen, 2.5 miles per hour would be normal. The Texas wagon train averaged nearer the larger number or faster. On level ground, a 20-mile day was excellent; the train's best was 33 miles to reach Throckmorton. On rough ground in the 19th century, a normal day was 10 miles. The conditions of the trail and rest stops for water and food dictated the travel whether one was a pioneer of a century and a half ago or a reenactor in 1986.

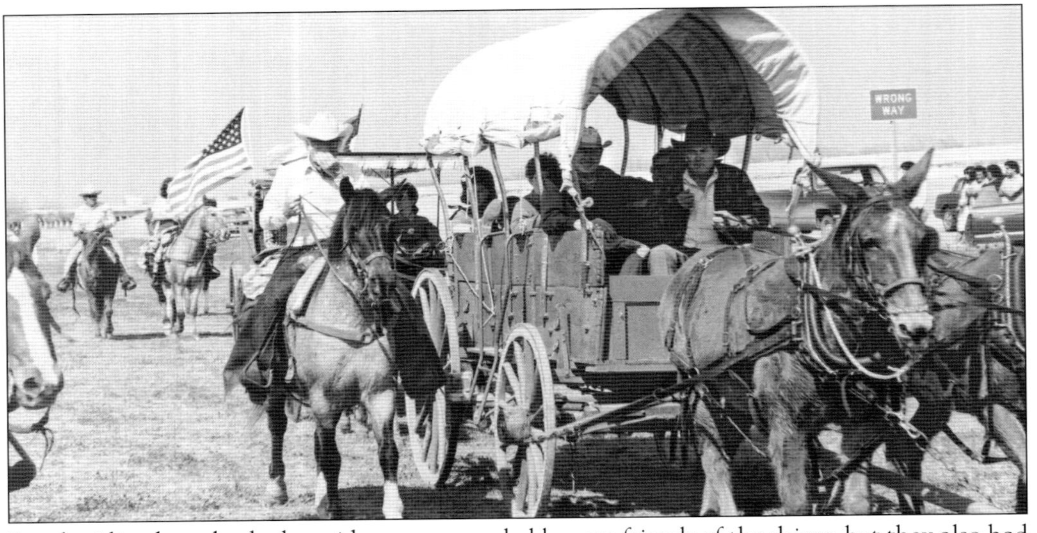

People riding horseback alongside a wagon probably were friends of the driver, but they also had an official role. They were called scouts, or outriders, and helped keep the horses on the wagon team quiet when anything spooked them. Trips through traffic in a town or city often made the horses jumpy, especially if someone honked a horn or a youngster yelled. The scout rode closer beside the horses to calm them in the event that they got nervous.

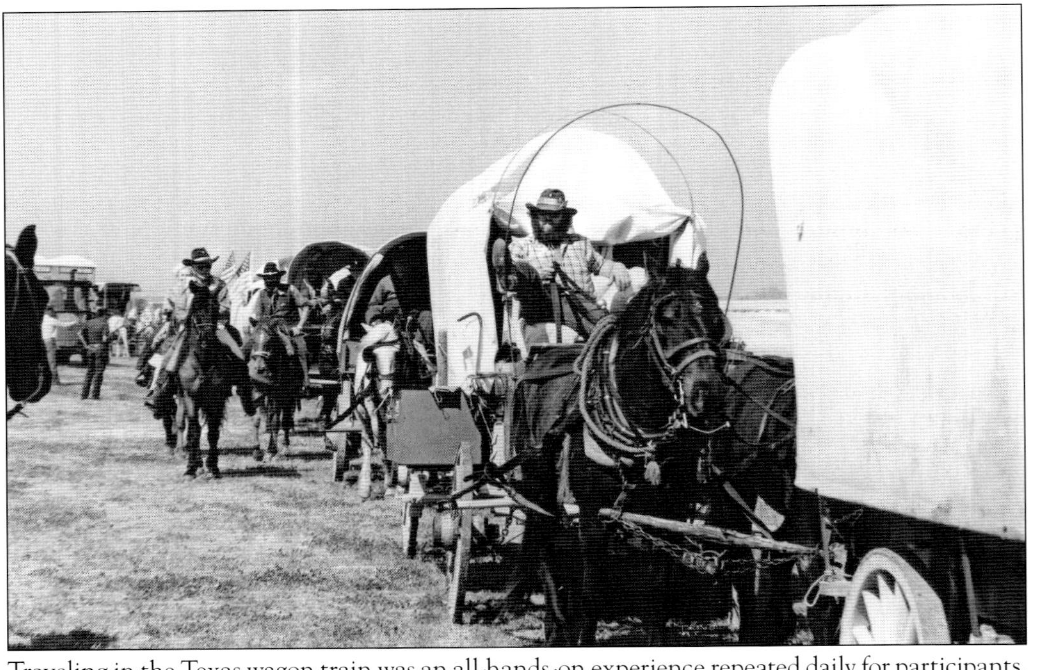

Traveling in the Texas wagon train was an all-hands-on experience repeated daily for participants. Here, the train has arrived in Robstown in central Nueces County and is pulling into camp on February 15. A week earlier near Luling on February 6, the Grandy-sponsored wagon turned over in the middle of the highway. Travis and Alene Reeves, aunt and uncle of the wagon master, were not seriously injured.

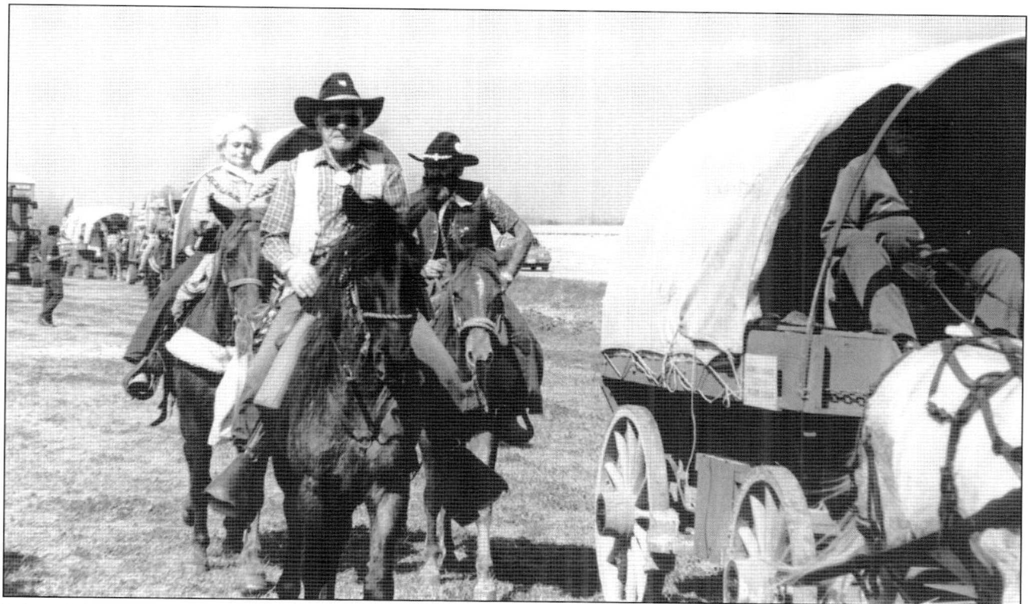

Many Texas counties are 30 miles square, which in the 19th century allowed farmers or ranchers to travel by horseback or wagon to reach the courthouse square in a full day. The county seat usually was located in the center of the county. A farmer/rancher could purchase supplies, handle business, or vote and drive home the next day. The distance the 1986 wagon train drove each day replicated this scenario.

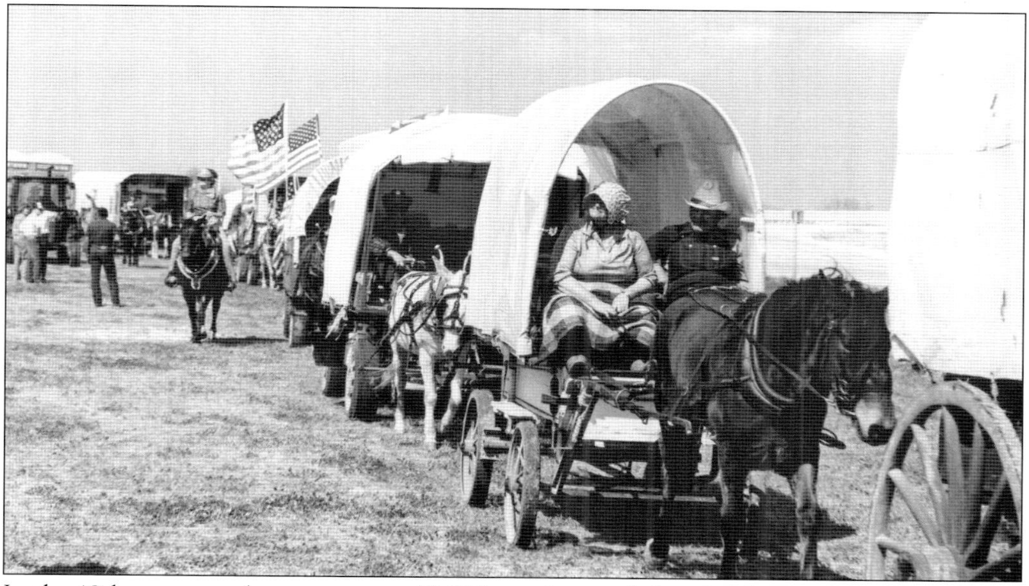

In the 19th century, when as many as 50,000 people traveled to California in 1849, overloaded wagons discarded items along the trail as animals tired or died. Hardships along the trail had to be expected for men, women, and children. Several husband-and-wife teams completed the entire trip in 1986 with the Texas train and wore pioneer clothing to please the crowds along the way. Many of them could look forward to a comfortable rest in their RVs, which were brought up to the campsite each evening.

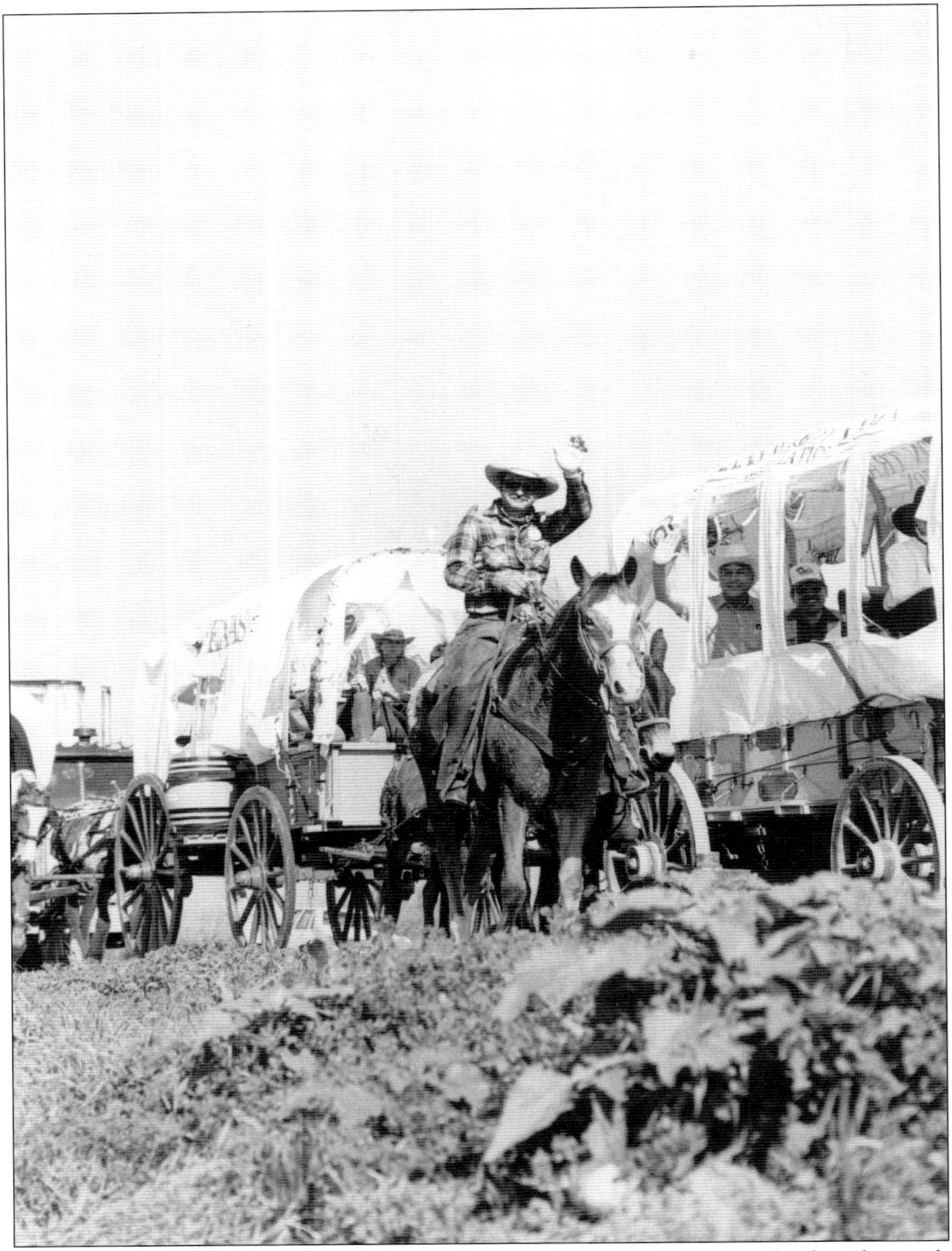

Note the "air-conditioned" feature of the windows on the wagon. Those proud to be riding with the wagon train give a friendly wave to the crowd. The train was headed to Robstown, which was established in 1903 and named for Robert Driscoll. Some participants took early retirement in order to ride with the train. Others even quit jobs to be able to partake of this once-in-a-lifetime experience.

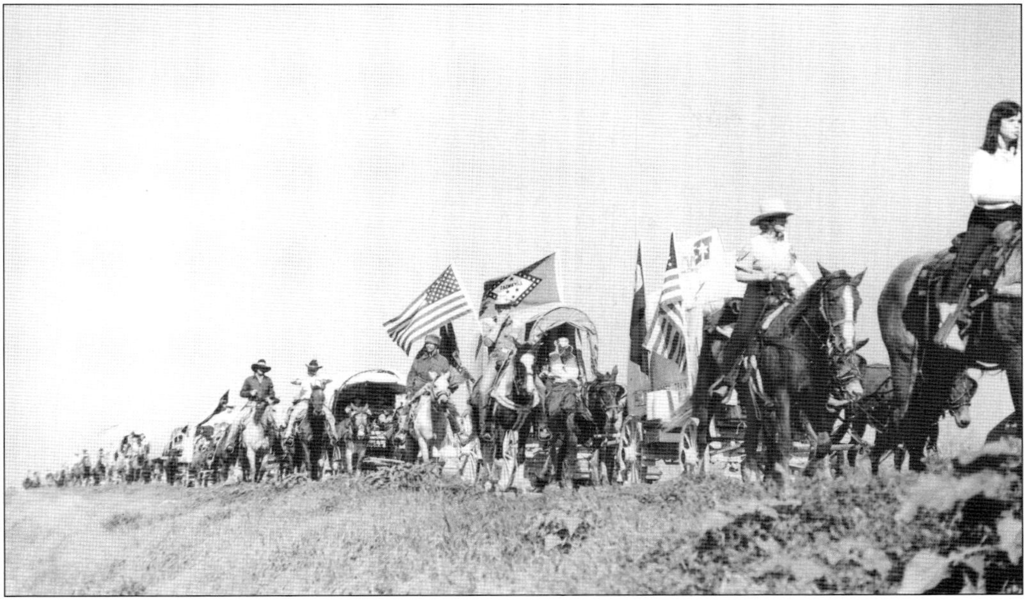

The logistics of the wagon train were impressive. The size of the event required rest stops every two hours for water and for wagon animals and riders to rest. The nightly circling of the wagons in camp was a slow ritual that townspeople enjoyed watching. The train remained authentic to its standards, because no motorized vehicles were allowed to travel with the train. They enjoyed space in the camp each evening, however.

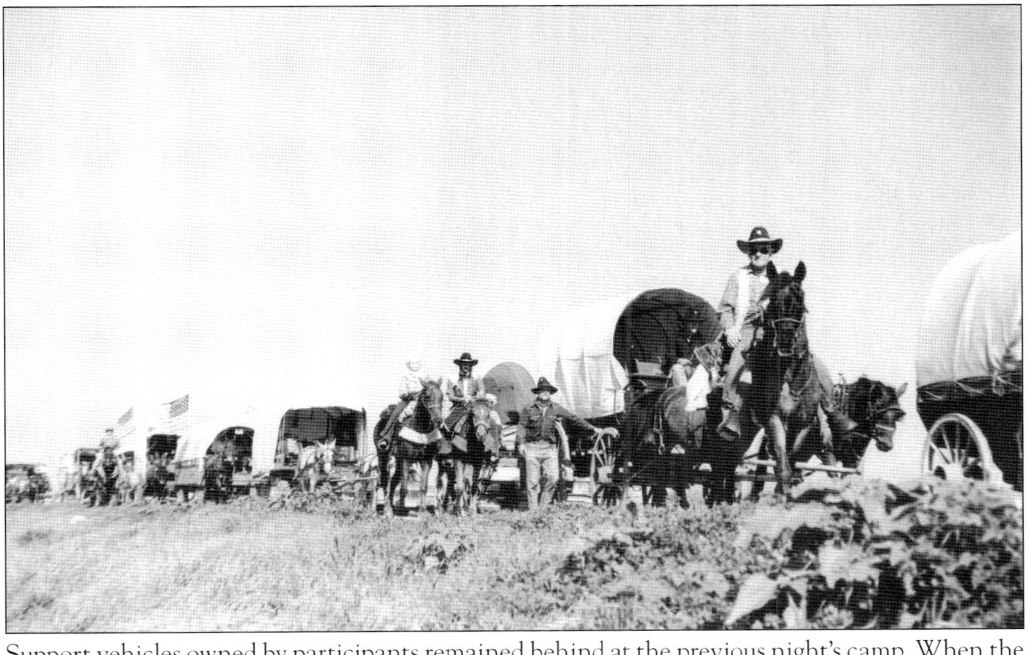

Support vehicles owned by participants remained behind at the previous night's camp. When the train had traveled its average of 20 miles to the next stop, drivers with support vehicles left their wagons and caught a shuttle back to the last camp, driving their vehicles to the new campsite. The train organization furnished two shuttles, but some towns volunteered buses as well.

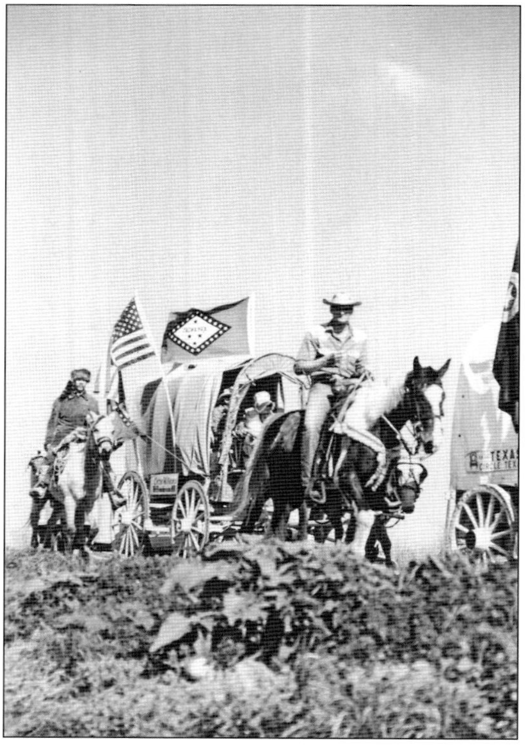

Previous campsites covered prior to this February 15 photograph included the Archie Roberts Ranch at Mendoza, Luling, Gonzales, Cheapside, Cuero, open camp, Goliad, Refugio, and Sinton. Gonzales and Goliad were two historic towns whose residents in 1836 fought the Mexicans in the Texas Revolution. On February 7, 1986, while the wagon train camped at Gonzales, the town fired the historic cannon that was the cause of the first shots of the Texas Revolution. It had also been brought to Sulphur Springs, and Jan France fired it for the kickoff ceremony. The cannon had been lost for a century, but was found in a creek bed and restored in 1936.

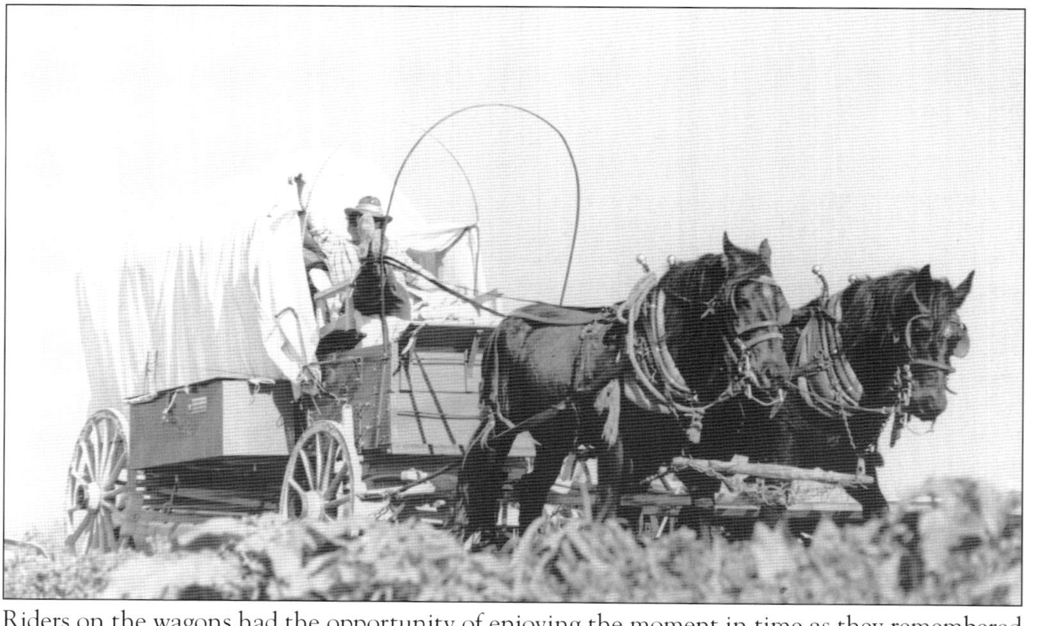

Riders on the wagons had the opportunity of enjoying the moment in time as they remembered the importance of what they were doing. History would come alive to them if they remembered the pioneers of the 19th century, who, in spite of hardships, found time to write in diaries and leave names and dates on rock outcrops or the sides of mountains. Some of the 1986 reenactors kept diaries too.

Horseback riders joined the wagon train for a day or two as the wagons arrived and passed through the various towns. Note the large American flag flying from the last wagon. Participants in the train stressed their patriotism for Texas and the United States as a major reason for joining the train. Horseback riders followed at the end of the train unless they were engaged in scouting for one of the wagons. No extra horses could be tied to the wagons in transit. They were left at camp and brought to the next campsite by trailer.

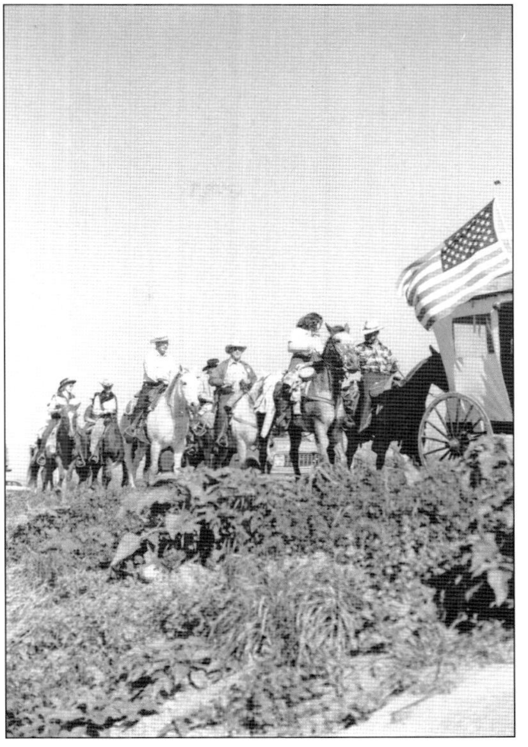

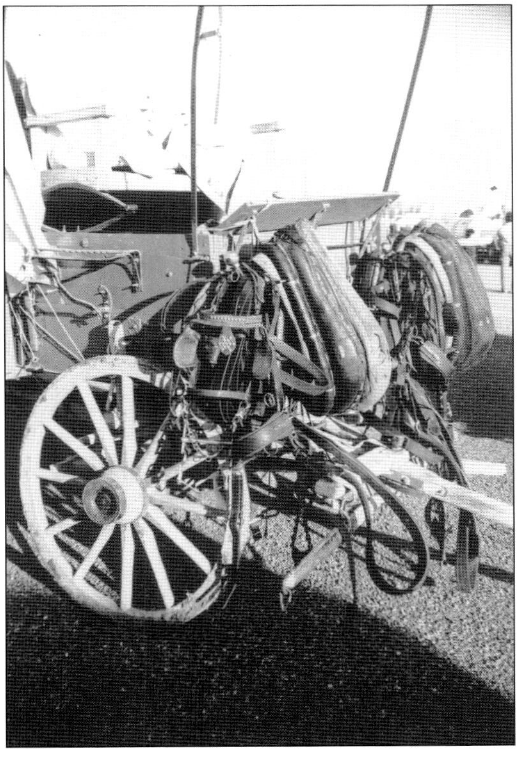

A lot of rigging existed for each wagon. Much manual labor was required to hitch the animals in the morning and unhitch them in the evening. From time to time, the gear needed repairs. Plenty of exertion on the trail came naturally for all hands. Folks did not need to think about an exercise program, unlike their friends who stayed home in the big cities.

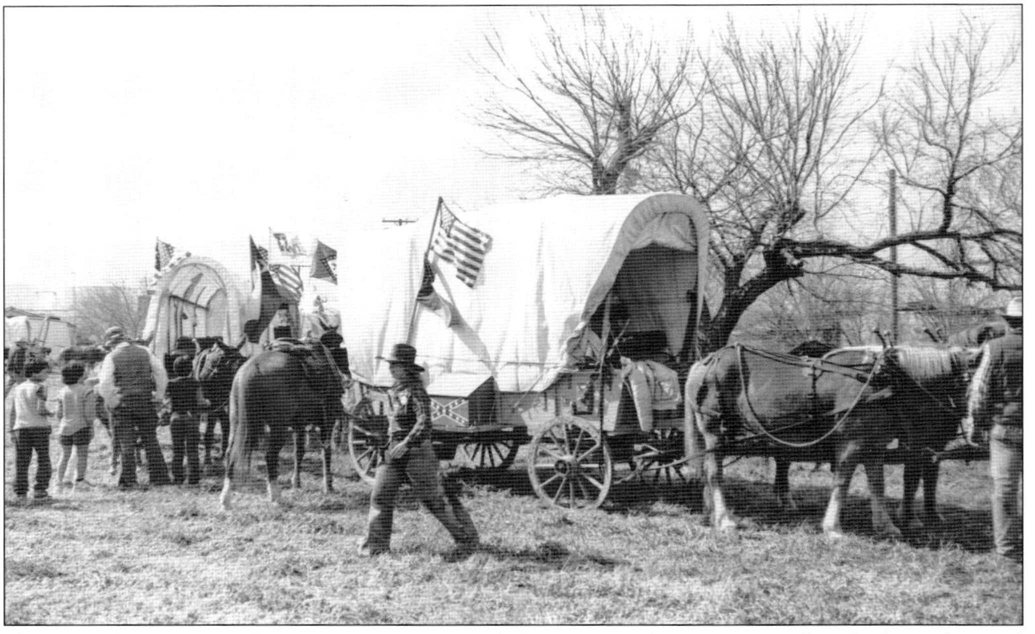

Photographer Dominick J. Cirincione snapped this picture during a water break along the trail as the train traveled to Kingsville for a layover of three days to let the riders and the animals rest and recuperate. Kingsville was named after the family that began the King Ranch. Richard King was a riverboat captain turned rancher who, with a partner, purchased land in South Texas in the middle of the 19th century.

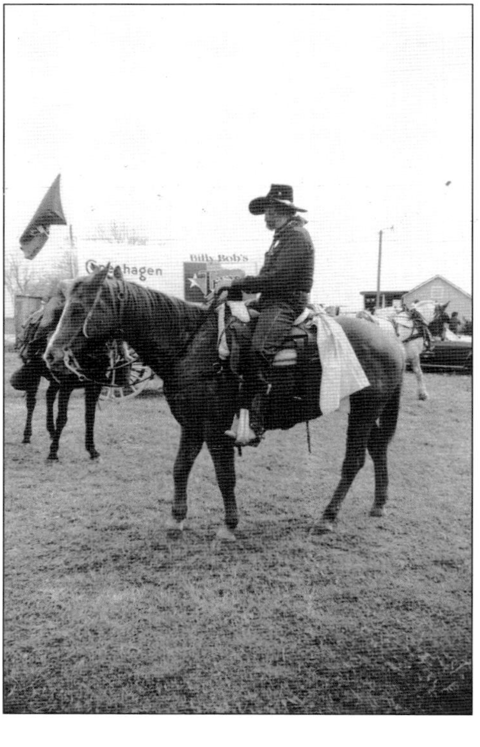

Kingsville was the next stop as wagon master Garry France mounted and got ready to lead the wagons out. Kingsville has a population of over 25,000 and is home to the King Ranch. It is the county seat of Kleberg County. After Richard King's daughter married Robert Kleberg, the ranch owners officially became the Kleberg family. Wagon master France, legally blind but a great horseman, used Vern Renz as his pacesetter and eyes. France rode beside Renz most of the time.

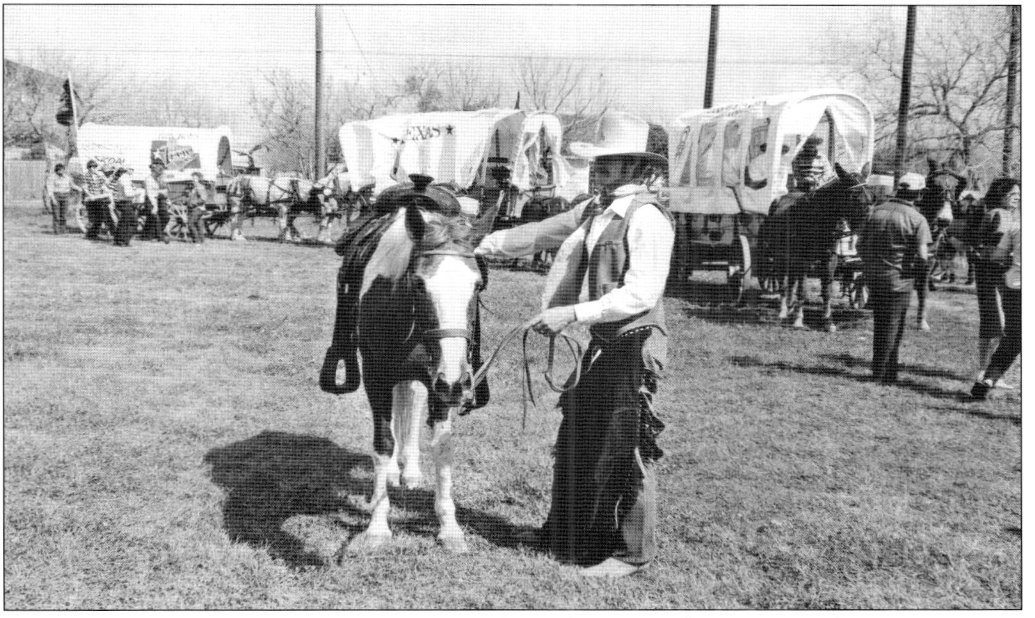

Taking care of one's horse at every rest stop along the way and at camp in the evening was a rider's primary responsibility. If one's mount needed a rest or developed a sore leg, it was possible to let it remain in camp and rest for a day or two. The rider could hitch a ride on a wagon or the stagecoach for the trip that day. After all, the camp was only 20 miles or so back, and a trailer could bring the horse up to the current camp. In all, 13,000 horses and mules were involved in the wagon train during its six-month trip.

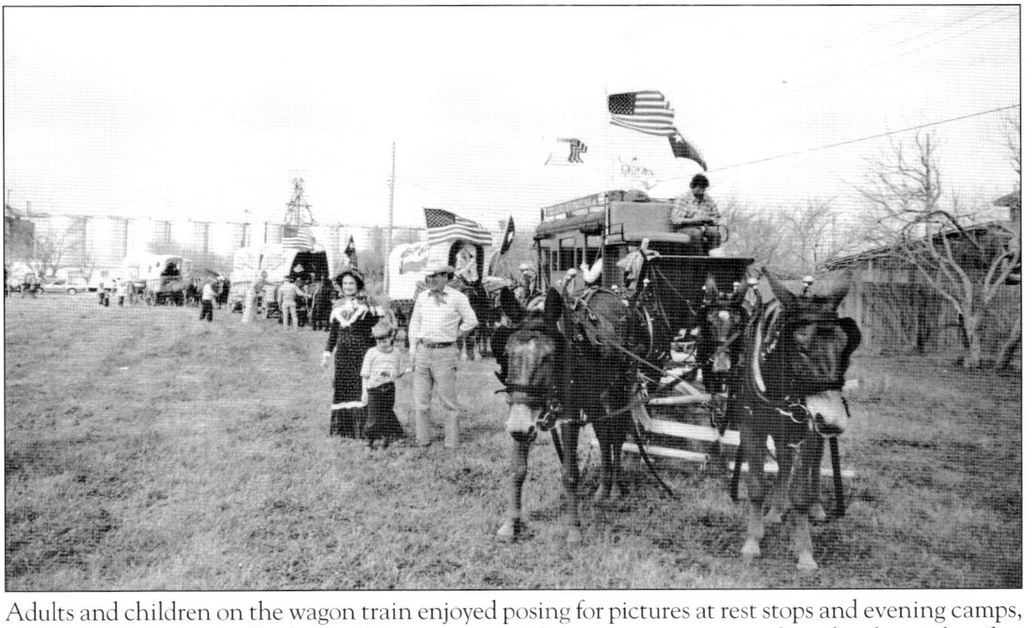

Adults and children on the wagon train enjoyed posing for pictures at rest stops and evening camps, especially if they proudly dressed like pioneers. These wagons were circling for the night after having driven from Robstown through Driscoll to Kingsville near the King Ranch. Santa Gertrudis Creek ran through the King Ranch, giving the name to the breed of cattle raised on the ranch.

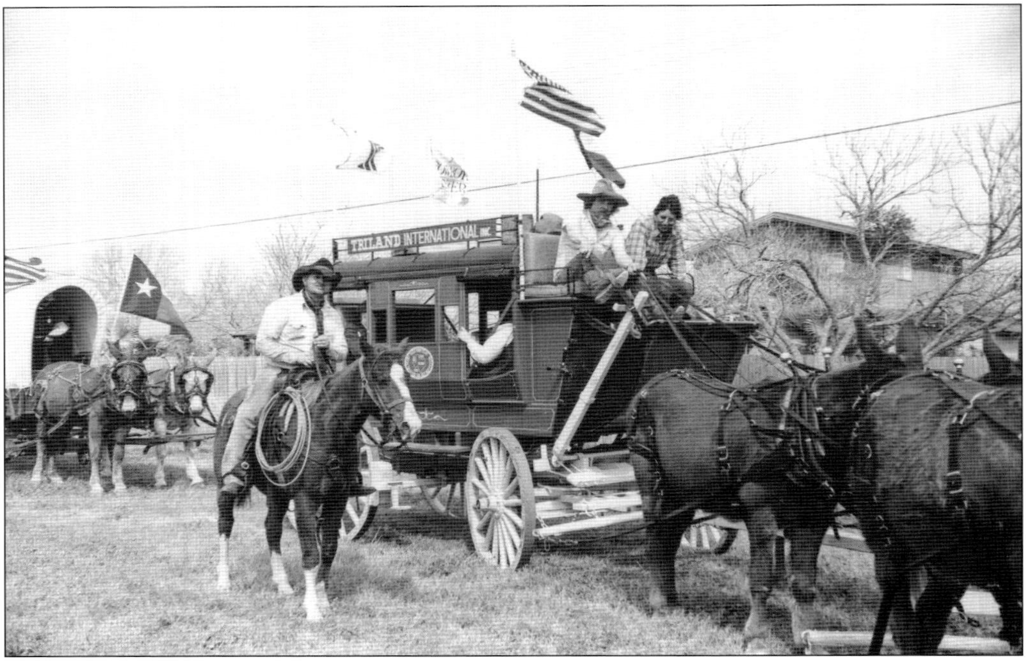

Land and commercial development group Triland International, Inc., one of the official sponsors, hired Rudy Nelson to drive the only stagecoach in the wagon train. Triland, along with other sponsors, contributed various materials for the train and its support staff of 45. The wagon train received no government grants. Shown by the train is Edward "Gotcheye" Gaston, who insisted upon the use of his nickname. A horse trampled him when he was a youngster and tore up his eye.

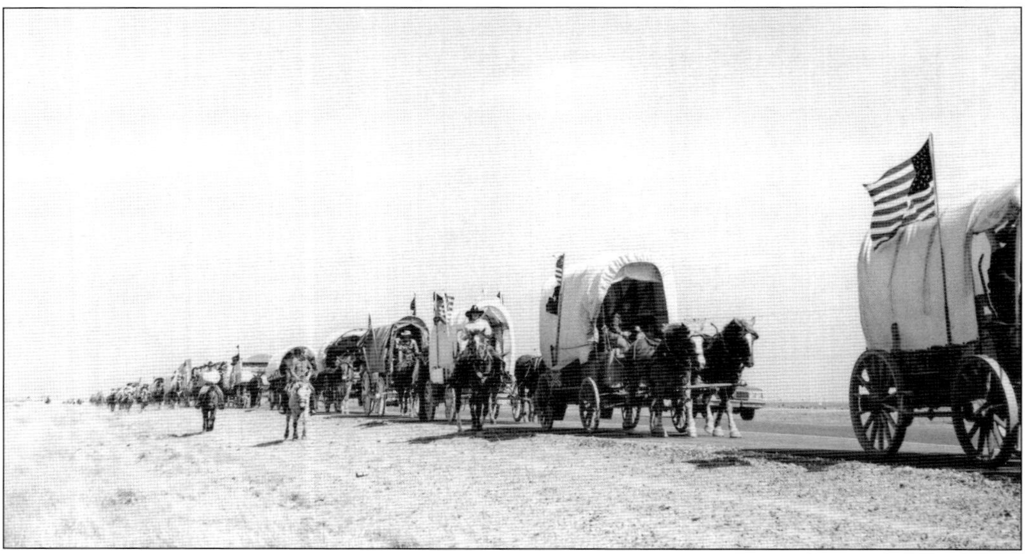

Folks driving the back roads and interstate highways of Texas during the six months that the wagon train traveled reveled at the impressive sights of the sometimes two- or four-mile wagon train trailing off into the distance. Many of the wagons flew US and Texas flags. Several of the participants had been a part of the 1976 US bicentennial wagon trains that converged before reaching Valley Forge, Pennsylvania.

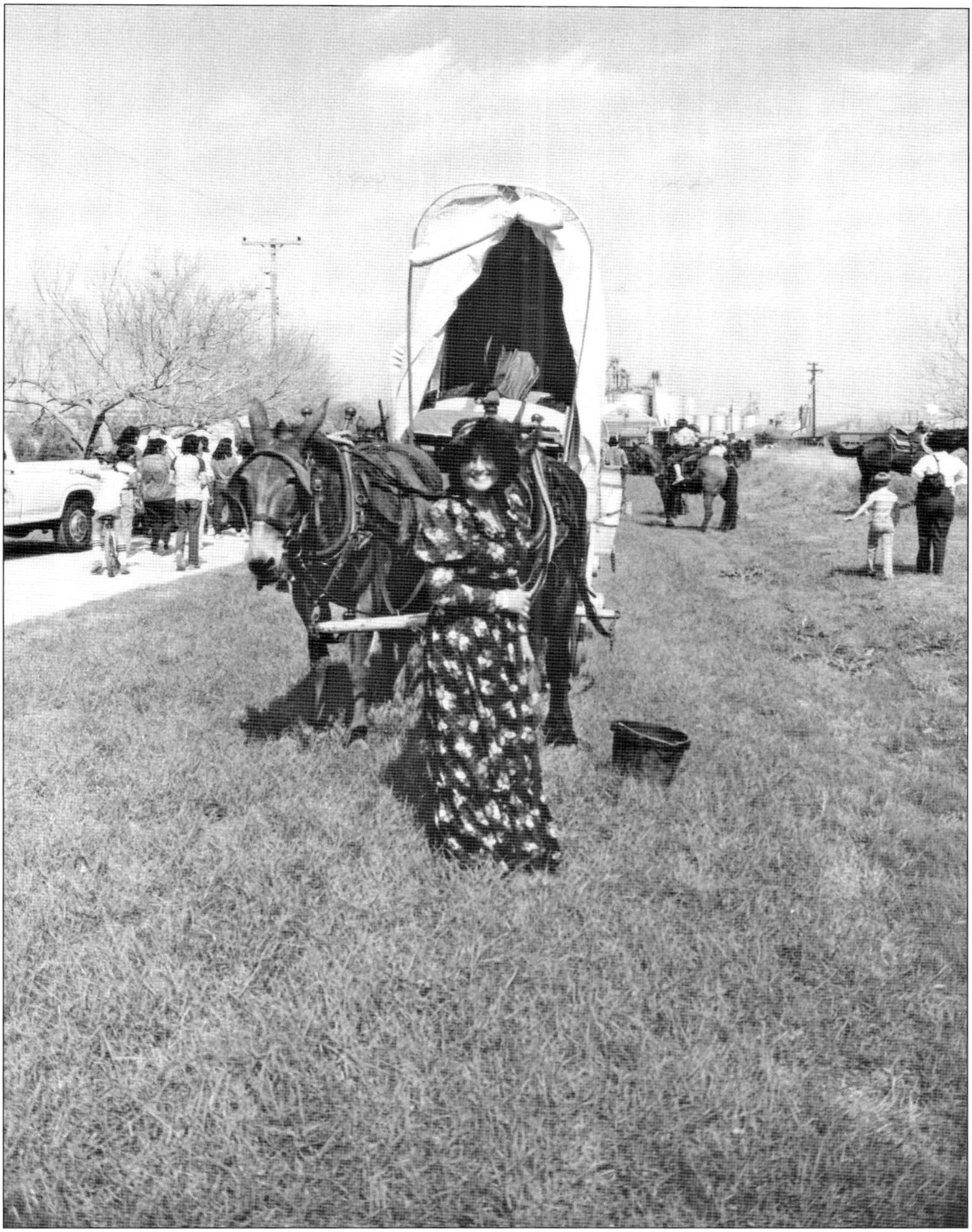

During a break along the trail, this participant in her pioneer dress is happy to pose for the camera. Riders in the train sometimes felt like actors in a pageant as they rolled into each town and waved to the citizens who had come out to greet them. Jan France, executive director of the train association, had replicas made of an antique dress housed in the Annie Riggs Museum in Fort Stockton and wore them. The dress featured denim riding pants that looked like a skirt. Having worked with every town and its committee for the previous three years, Jan had invited officials to join her for a ride on the train as thanks for their long, hard planning.

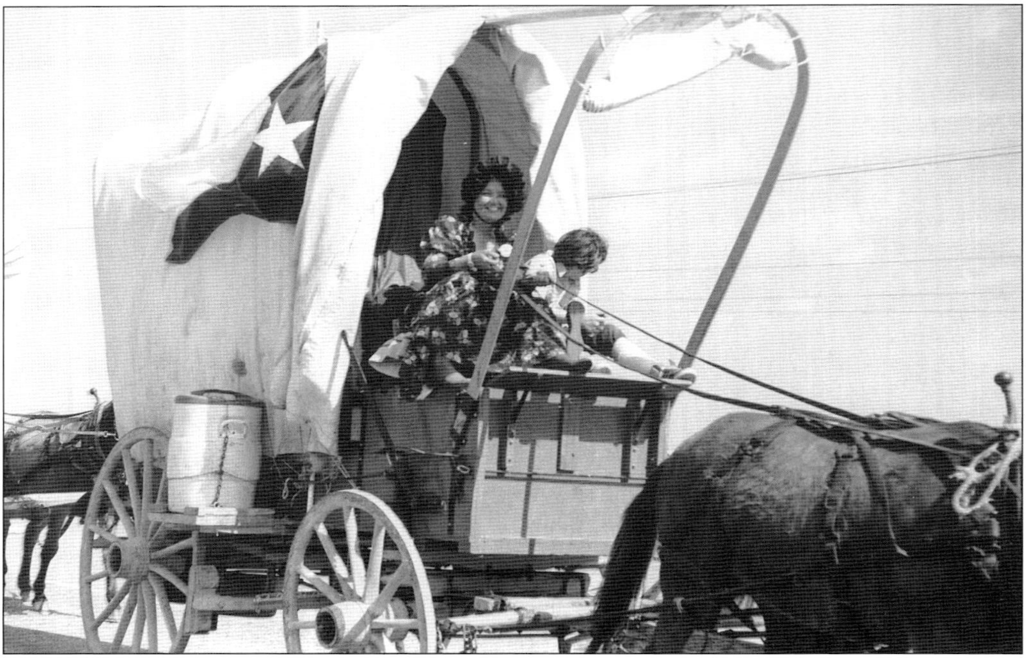

With her posing over, it was time for the pioneer-dressed lady to get back on board her wagon and share the exhilarating experience with a family member. It was obvious to all who saw her that she was enjoying the ride. Here, the train is traveling near Bishop in southwestern Nueces County. In the 1920s, it was known as the "Cotton Capital of the Coast."

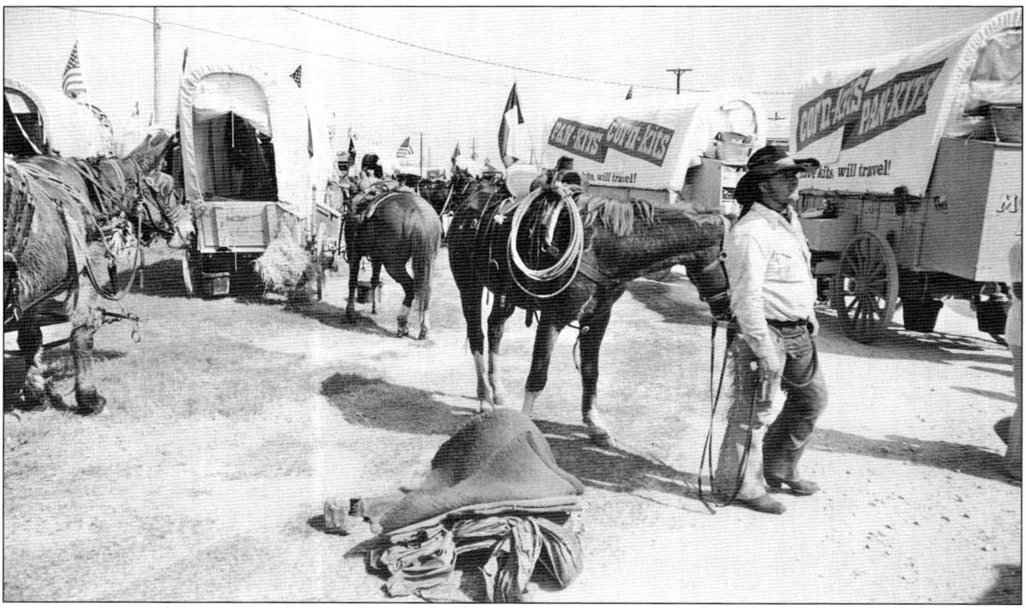

The two Morrison Milling Company Corn-Kits wagons are circling with the others to set up camp in Kingsville. A cowboy outrider is contemplating where to go with his horse. Sometimes in camp, volunteers pitched in to help a driver whose wagon had been damaged by runaway horses. Often they worked until late at night to be ready to go by the next morning.

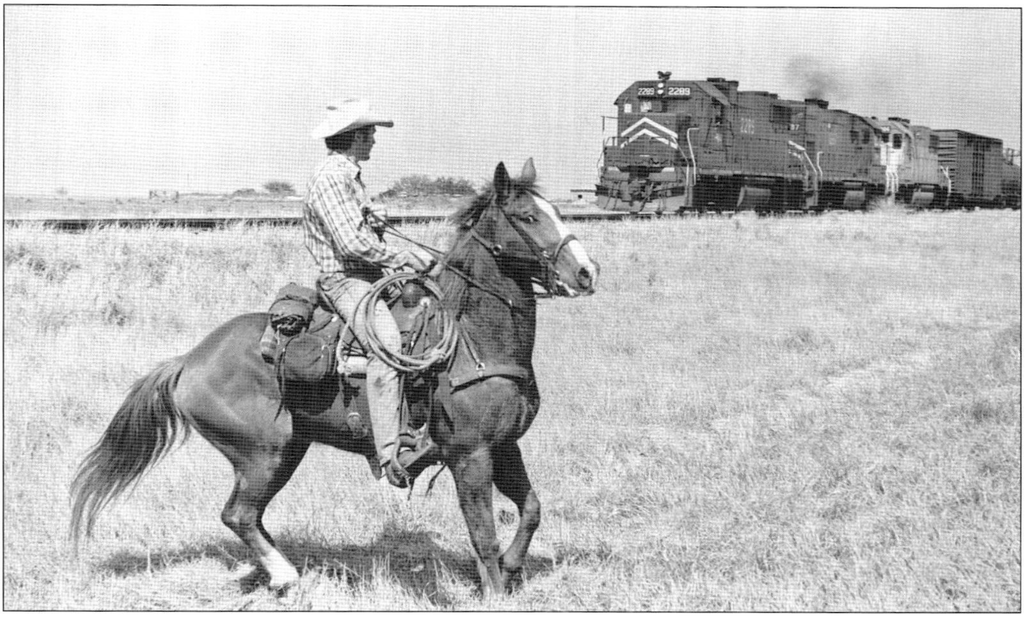

A flesh-and-blood horse meets what many first called an iron horse, with the result that the former was on the verge of bolting at full speed. One blast from the iron horse would result in a horse and rider in panic mode. Note the horse's eye and posture. The noises coming from the train are making him very uncomfortable. Many a horse bolted during the trip.

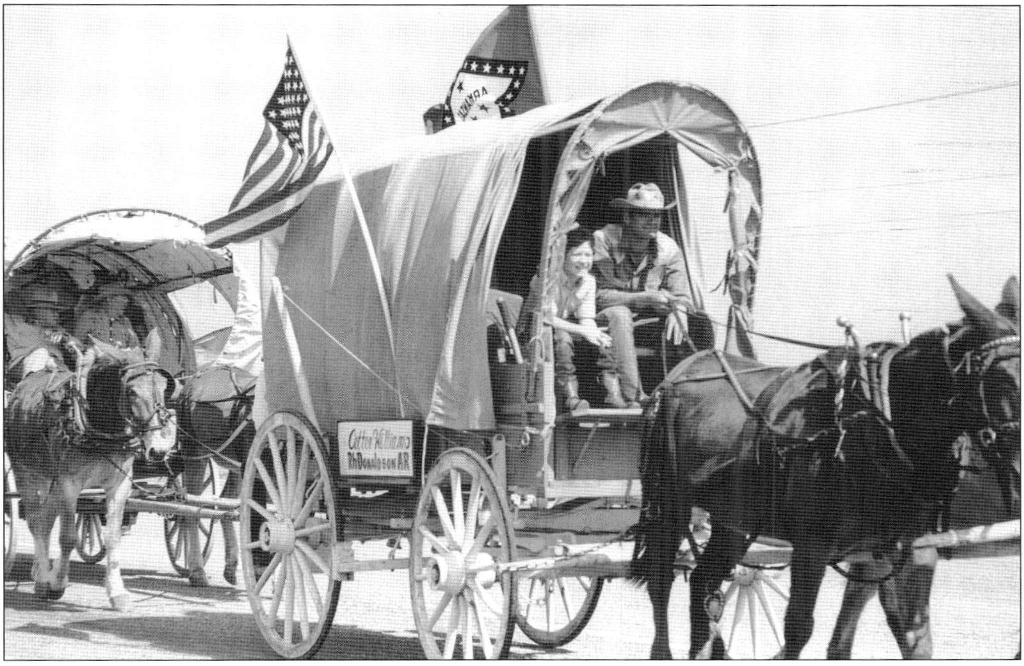

The flag to the right is the Arkansas state flag. All states were invited to send someone to participate in the wagon train. Cotton Williams, who had represented Arkansas in the US bicentennial with a wagon, also participated in the Texas wagon train as the official Arkansas representative.

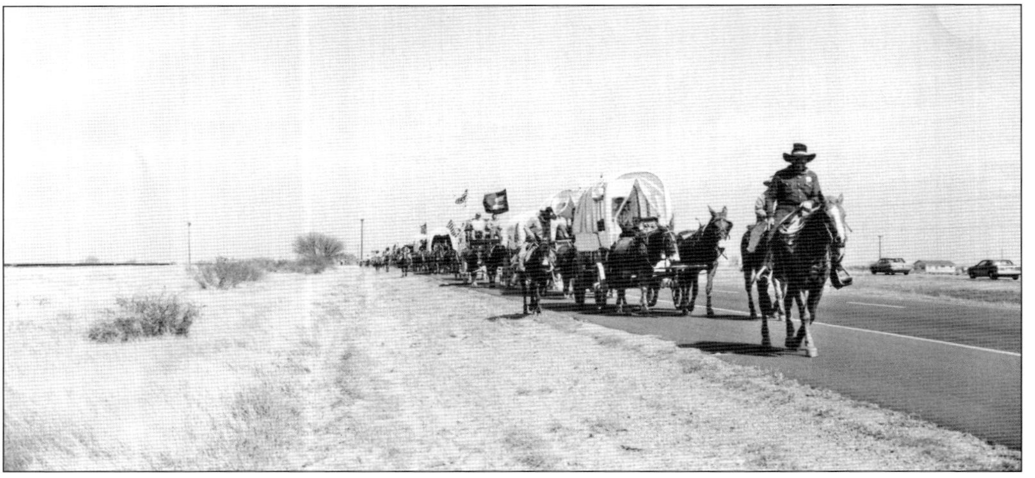

In real life, the wagon master called the shots in the Old West. The wagon train started and stopped by his orders. He was the boss. When the beaver fur trade ended, mountain men familiar with the trails out west became wagon masters to lead pioneers to Oregon. One estimate is that over a 30-year period between 1840 and 1870, some 300,000 migrants headed west by wagon train on one-way journeys. The East Coast wagon builders were kept busy until the railroad linked the eastern and western limits of the United States.

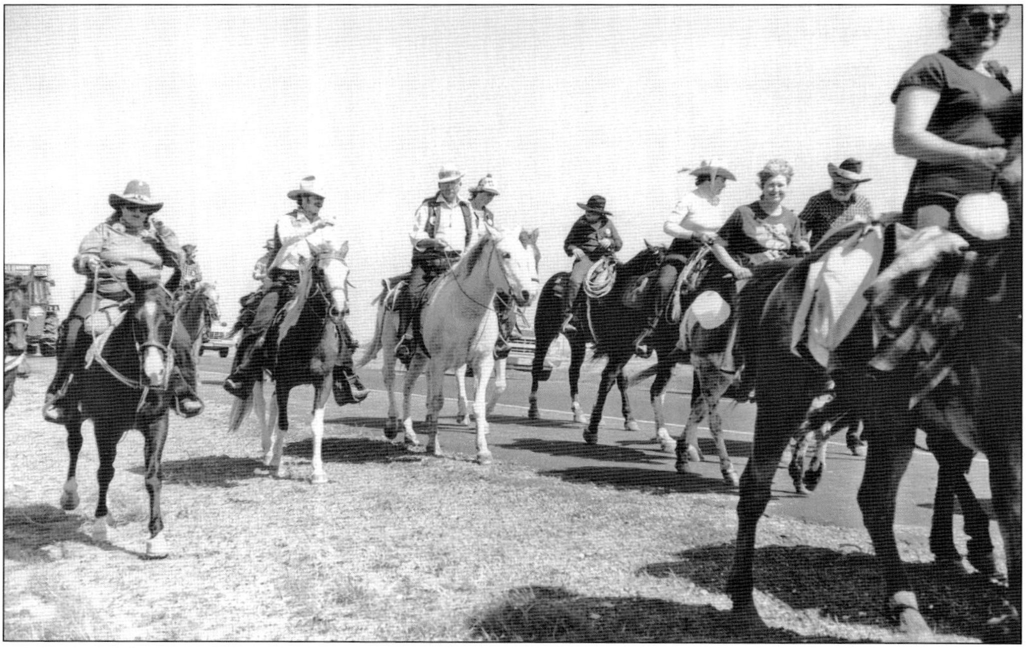

In many of the towns in 1986, riders from that community and their horses joined at the end of the train so that they could wave at their friends, accumulate memories, and tell their grandchildren that they took part in this historic ride. The wagon train organization limited the horseback riders on any one day to 300. Official outriders rode alongside the horseback riders at the back of the train to help them in case anyone's horse became restless. Chief outrider Viola Cook, also chief outrider in 1976 in the bicentennial wagon train, had help from Jo Anne Thielemann and Jeff Shepherd.

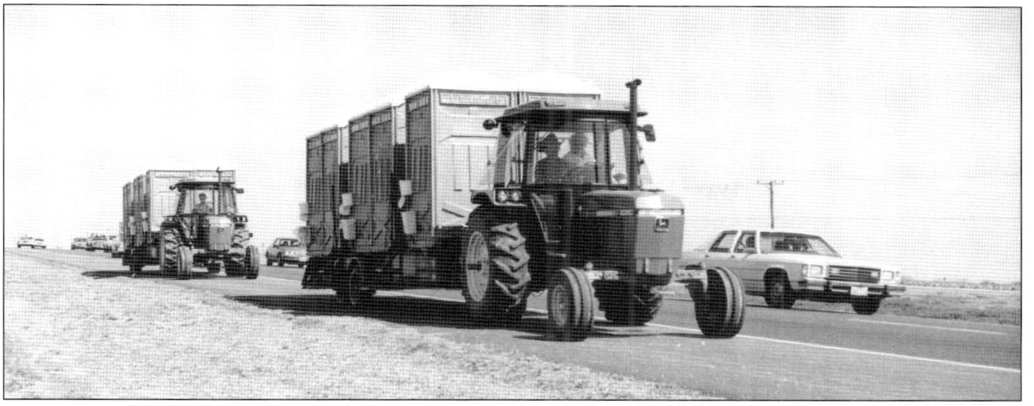

Two of the four large tractors carrying blue portable toilets were traveling the interstate to arrive at the evening's campsite ahead of the train. With at least 200 riders, support staff, and hangers-on with the train on any day, the facilities certainly were needed and welcomed. These were modern conveniences that those arrivals to Texas in 1836 never enjoyed. Folks called the potties the "Blue Room." One participant even wrote a song about the blue room that the campers enjoyed hearing at one of their evening shows.

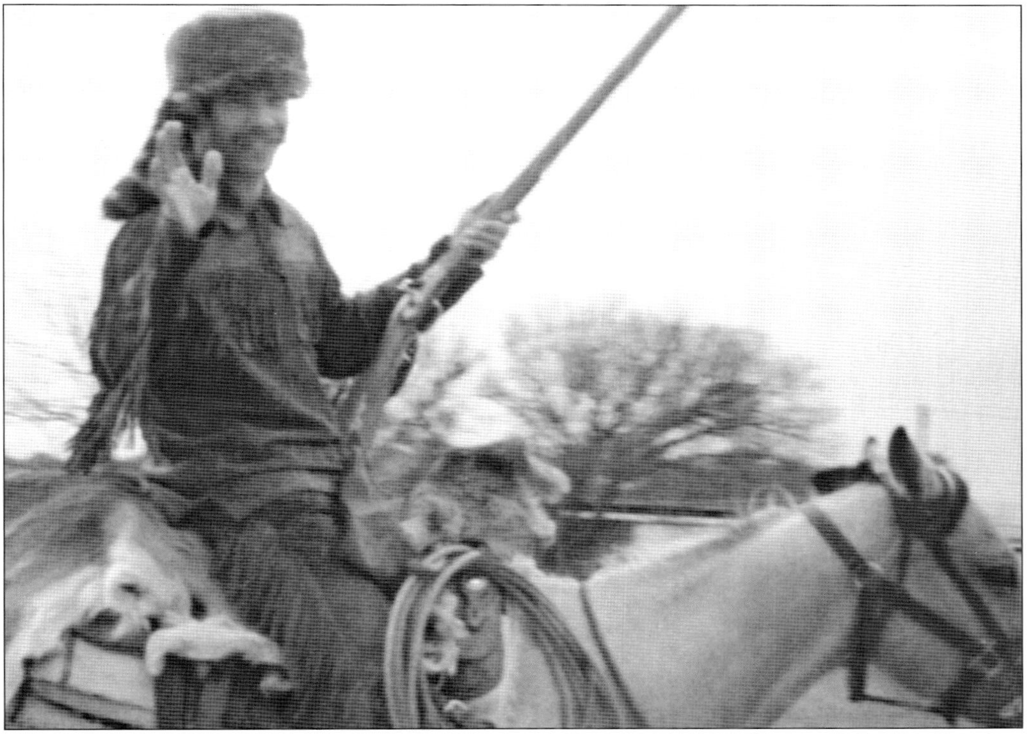

This is not Davy Crockett or Daniel Boone, even though he looks like it with his coonskin cap. Riders enjoyed being as historically authentic as possible. After all, their wagon train was a 150-year step back into the past, and their clothing might as well be, too. Planning from the beginning made sure that the wagon train was in San Antonio on Texas Independence Day, March 2. The train circled the Alamo, where the most famous battle occurred and where 187 Texans died defending freedom. (Courtesy Azle Historical Museum.)

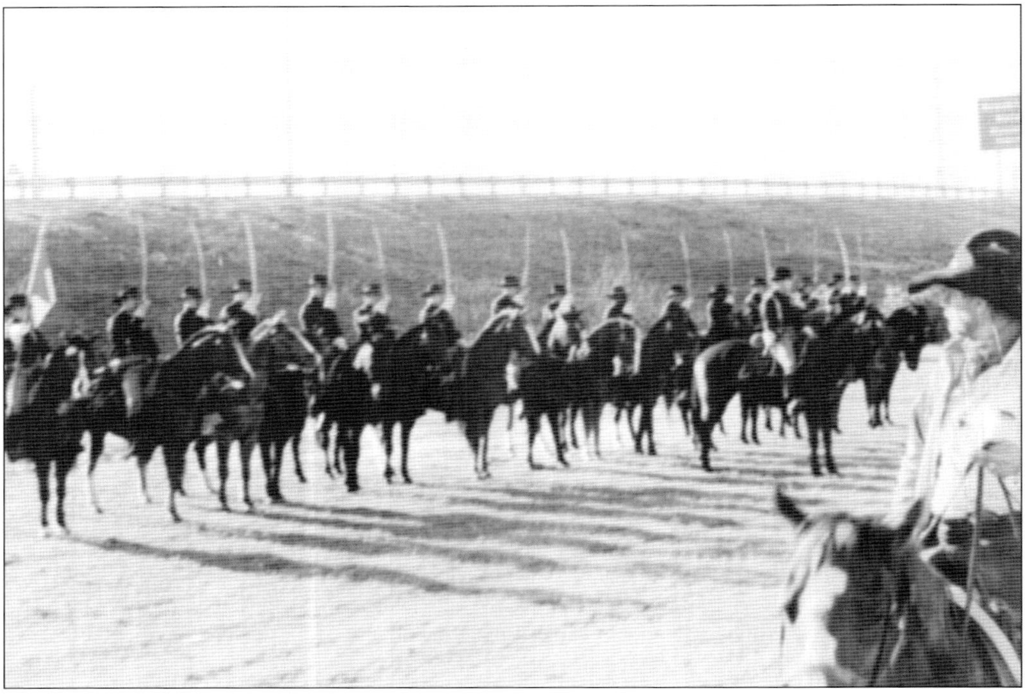

The 1st Cavalry Division Horse Platoon lined up in San Antonio in preparing to march around the Alamo with the wagon train. At the beginning of the journey, at important points in between (like the Alamo), and at the end, the Fort Hood unit came to support the train. (Courtesy Quentin McGown.)

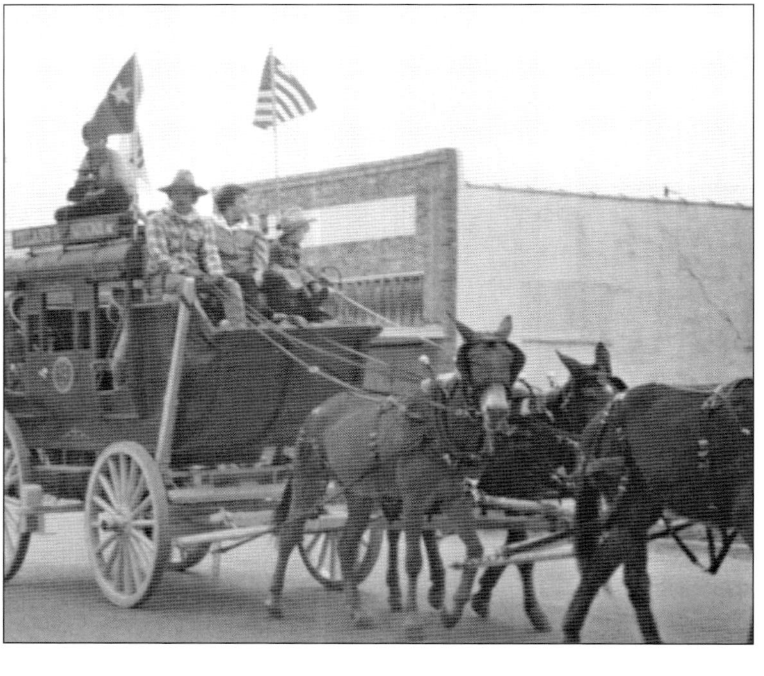

Rudy Nelson enjoyed having company as he drove the lone stagecoach of the train. Here, the train is passing through the town of Menard on March 14. In the days prior to reaching Menard, the train had camped at the Lyndon B. Johnson State Park at Johnson City, Fredericksburg, Kerrville, Hunt, and three ranches—Felix Kline Ranch, YO Ranch, and the Tillman Ranch near Junction. (Courtesy Azle Historical Museum.)

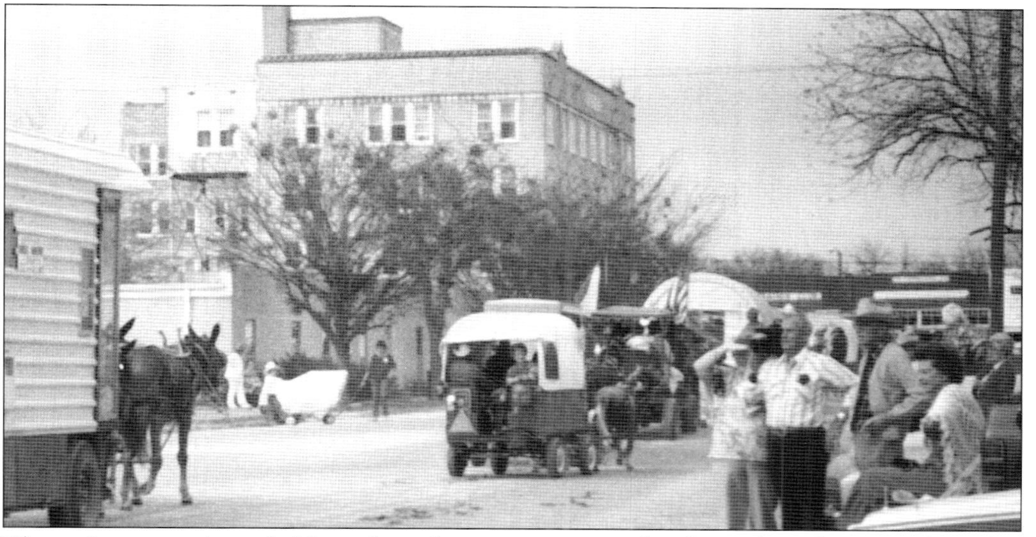

The train passes through Menard on the way to its stop for the night. The Spanish settled Menard, building a mission and presidio, but they abandoned it by 1758. Indians used it as a camp. Later, settlers came through looking for a lost silver mine. By 1867, Menardville had a trading post and was a stop for the cattle drives. Menard County was organized in 1871. (Courtesy Azle Historical Museum.)

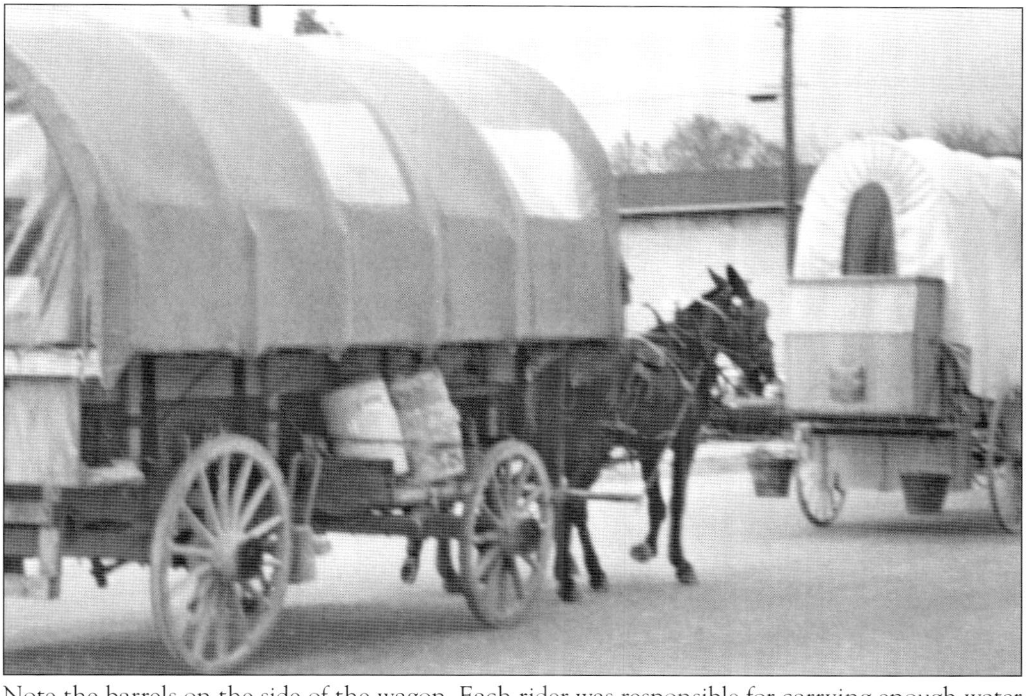

Note the barrels on the side of the wagon. Each rider was responsible for carrying enough water for himself and his animals for one day. The wagon train staff supplied a 6,500-gallon tanker truck with water for refilling of barrels in camp. Most towns supplied water for the camp water wagon. A Purina vehicle drove the entire route to offer feed for the owners to purchase for their animals. (Courtesy Azle Historical Museum.)

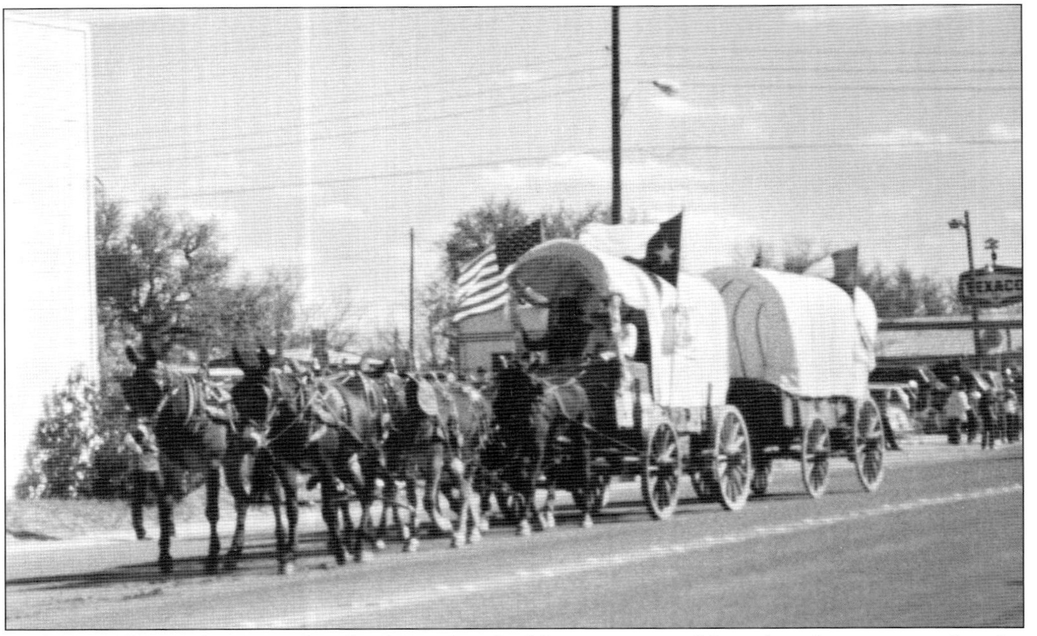

Both a US flag and a Texas flag fly above this double-wagon unit. Note that three teams of mules are necessary to pull the two wagons. Participants in the train commented later that upon many occasions they simply choked up as they experienced the appreciation from spectators in each town and remembered the history they were creating. (Courtesy Azle Historical Museum.)

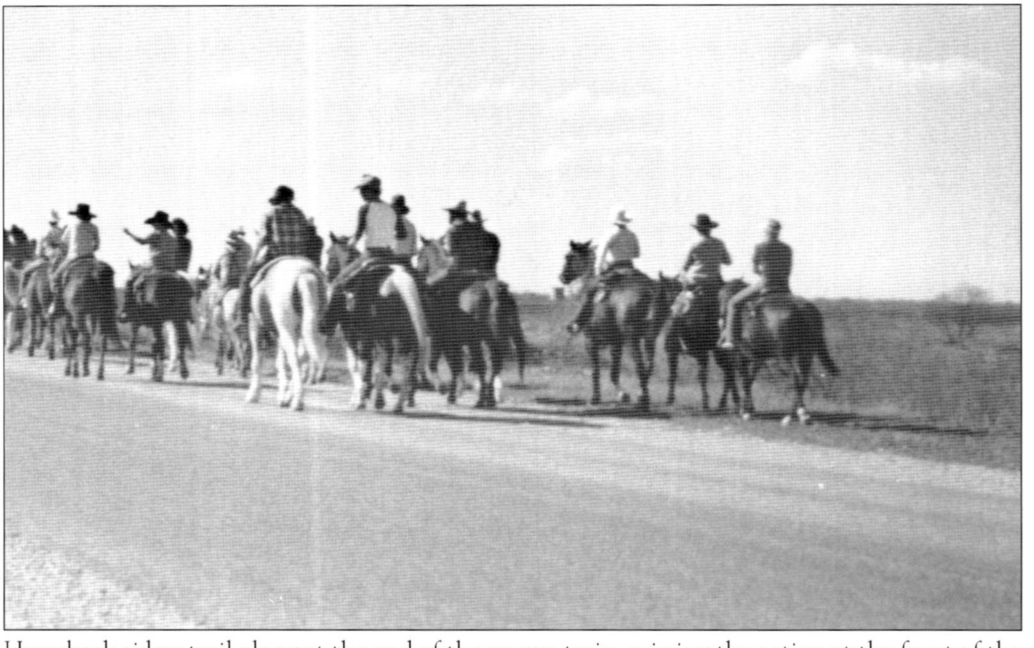

Horseback riders trail along at the end of the wagon train, missing the action at the front of the train when it pulled into a new town but experiencing all the dust the horses kicked up. Viola Cook, who was head outrider in the US bicentennial wagon train, served as head outrider for horseback riders to help keep the horses and their riders settled. (Courtesy Azle Historical Museum.)

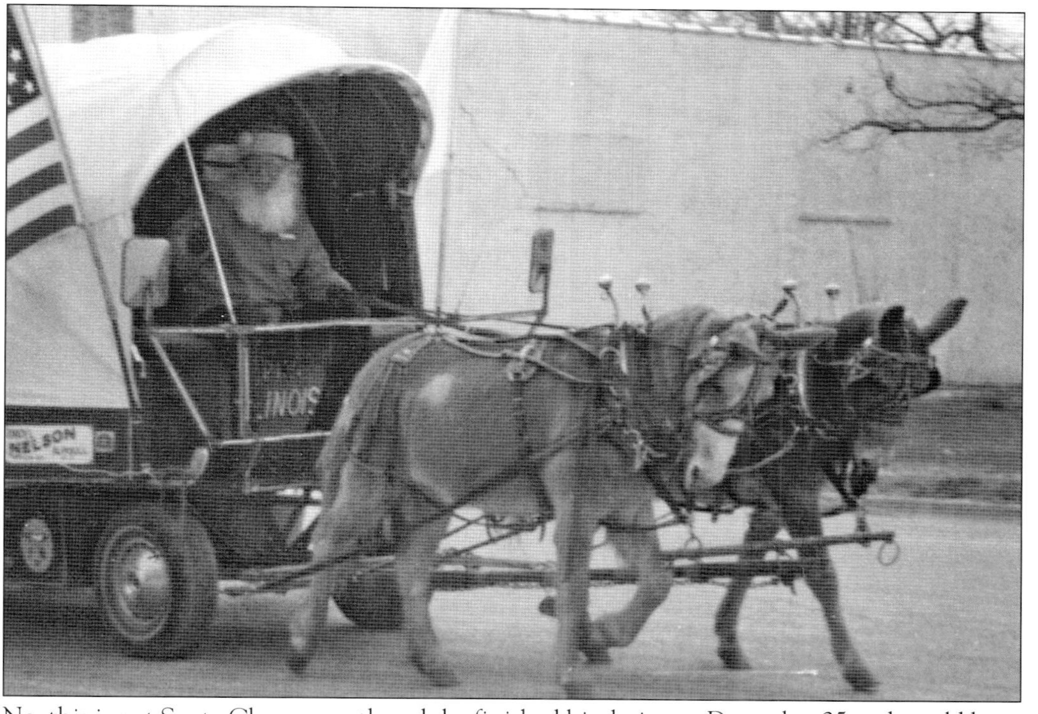

No, this is not Santa Claus, even though he finished his duties on December 25 and would have had plenty of time to join the train that spring of 1986. Macy Nelson, the man in the white beard, was not the real St. Nick, but folks called him "Santa" anyway. He hailed from Alpha, Illinois, not the North Pole. (Courtesy Azle Historical Museum.)

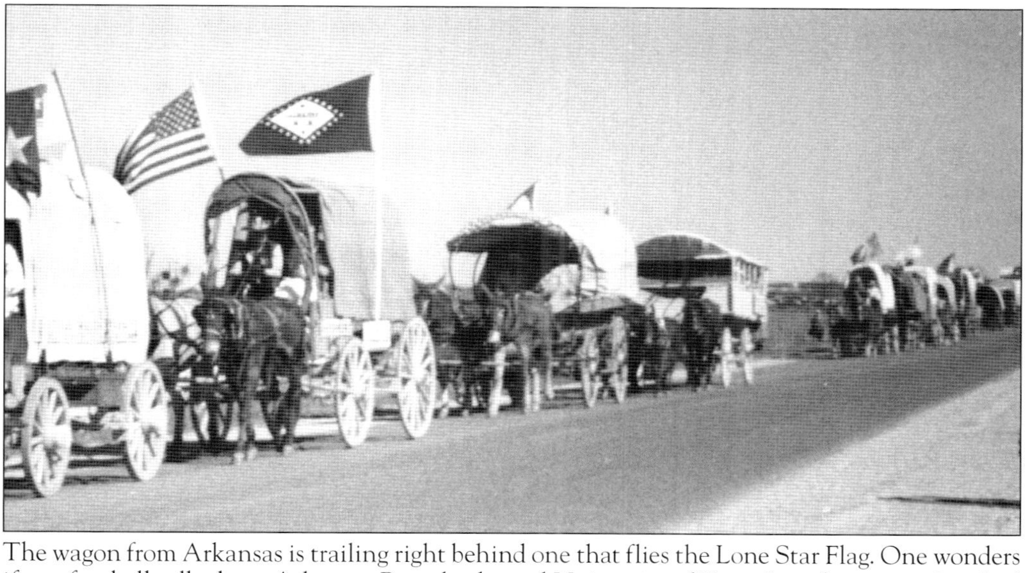

The wagon from Arkansas is trailing right behind one that flies the Lone Star Flag. One wonders if any football talk about Arkansas Razorbacks and University of Texas Longhorns was bandied back and forth. In her early planning for the Texas wagon train, Jan France knew that most of the 1936 centennial activities centered in Dallas. She wanted the 1986 observance to include not only all of Texas but other states as well. (Courtesy Azle Historical Museum.)

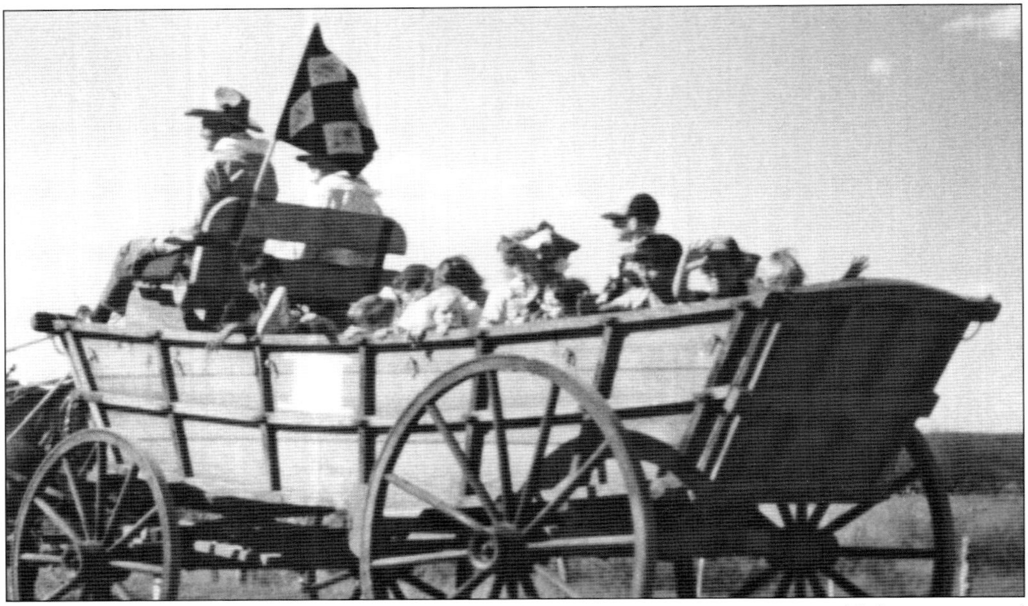

Spectators along the streets in Menard probably did not expect to see a "convertible" open-topped wagon, unless this was one that joined for only the one day from the town itself. All those kids aboard probably did not care, because they were enjoying the ride. Two weeks later, when the train reached Balmorhea on March 30, it was Easter Sunday. The town was only three blocks long when they were there, but it held an Easter egg hunt for the children. (Courtesy Azle Historical Museum.)

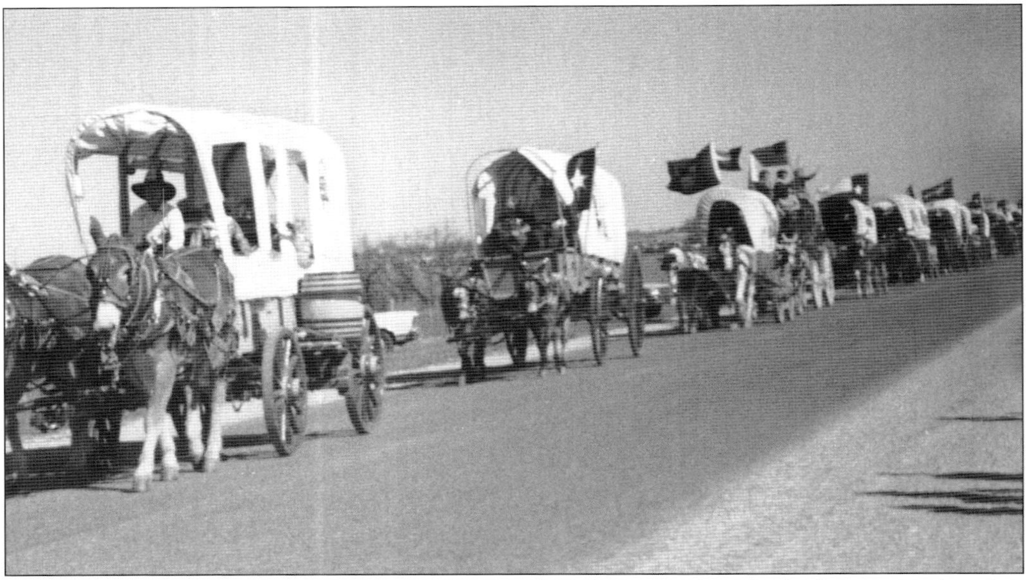

Imagine how automobile or pickup truck drivers felt if they turned on the highway to realize that they needed to share the road with a long string of canvas-covered wagons drawn by mules or horses. Anyone unaware that the wagon train was coming, however, would have been unusual. People in each town anticipated the wagon train's visit for weeks, if not years. (Courtesy Azle Historical Museum.)

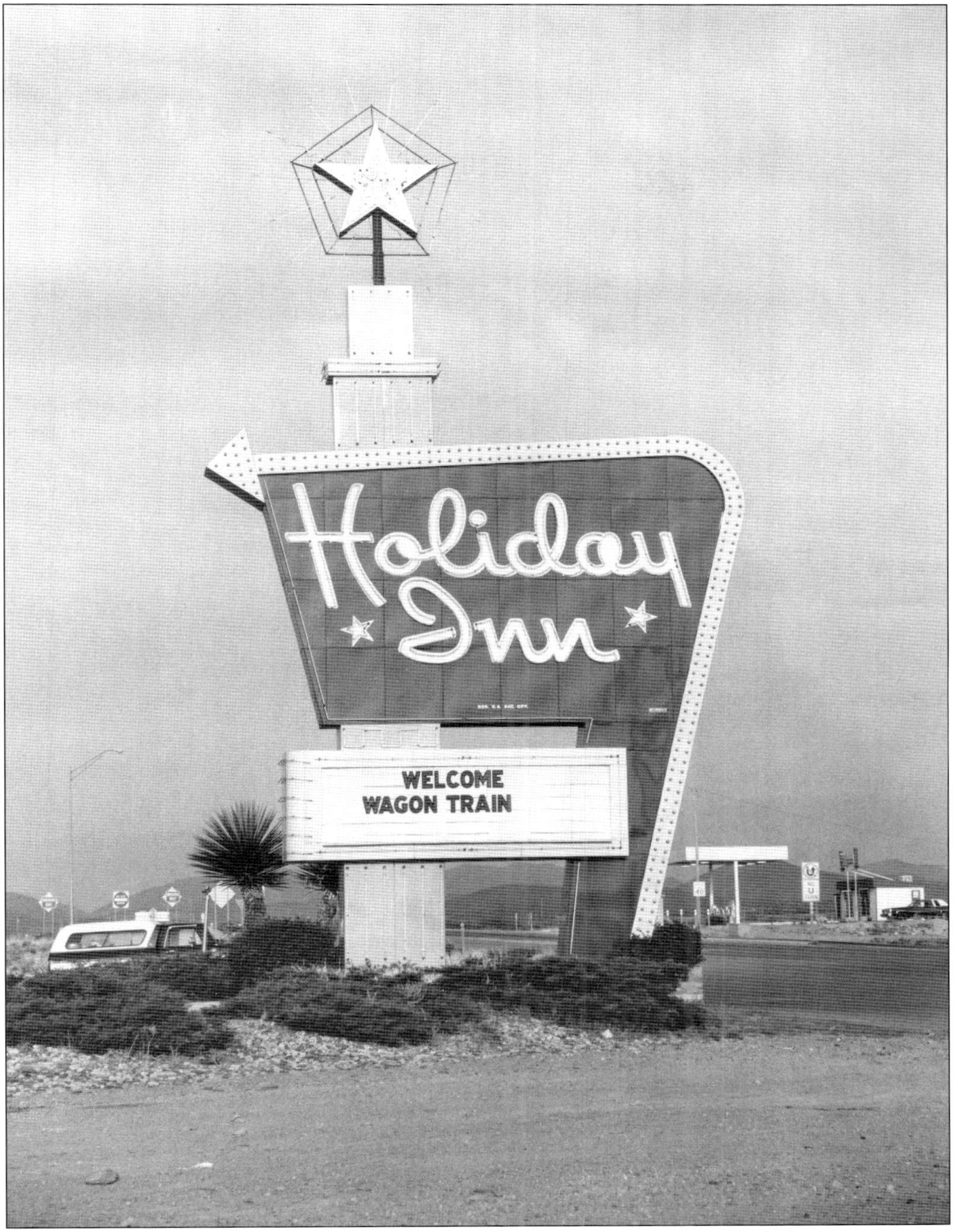

This is a typical sign welcoming the wagon train. Whenever the wagons circled near a town for the night, townspeople often put on the feed for the participants—barbecue, drinks, and music to celebrate the visit. This Holiday Inn was located in Van Horn. The train made a two-day stop there April 3–4 after passing through McCamey, Fort Stockton, Balmorhea, and Kent the previous few days. Kent had a population of 17 people, but they served cake and ice cream to everyone on the train.

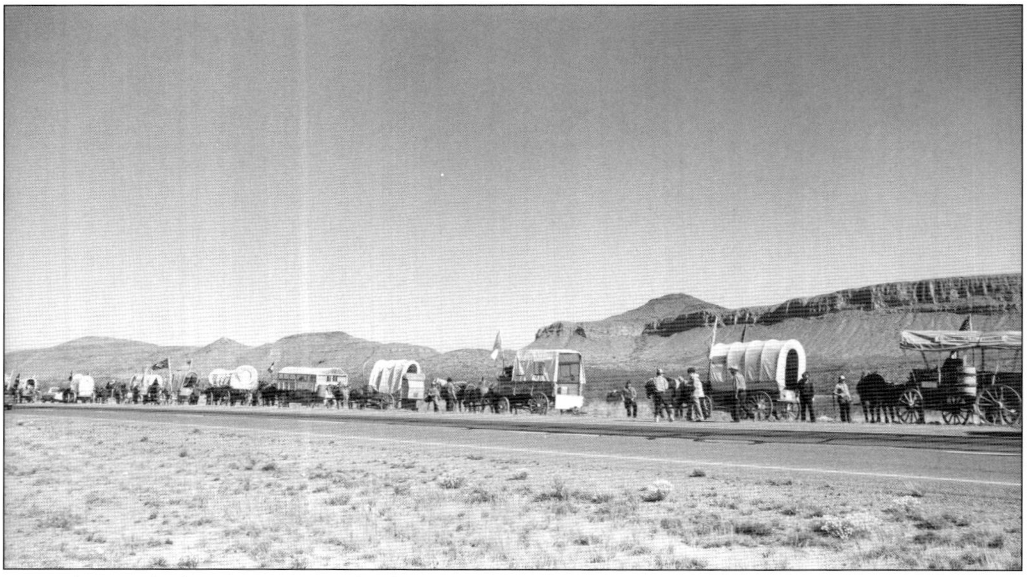

By early April, the wagon train had nearly reached the Big Bend area of Texas, so it saw less rainfall. Hot, dry weather could cause wooden wheel spokes to loosen, as water will tend to tighten the wooden wheel joints as the wood expanded. The rustic background contributed to the wagon train experience for the participants. Some of the best photographs of the trip have mountains in the background.

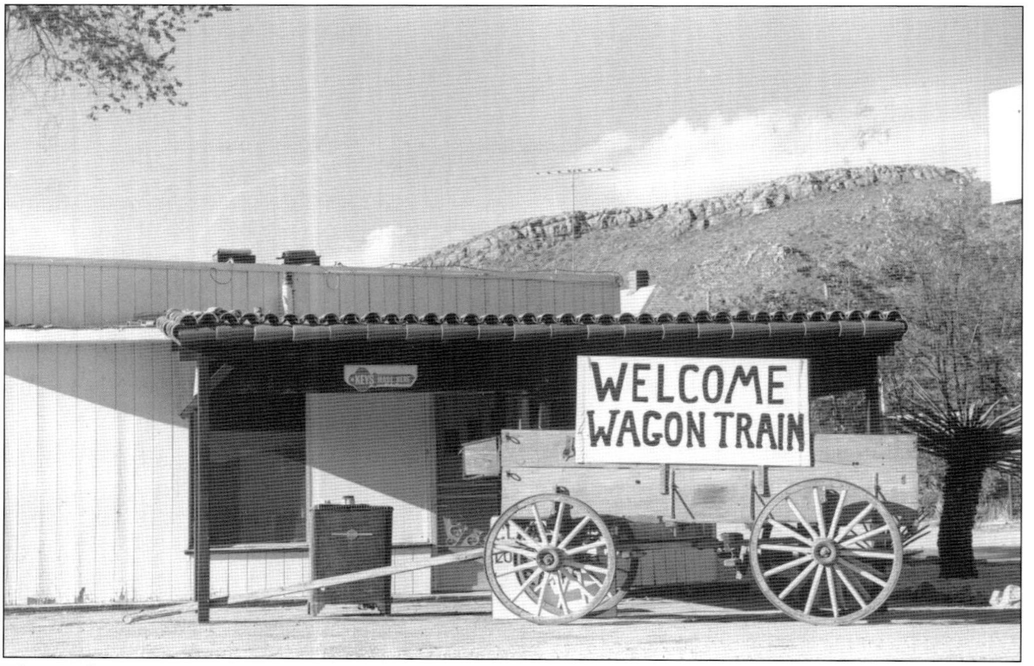

This welcome sign is appropriately on a wagon in Sierra Blanca, with Sierra Blanca Peak rising behind it. Some towns provided food for all the members of the wagon train. A food concession was available, however, as a part of the services the Texas Wagon Train Association provided. Each rider or driver paid his or her own expenses along the way.

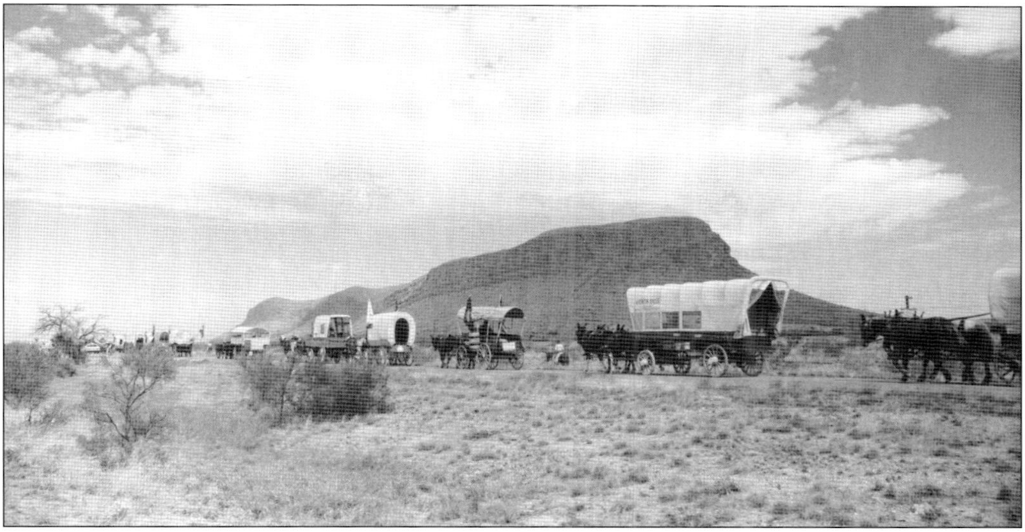

Sierra Blanca Peak provides a fitting background for this scene, which is reminiscent of old-time Westerns. The train is leaving Sierra Blanca en route to Fort Quitman for an open camp. An open camp meant that the campsite would not be near a town and provided no facilities except what the train furnished. Fort Quitman camp was a former talc mill, and all animals the following morning were white, making their harnesses and saddles slip all day. Animal sweat turned into a white, gooey paste. It took days to clean the animals and tack.

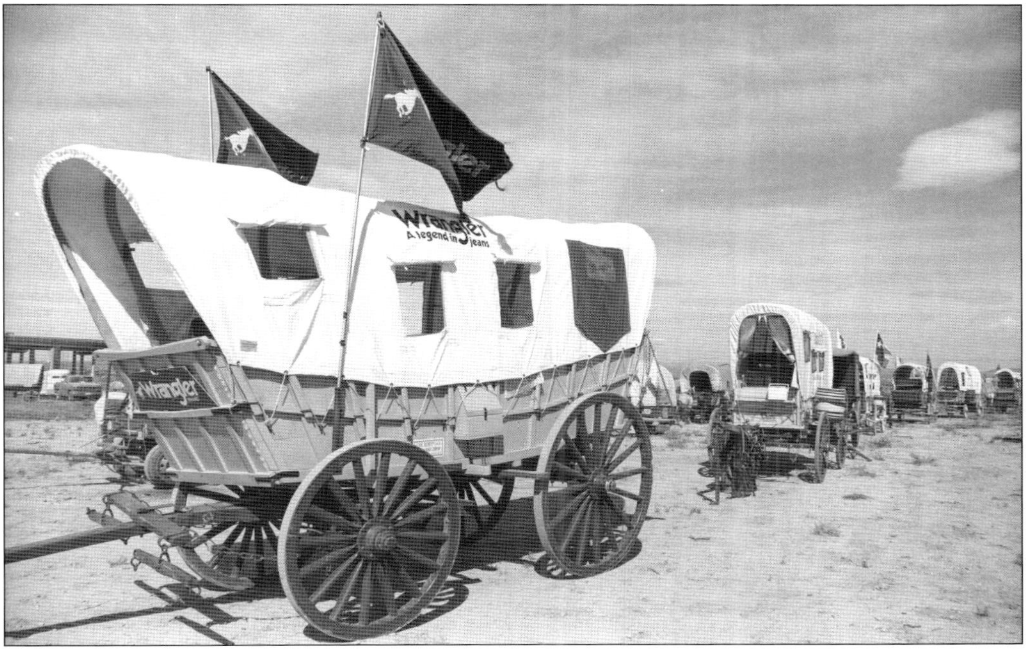

This wagon traveled the full 3,228 miles around the state and is now located in Grapevine, Texas. In this image, animals have been unhitched, and the wagons are circled around in camp. The train arrived in Sierra Blanca in Hudson County on April 6. The town, established in 1881 at the junction of the Texas and Pacific Railway and the Texas and New Orleans Railroad, was named after Sierra Blanca Peak nearby.

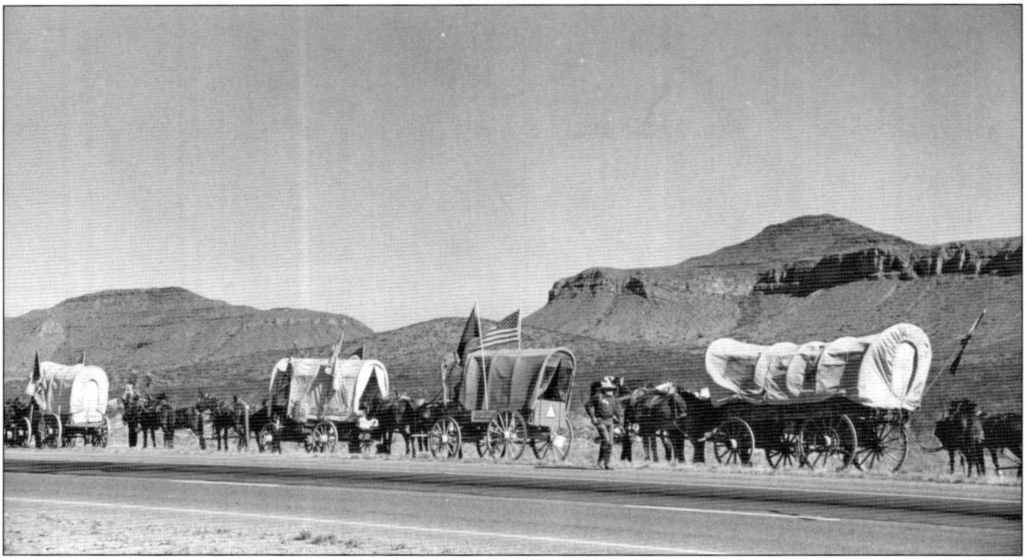

Folks who think that Texas has a totally flat terrain should have been with the small group of wagons and die-hard riders who made it to the Guadalupe Mountains of far West Texas. For many days before arriving there, the participants worried that their animals would not be able to pull the wagons up the inclines. They made it, though, and were the first wagons to go up Guadalupe Pass. The Butterfield Stage Line used to go down it. The wagons prepared in advance with ropes tied on and extra outriders to help as needed. Near the top, several wagons vied to reach it first.

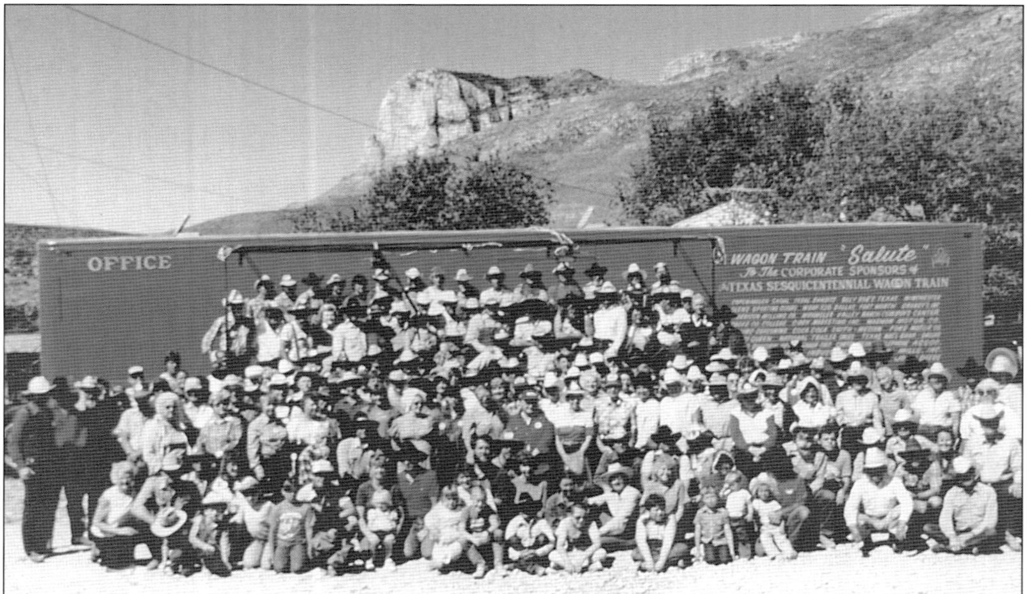

When the wagon train had traveled almost to its farthest point west away from towns and civilization in the Guadalupe Mountains, the core group of participants was down to its smallest number of people. The train was down to only 30 wagons. With the mountains in the background, the people are gathered in front of the 18-wheeler that served as an office. (Courtesy Texas Wagon Train Collection, North Fort Worth Historical Society.)

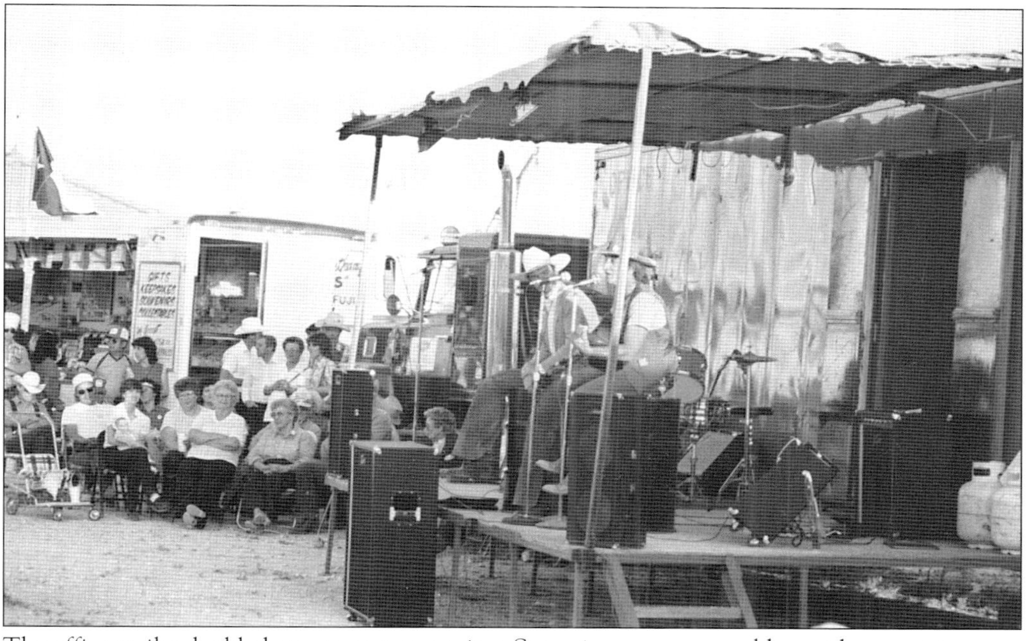

The office trailer doubled as a stage at campsites. Sometimes, towns would provide entertainment; at other times, participants would have a talent show of their own. Here, far away from population centers, the wagon train "family" provides its own show while camped at Guadalupe Peak. (Courtesy Quentin McGown.)

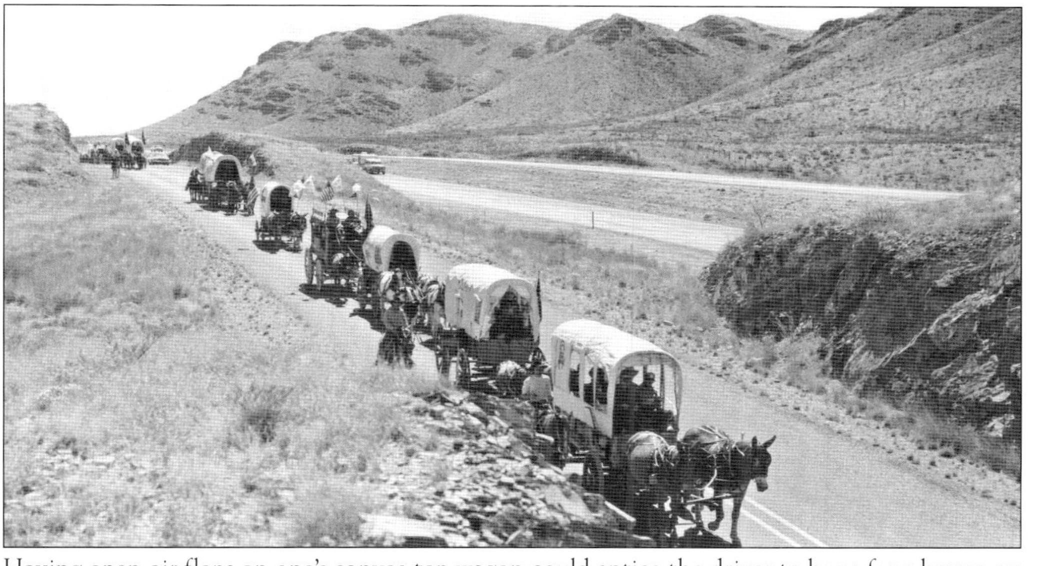

Having open-air flaps on one's canvas-top wagon could entice the driver to hope for a breeze on a hot summer day in Texas. The six-month trek from January 2 to July 3, 1986, faced all types of weather, but the train kept going. The route was planned in advance to allow enough time for rest and repairs—always on schedule, always on time. If a wagon broke down during the day, the others went around it, keeping the schedule. There was support following the train every day, with a trailer for the animals and help for the people. This route along Interstate 10 near Allamore on April 5 was one of the most scenic of the trip.

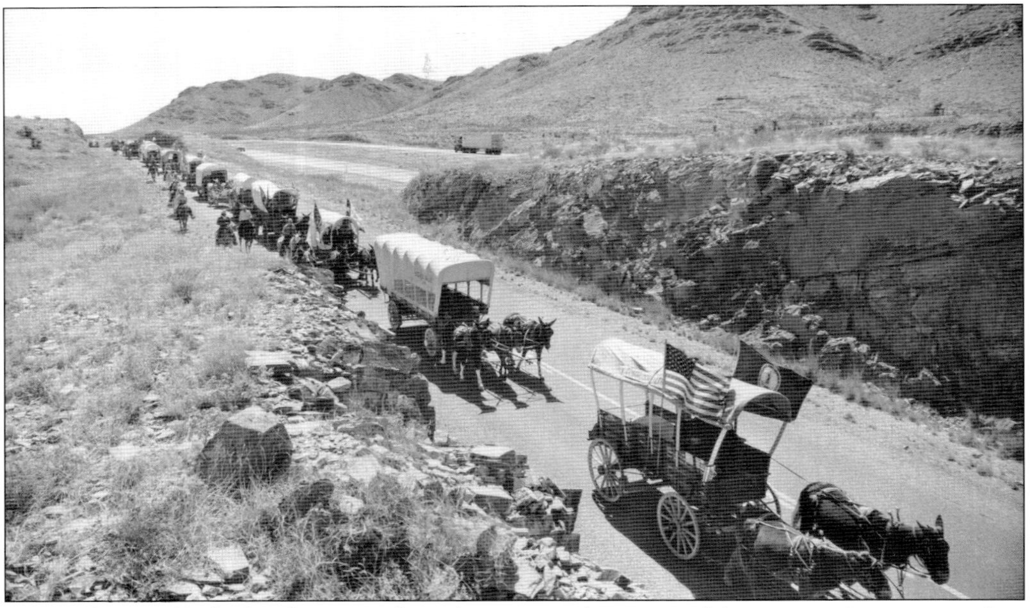

Notice the 18-wheeler heading away from the train in the center of the picture. A century earlier, mule trains with canvas tops like these carried much of the nation's freight. Minus the truck and the interstate highway, this scene is what many a Western movie portrayed of pioneers moving westward. This is the ultimate visual image of the West. Imagine experiencing it for days while sitting on a bench, holding the reins, and gazing over the rumps of one's horses.

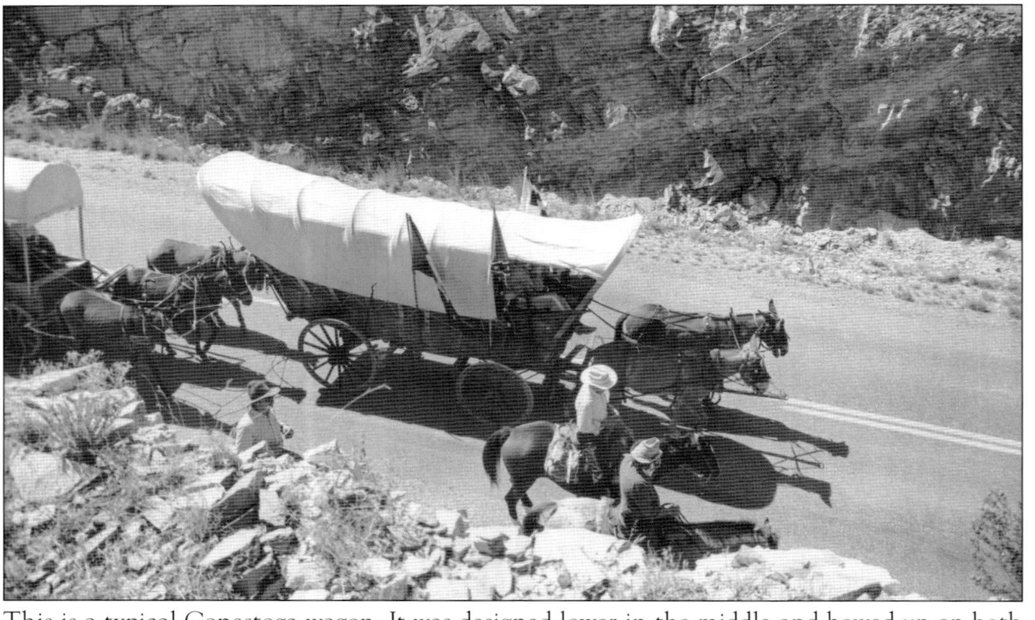

This is a typical Conestoga wagon. It was designed lower in the middle and bowed up on both ends to keep heavy loads of merchandise from shifting and putting a strain on the rear or front while going up or down hills. The inclines around Allamore provided that kind of terrain. The community began in 1885 as a railway section house and was named after the wife of an early settler.

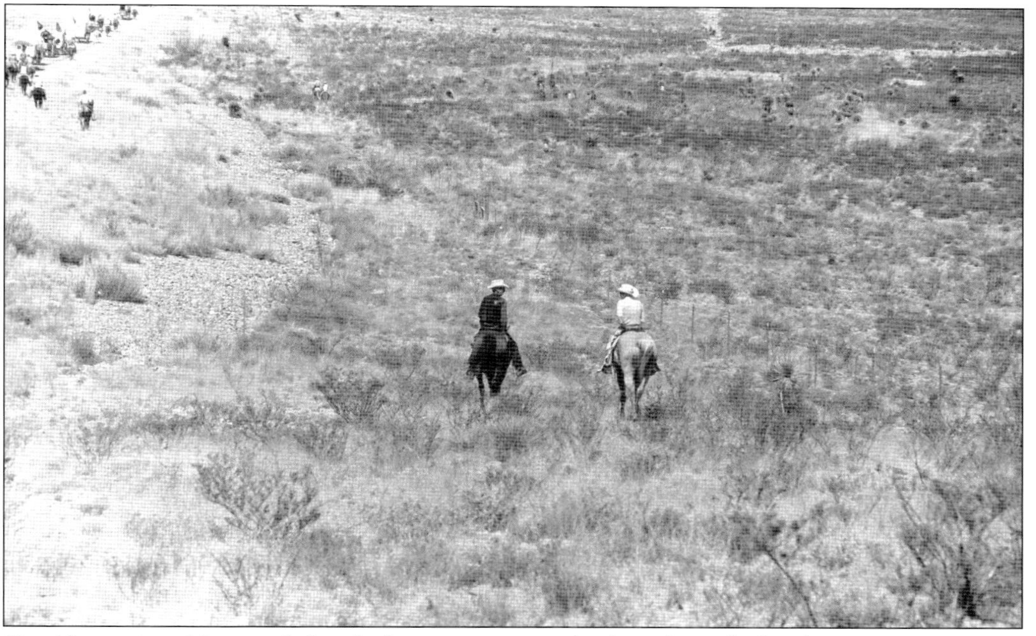

Outriders enjoyed lagging behind a bit sometimes and riding through the changing terrain. However, rattlesnakes became a problem in some areas where the train traveled. Folks needed to be careful where they stepped in campsites and watch for the rattlers. Even the elapse of a century or more from the early pioneers' experiences did not change that fact in Texas.

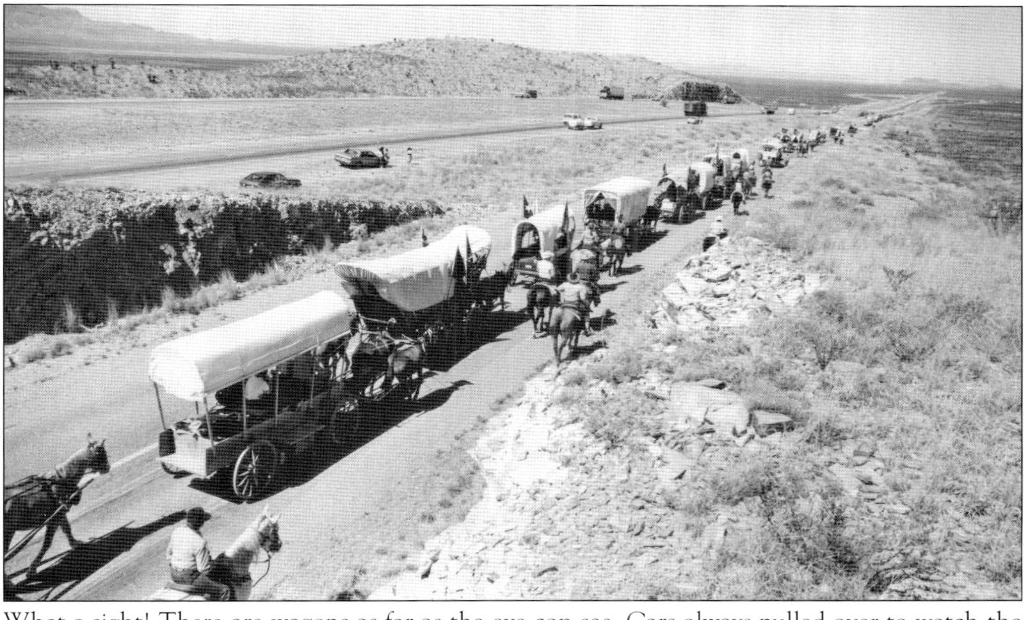

What a sight! There are wagons as far as the eye can see. Cars always pulled over to watch the wagon train go by. Those with imaginations should wipe away the paved roads and visualize the wagon train rolling alone in open country. It is as close as people today in the 21st century can come to experiencing a wagon train in motion. Most wagons left today are viewed in museums or during special events like rodeo parades or pioneer days.

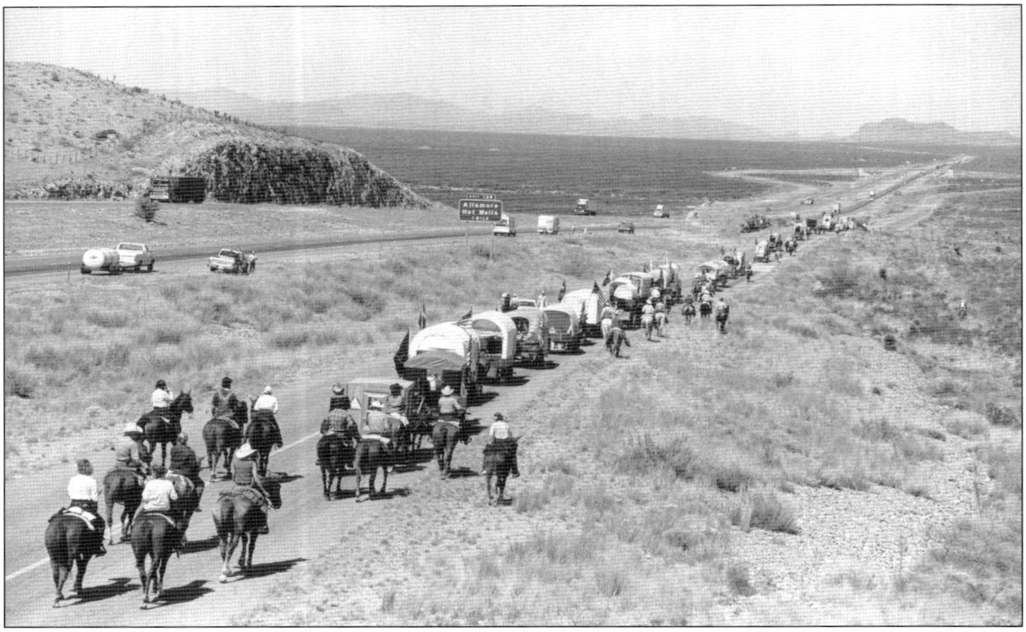

Access roads alongside interstate highways often provided the perfect place for the wagon train to mosey along in its four-miles-per-hour speed. Mountains in the background and the desertlike terrain indicate that the train was on Interstate 10 east of El Paso in West Texas. The highway sign informs drivers that the Allamore and Hot Wells exit is ahead.

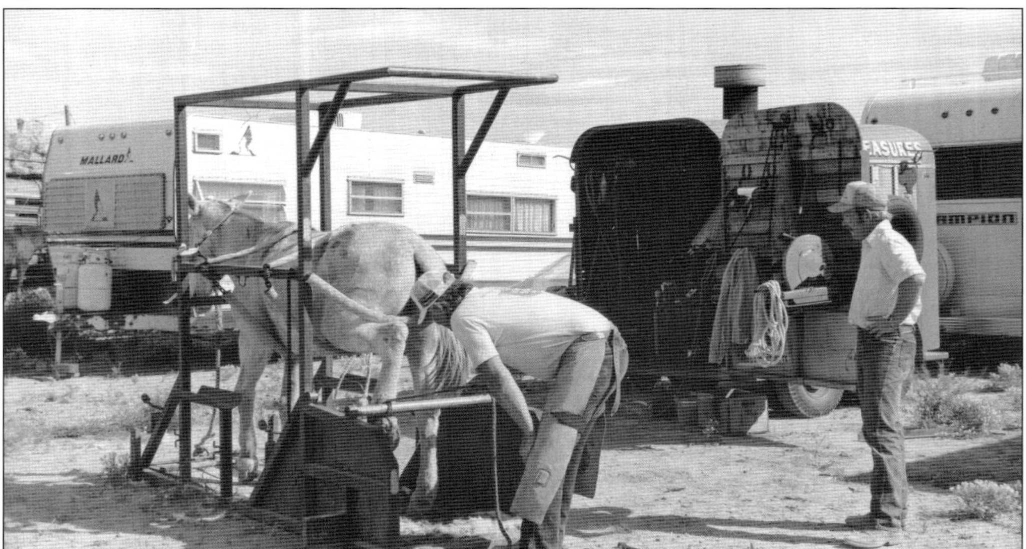

Horseshoe replacement services followed the wagon train. While the wagon train association provided for the availability of a professional farrier, those who used his services were responsible for payment. Boyd Ivey from De Kalb was the official blacksmith for the train. His was a job that had continued with little change from a century earlier. Boyd Ivey was also on the 1976 bicentennial wagon train to Valley Forge, Pennsylvania, where he shod the horse of Jan France several times. She asked him to be official blacksmith for the Texas train.

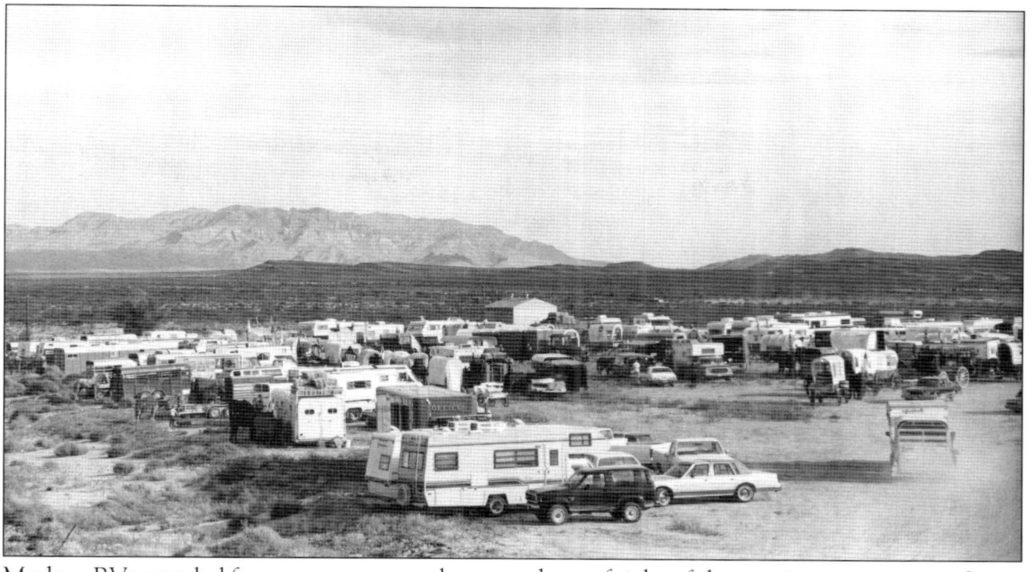

Modern RVs traveled from camp to camp but stayed out of sight of the moving wagon train. Some of the drivers of authentic wagons roughed it and slept in their wagons, on the ground, or in tents or teepees nearby. Others had support people arriving at camp earlier than the train to provide all the comforts of home. Wagons and horses circled each evening to camp and were not mixed in with the modern vehicles. Also, rules of the Texas Wagon Train Association said that support vehicles could be nowhere in sight when the wagon train traveled. Wagon train staff and personnel moved their trailers from camp to camp, or they rode the shuttle to get their own rigs.

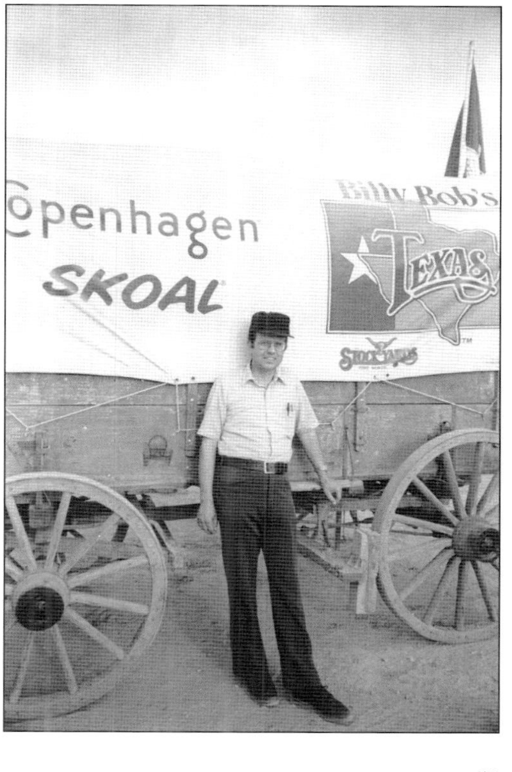

Dominick J. Cirincione is leaning against a wagon that advertises Copenhagen and Skoal tobaccos and Billy Bob's Texas nightclub. Cirincione, then an employee of Bell Helicopter in Fort Worth, drove or flew to photograph the train on weekends.

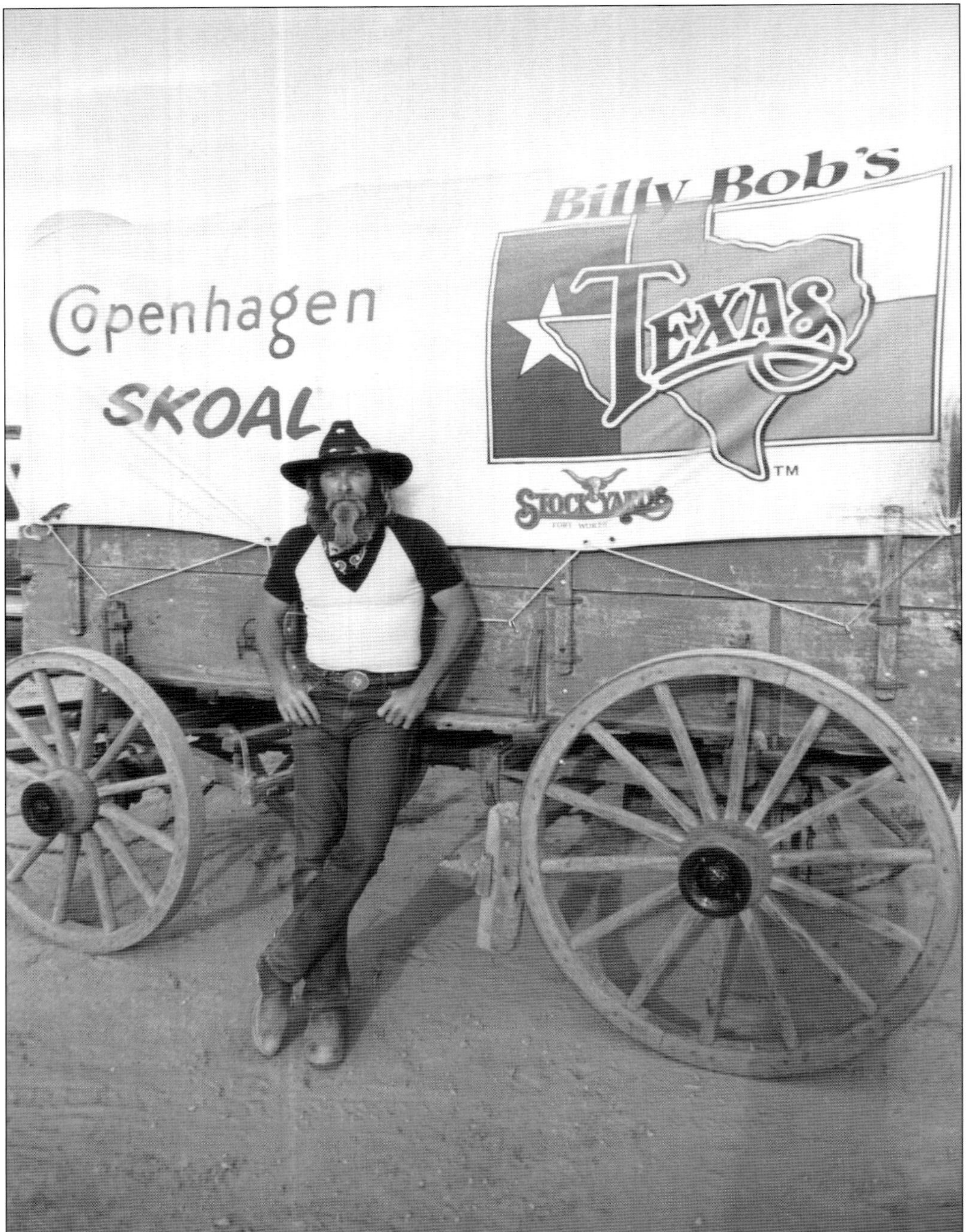

John "Buffalo" Chester of Sulphur Springs served as assistant camp jack for the train. Not pictured is West Pearce, head camp jack from Silver City, New Mexico. Pearce looked over the site for each night's camp and was in charge of organizing the parking and smoothing away any problems involved. He and his workers enforced camp rules of no alcohol, no drugs, no firearms, no littering, and a quiet camp after 11:00 p.m. Rules even allowed no dogs except for the brief participation of the 1st Cavalry Division's mascot, Missy.

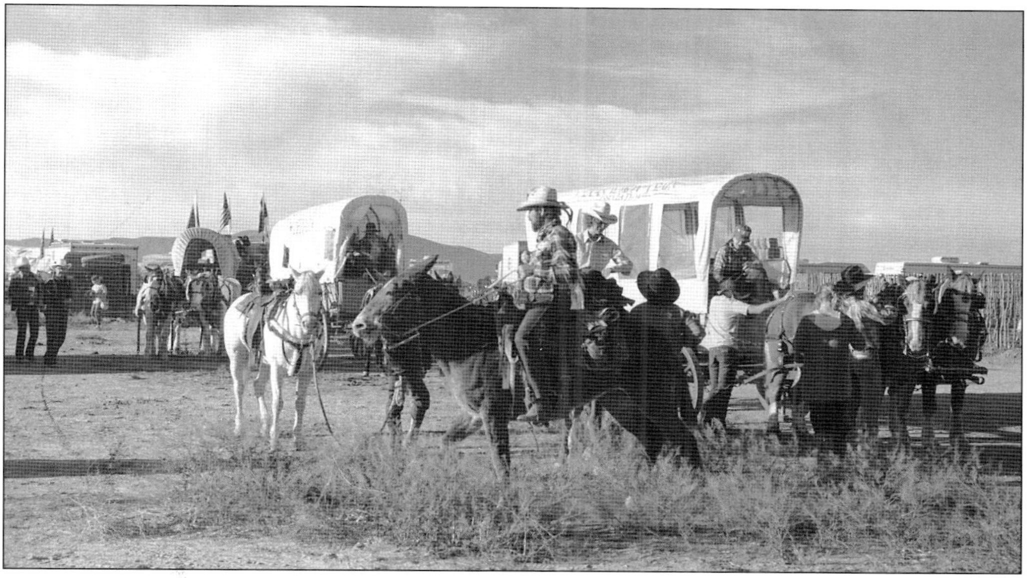

Mornings came early for wagon train participants as they rose at 4:30 or 5:00 a.m. to water and feed their animals, eat breakfast, and harness two or four horses or mules. In several towns, a local Dairy Queen provided a free breakfast. The train began leaving at 8:00 a.m. but, as the days got longer, pushed the time up to 7:30 a.m. and then 7:00 a.m. to arrive in camp before the heat of the day and to leave while it was cooler. That call from wagon master Garry France of "Wagons, ho!" came earlier and earlier.

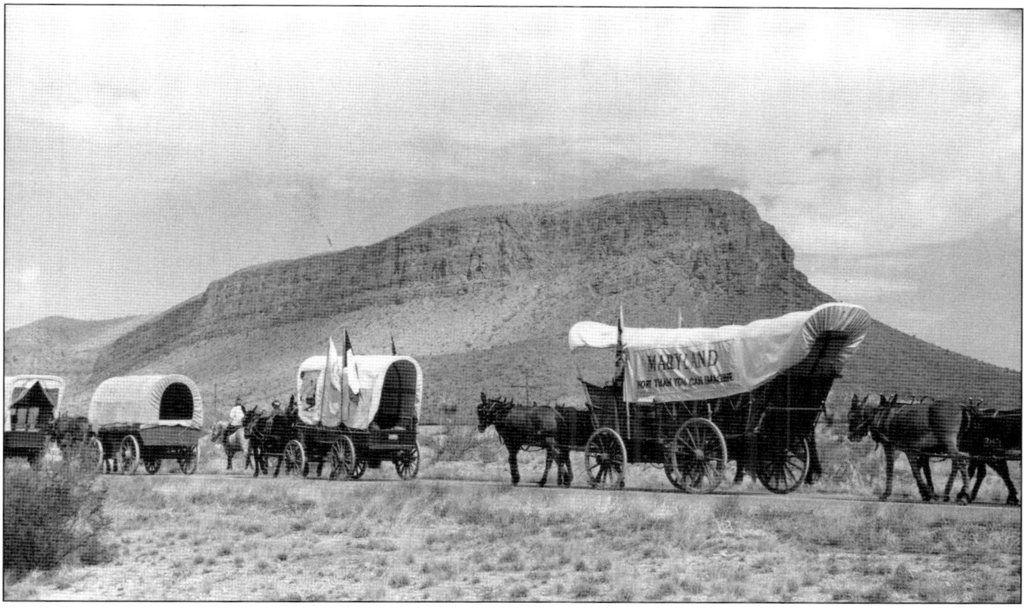

On the side of this Conestoga wagon is the message "Maryland, More Than You Can Imagine." Jim Saylor from that state drove the wagon. In newspaper articles about the wagon train, numbers vary as to how many states were represented. The difference comes from whether it is the number of states from which wagons or riders came. The largest number cited is that participants came from 27 states.

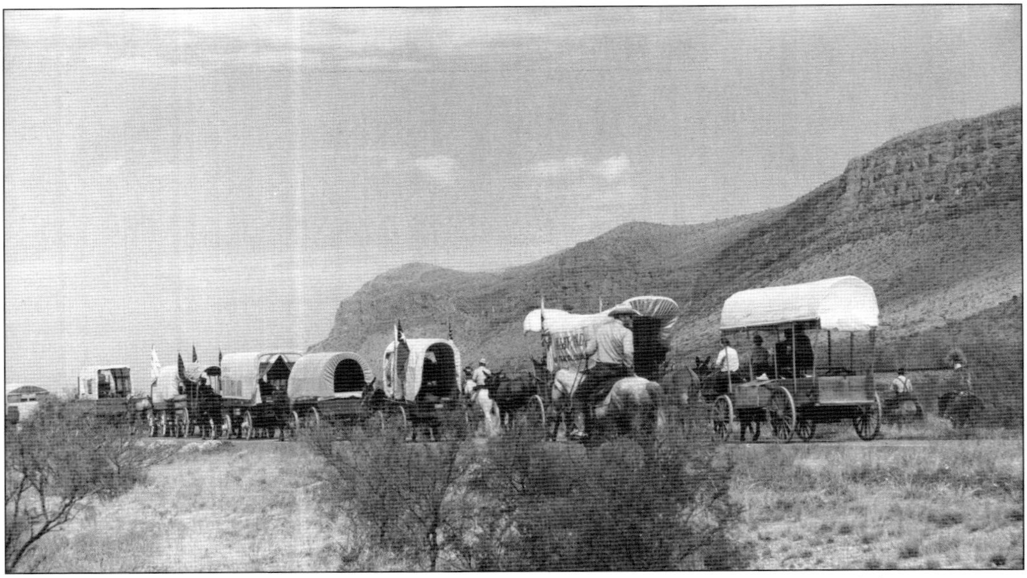

Participants in the wagon train saw themselves as reliving a journey that some of their ancestors made several generations back, when they first came to Texas. They were a 20th-century group of reenactors making its own history in order to help fellow Texans never forget what happened a century and a half earlier. Patriots overthrew an oppressive government that was trampling on their rights as citizens. The slogan developed in 1983 was "Circle Texas for the Past and Future."

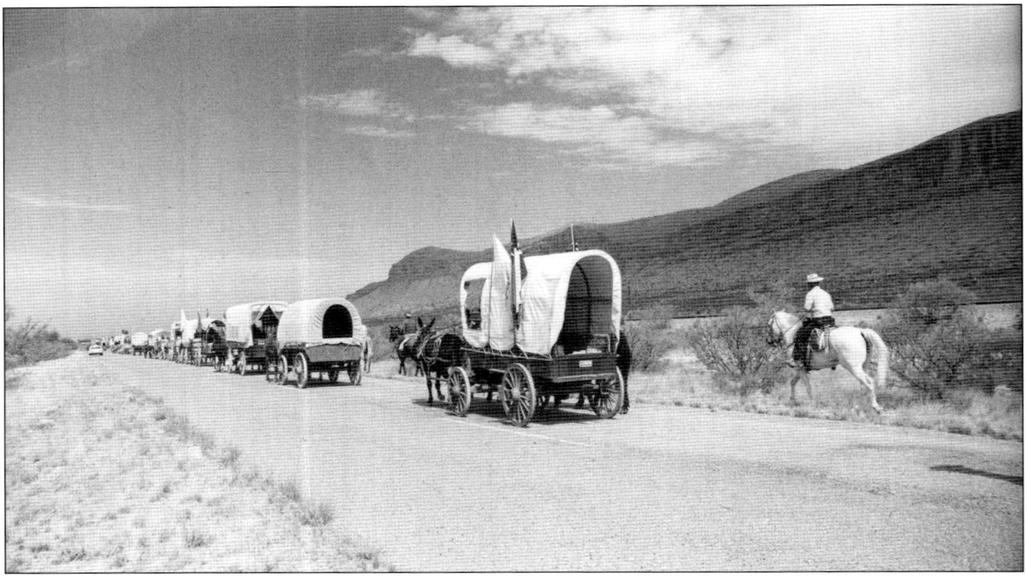

This long shot shows the large number of wagons in the train. Excitement always remained high as the train traveled along the highways and through towns and cities. Cars continually pulled over to observe the parade of wagons roll by. As intended, large numbers of Texans throughout the state were able to experience the Texas Sesquicentennial Wagon Train. It became the largest and most attended event that took place in the state during the entire sesquicentennial year. The train received no state remuneration, which shows what determined Texans can accomplish.

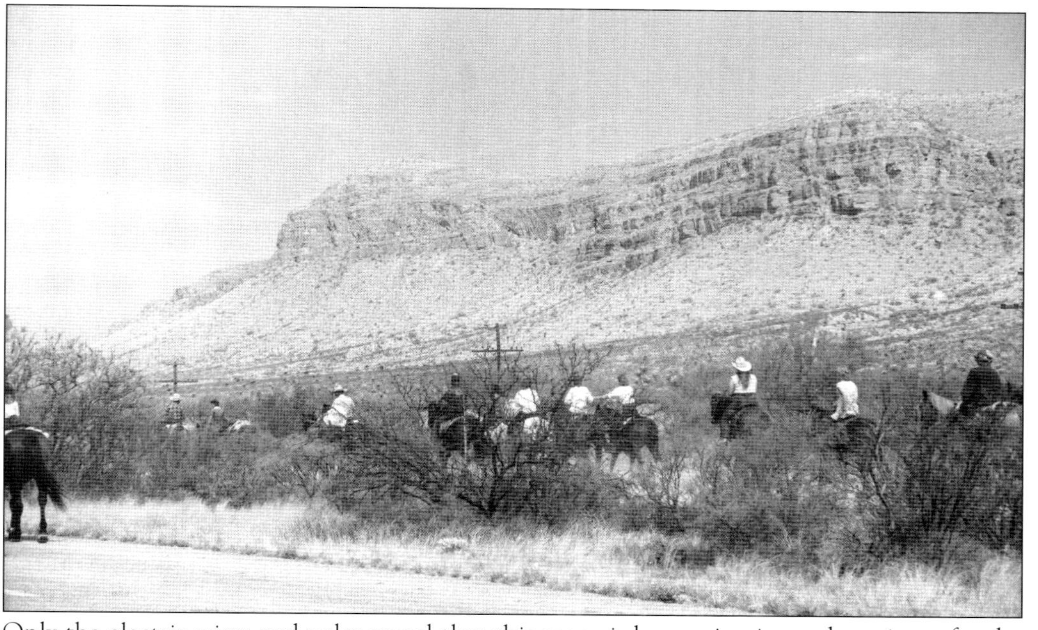

Only the electric wires and poles reveal that this scene is happening in modern times, for the setting is pure Western imagery. Those riders must not so forget themselves by enjoying the scenery that they neglect to watch for rattlesnakes. The country in which they ride provides the perfect setting for rattlers. Quick movement on the ground by a snake or other varmint could spook the horses and provide trouble for the rider. Official outriders are there to help.

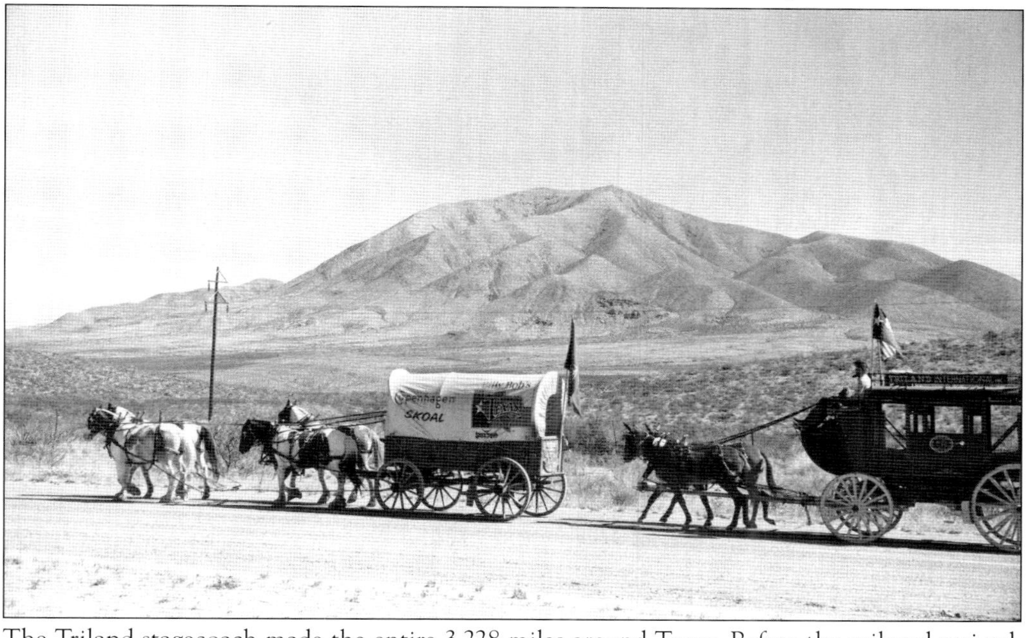

The Triland stagecoach made the entire 3,228 miles around Texas. Before the railroad arrived, the stagecoach was king of the road for passenger service. Even after the first railroads crisscrossed the country, stagecoaches for a few years still carried passengers to outlying areas where the trains did not reach. Driver Rudy Nelson enjoyed taking passengers up on the high perch with him.

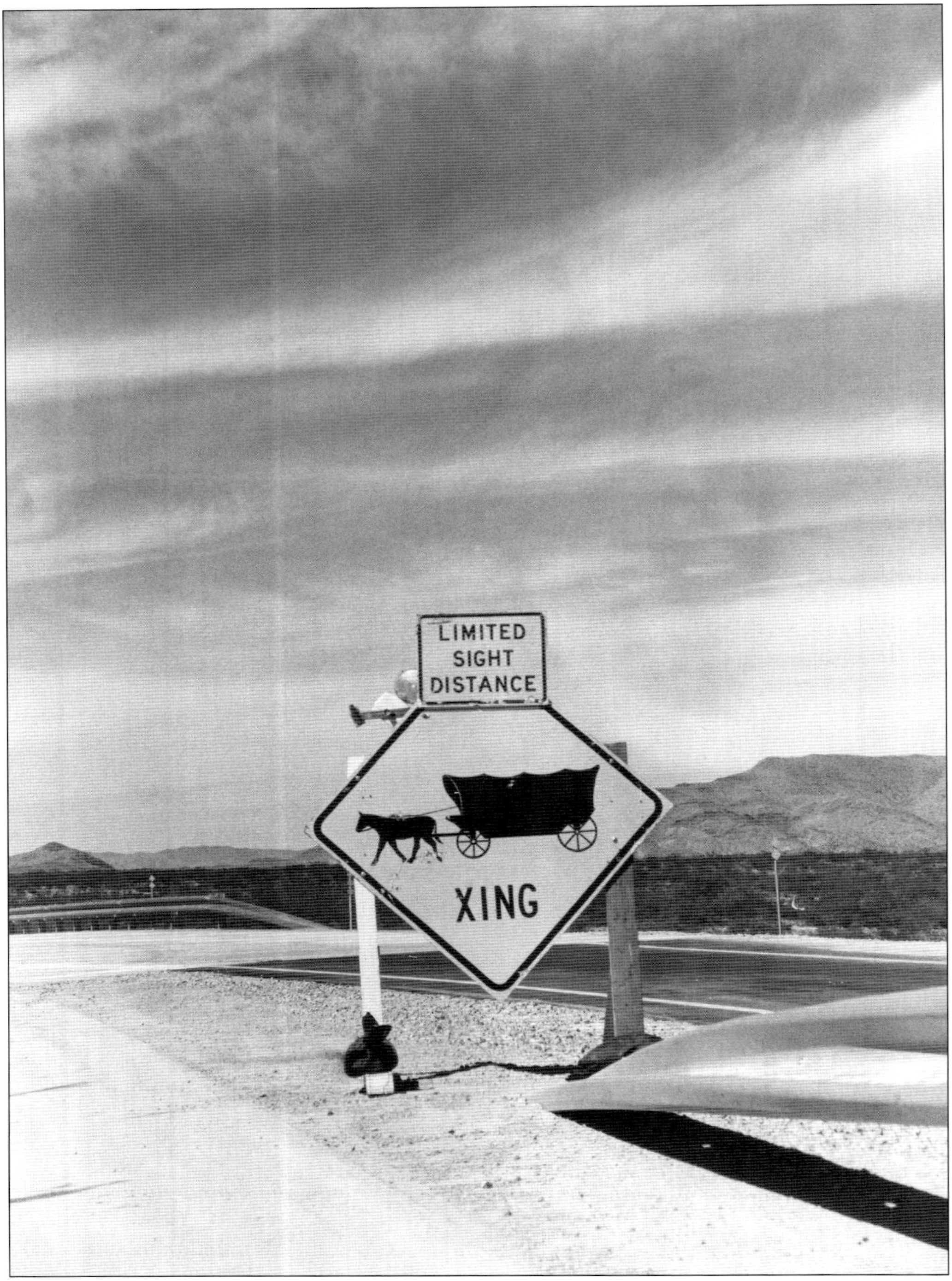

The Texas Highway Department created these signs for the wagon train personnel to place at intersections when the train was coming through. Any tourists traveling through Texas who were unaware of the special celebration and the train's journey probably did a few double takes after seeing this sign. However, people kept stealing them for souvenirs, so the state quit making them.

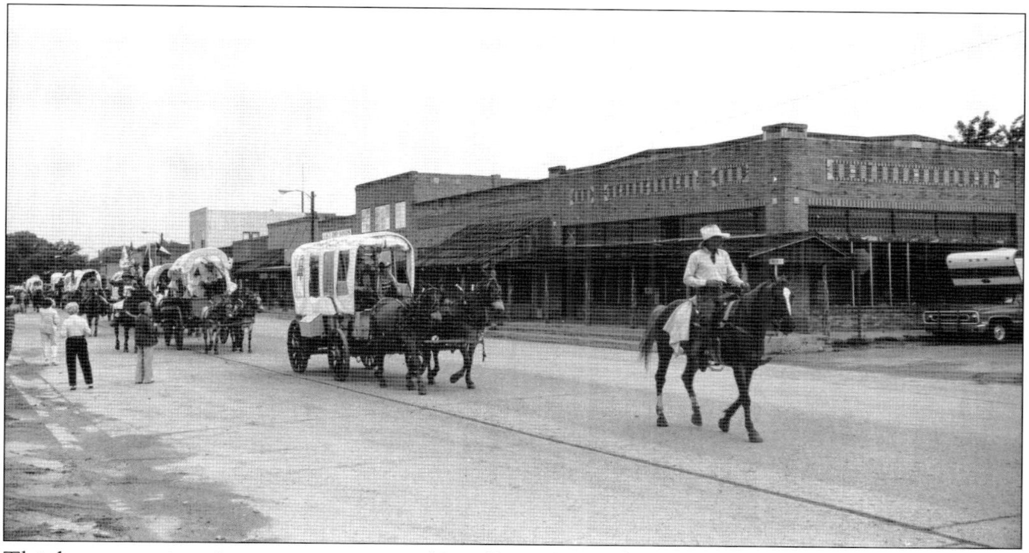

This horseman is assistant wagon master Vern Renz. Here, the train travels through Turkey, Texas, the home of Bob Wills, country-and-western singer and bandleader. Ladies coordinated food from Turkey and surrounding areas to provide 975 plates to the participants in camp that night. The wagon train folks were fed and treated like VIPs at most of the stops. Then, of course, the evening gathering around the campfire provided lots of music. Wagon master France once commented that they "waltzed across Texas" because so much took place along the way as well.

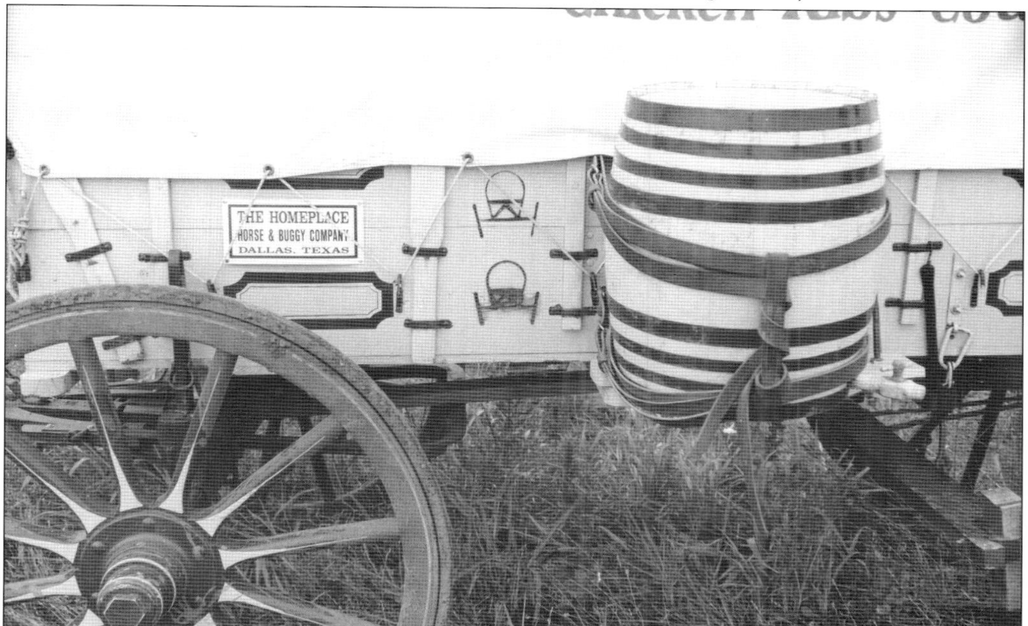

This wagon from Dallas has completed 2,000 miles. It has been branded two times with the official Texas wagon train logo on the side of the wagon to the left of the water barrel. If this particular wagon makes another 1,000 miles (which it did), it will receive another logo brand. Drivers strove for this mark of distinction on their rigs.

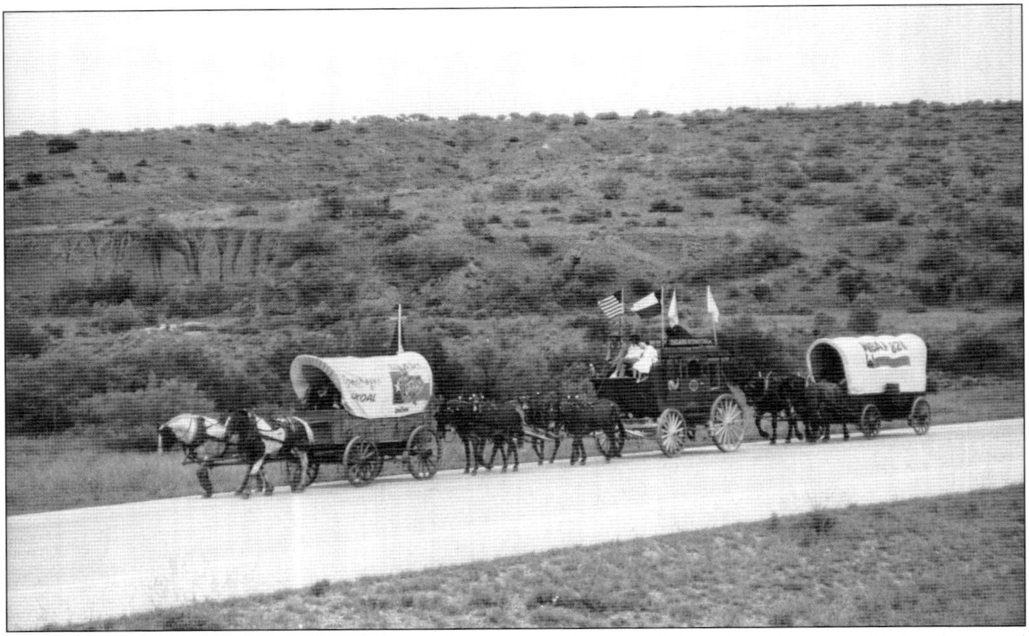

Matador was the next stop after Turkey. The train had reached the Texas Panhandle by then and saw stops in Amarillo, Claude, Ashtola, Clarendon, Brice, and Turkey during the third week of May. At the edge of the Panhandle, a group of people decided to dress like Indians and charge the train. The train was alerted ahead of time that it was going to happen and had permission from the wagon master. Extra outriders looked out for teams that might spook. Fortunately, the drivers were pretty well accustomed to the road and held their animals in check. A nice historical reenactment, it was fun and without incident.

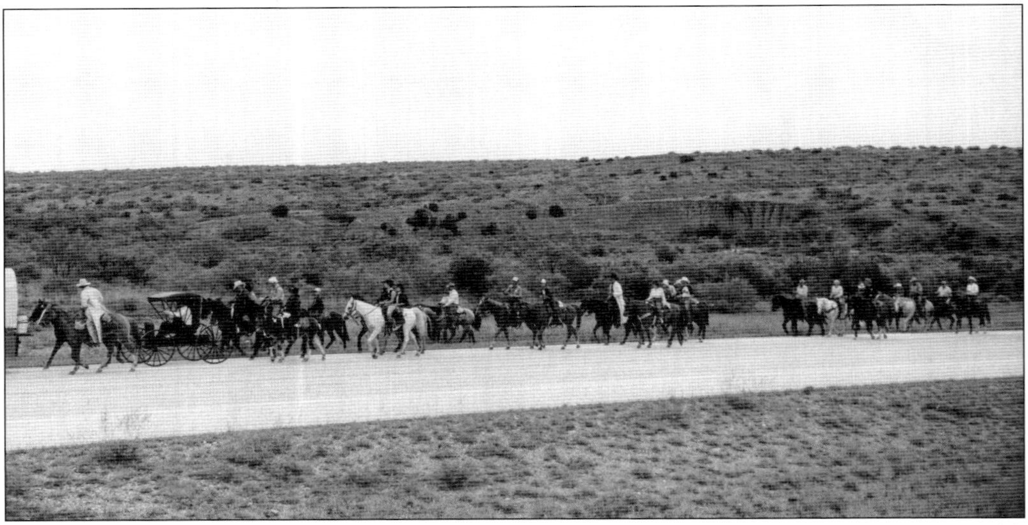

At the extreme left of this picture, behind the man on horseback dressed in white, is an old-fashioned surrey, which joined the train on May 26. Because drivers and wagons that started early had their places in line, any newcomers for a day or two had to take a place at the back of the train. "First come, first served" was the order of the day. A core group of 30 wagons plus support staff made the entire trip.

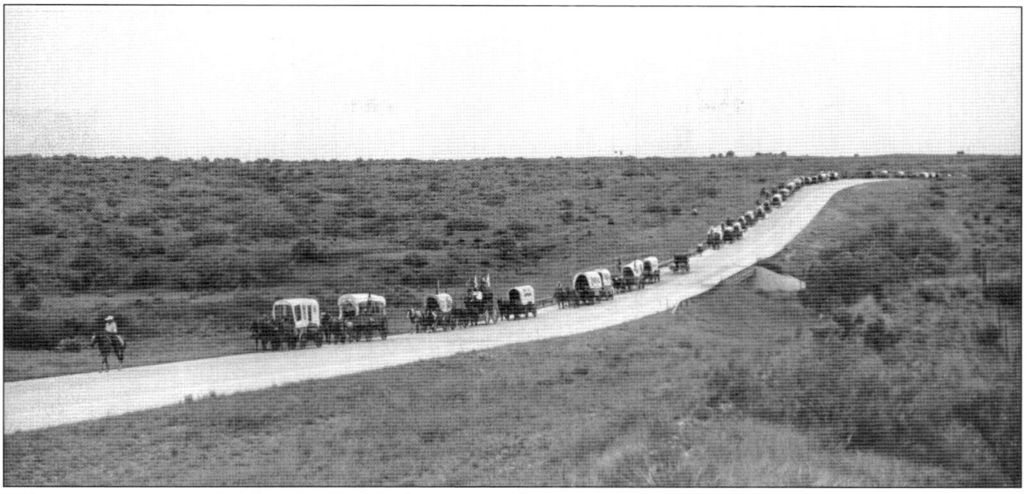

What an impressive sight of wagons this scene shows as far as the eye can see. To organize and run a wagon train of this size for 3,000 miles around Texas took uncommon motivation and determination. Western heritage still is strong in Texas. The state may have advanced to the 21st century, but its people still reach back to their Western roots for inspiration and their values system. Near Tahoka, a 101-year-old man who had been a driver of a freight wagon between Big Spring and Tahoka was invited on the head wagon and even drove the team for a while. His son, grandson, and great-grandson rode along as he took the reins. He lived to age 106, and he even later wrote a letter only addressed to "Jan France, Texas"—and she received it.

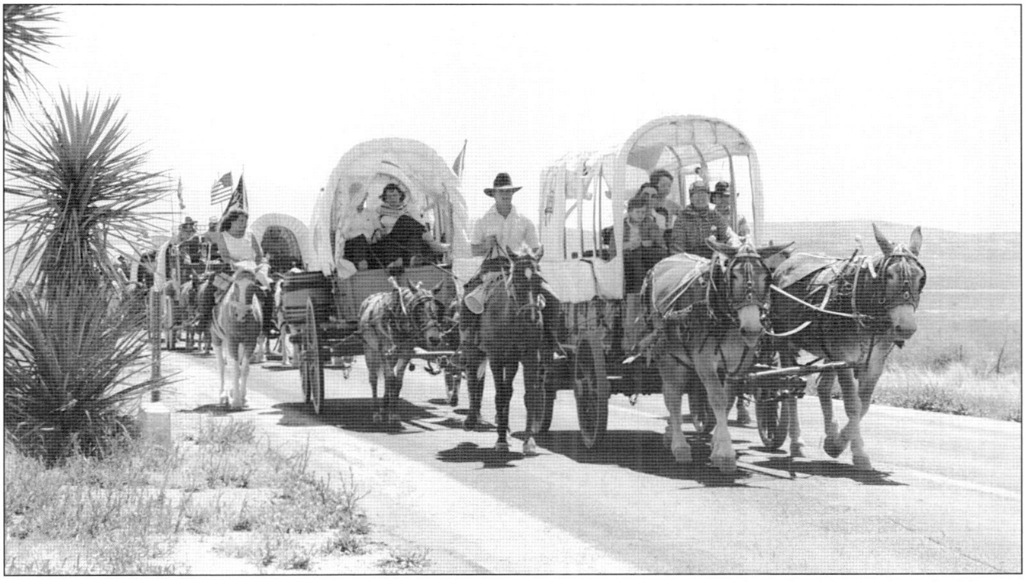

This was the lead wagon each day that headed out first. Jan France, left, holding the child, sits by her codriver, Ina Nell "Woody" Wood. Children of each town's dignitaries liked to ride in the lead wagon. On horseback to the left is Jo Anne Thielemann, official representative of the State of Florida, and next to the lead wagon is outrider Tommy Underwood. Seen through the window behind Woody is the wagon master Garry France. For safety reasons, every wagon had to have an outrider to assist the teamster in case of problems or to stay with the team during rest breaks. (Courtesy Ina Nell Wood estate.)

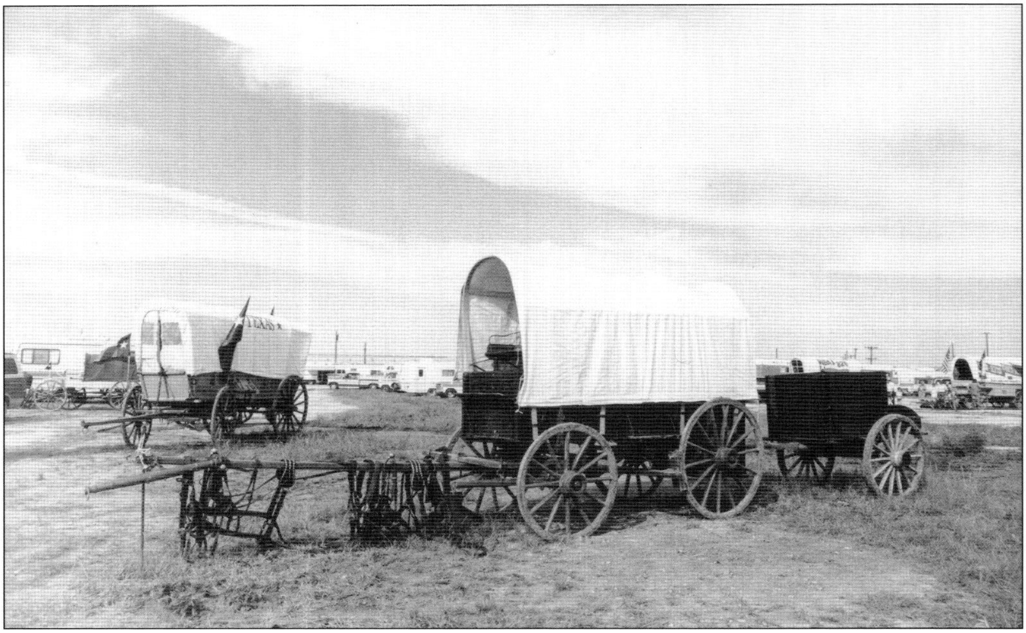

By June 7, the train had camped over the previous 10 days at the Pitchfork Ranch, the 6666 Ranch, Benjamin, Rochester, Haskell, Stamford, Hawley, and arrived in Abilene for a three-day camp. Wagons were parked away from modern RVs, as can be seen in the background. This wagon pulls what chuck wagon referred to as a "hooligan cart." It simply is a trailer for extra supplies.

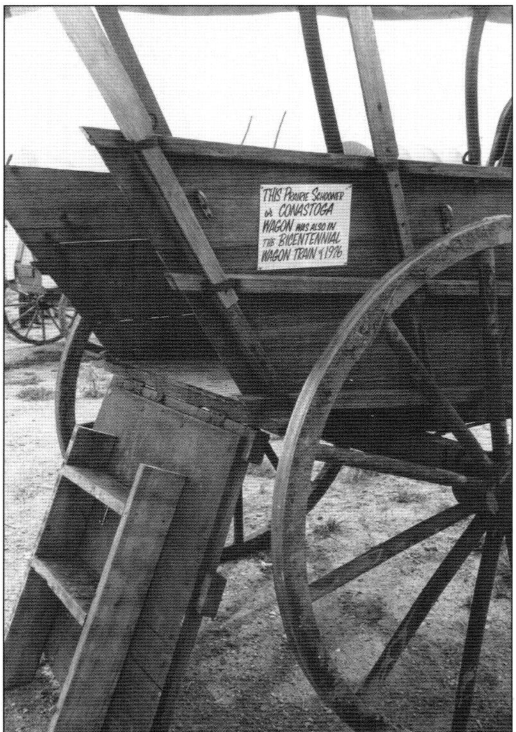

This wagon traveled in the 1976 train commemorating the bicentennial of the United States as the official representative of the State of Virginia. A true Conestoga wagon, it is designed after the original ones built in Pennsylvania's Conestoga Valley near Lancaster in the 18th century. Albert and Alice Nicely hauled this wagon to Texas from Lexington, Virginia, in a trailer to participate in the Texas train. Everything was original on it except for a rear view mirror and a hydraulic brake, which were required additions for safety.

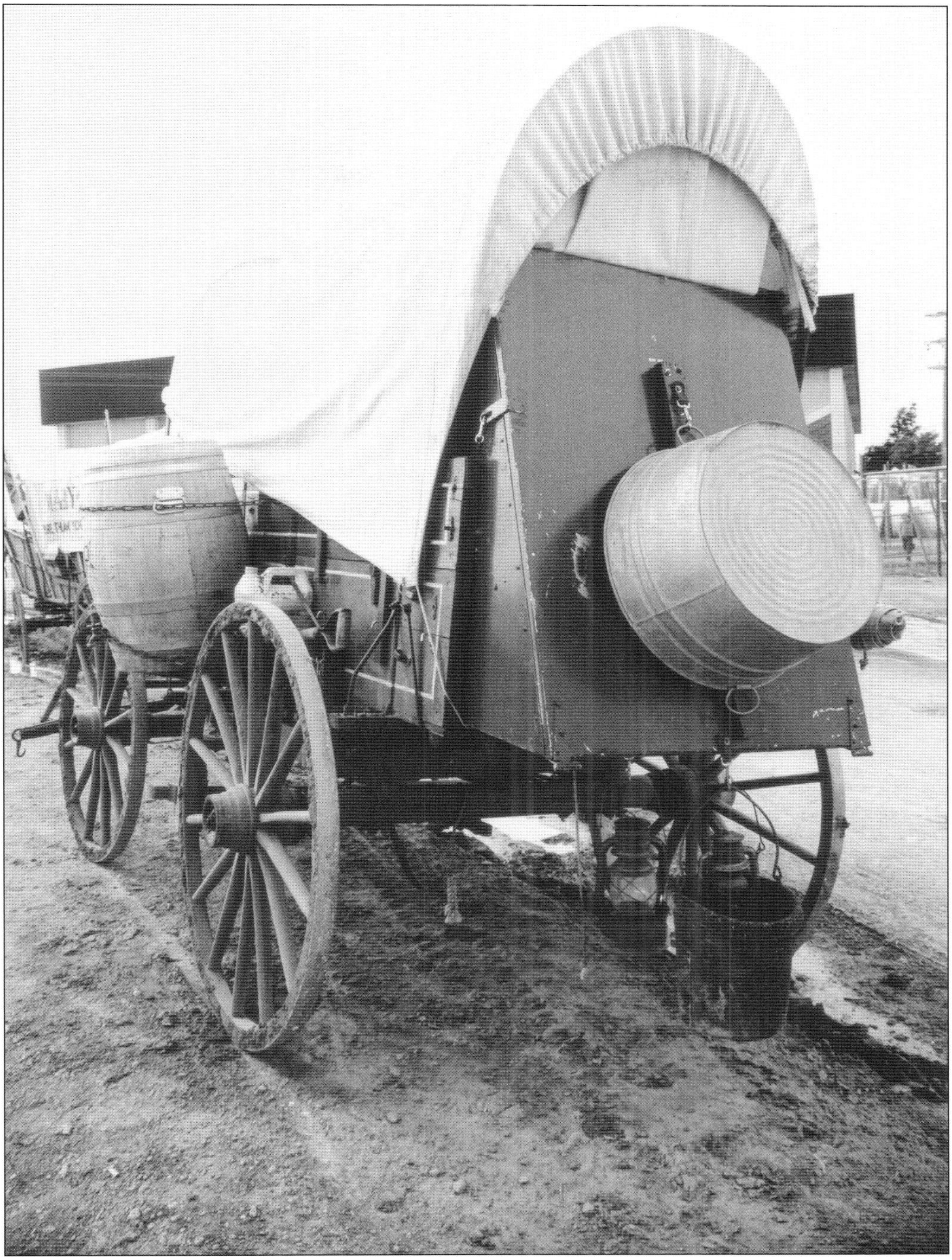

This Conestoga wagon was a chuck wagon whose tailgate could be let down. The washtub most likely was used to wash dishes, not bodies. Many towns arranged showers in school gymnasiums and other places for the wagon train folks, who were very appreciative of the service. They felt that they truly were pioneers when they had to forego a bath for two or three days. A hot Texas summer with no air-conditioning suggests the old days.

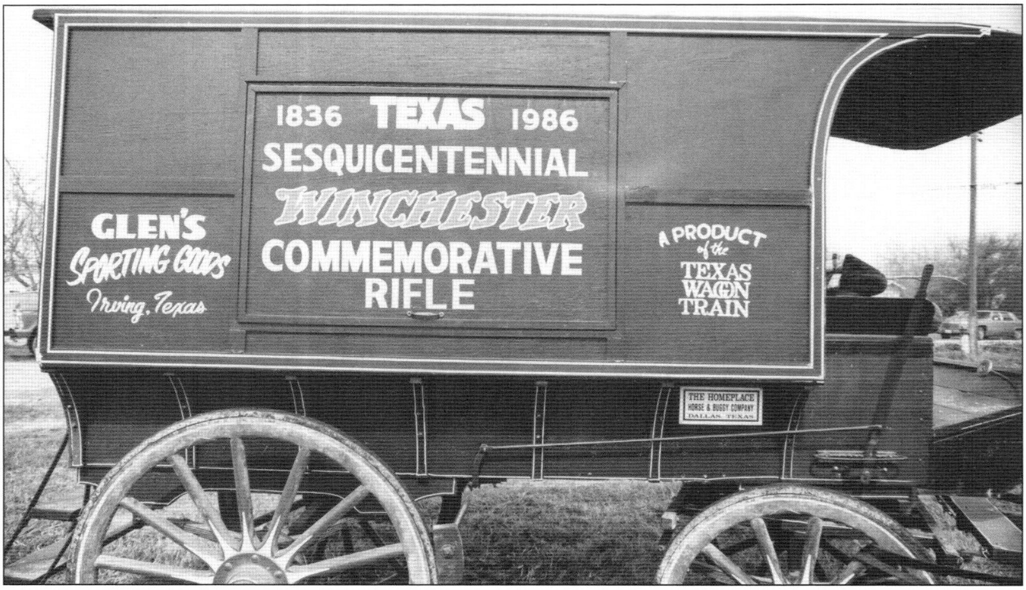

This wagon represents an old-time ambulance, a doctor's wagon, or perhaps a delivery wagon. For the train, it boasted large sponsor advertisements and a small sign noting the restoration completed by Homeplace Horse and Buggy Company of Dallas. Charles Oliver, president and CEO of the Texas Wagon Train Association, owned the company that restored wagons like this one. He often was on the road raising money to keep the train moving. For those who today in the 21st century want to see more unique vehicles like this one, a wagon museum exists on East Exchange Avenue in the Fort Worth Stockyards.

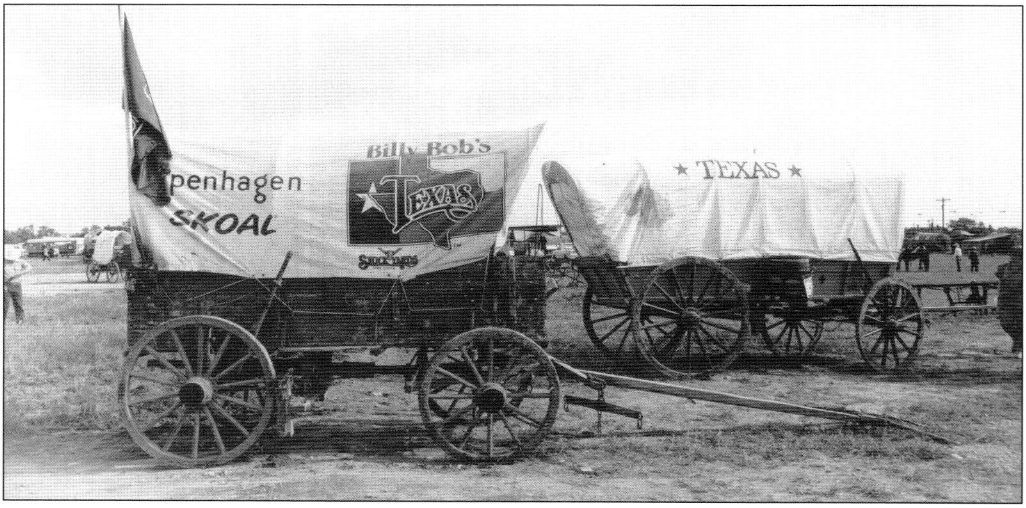

Leo Miller drove the Copenhagen/Skoal wagon. His daughter Carol, who had been separated from him for 35 years, found him because of the wagon train. She joined the train and rode on the wagon with him. Abilene, where this photograph was taken, was named after the cow town on the cattle drives, Abilene, Kansas. The Texas Abilene had its ties to cattle as well, for cattlemen established the town in 1881 as a shipping point for their livestock on the Texas and Pacific Railway. Participants Mike and Shawna Lowery married at the Ray Boeshart Arena in Abilene. Boeshart himself rode with the wagon train for many miles.

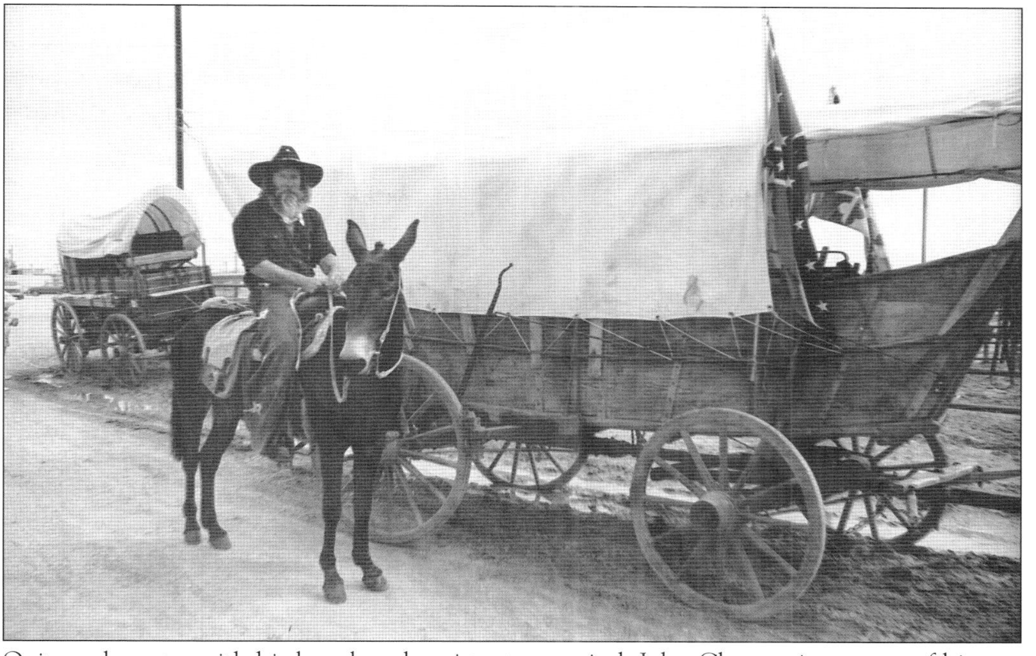

Quite a character with his long beard, assistant camp jack John Chester sits on one of his two mules. J.R. Newton also helped camp jack West Pearce. Their job was to help people get settled in camp. Sometimes, if one wagon had runaway animals, the excitement would spook other teams. This could occur on the road as well as in camp. The camp jacks, as well as other campers, pitched in to help.

Someone drew a picture of Chester's two mules, who pulled his wagon. The spit and polish of the wagons and mules or horses usually found in a modern Western parade was noticeably missing from the wagon train. Long days on the road exposed to all kinds of weather and terrain produced the look of working wagons, tired horses and mules, and dusty cowboys.

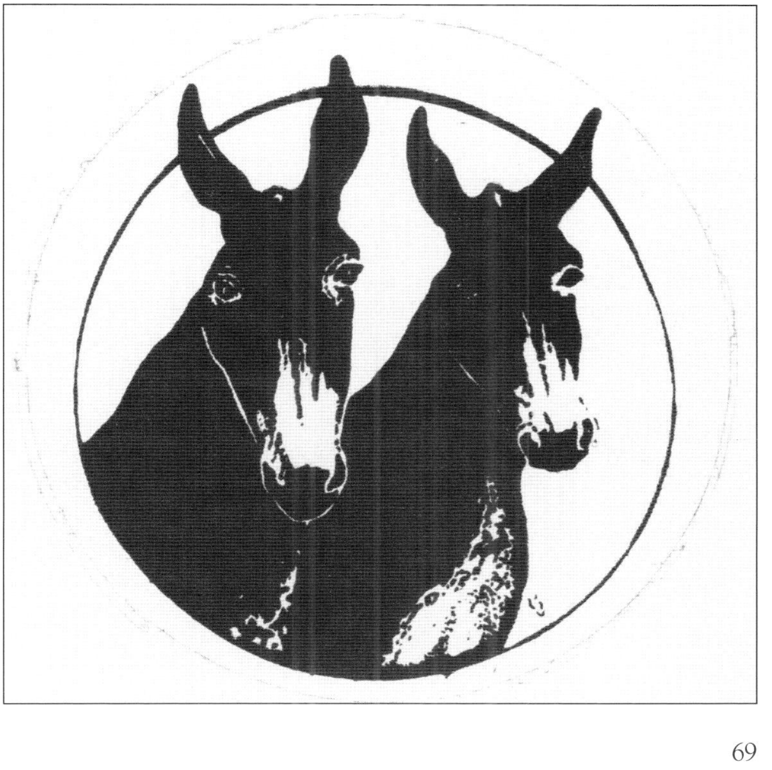

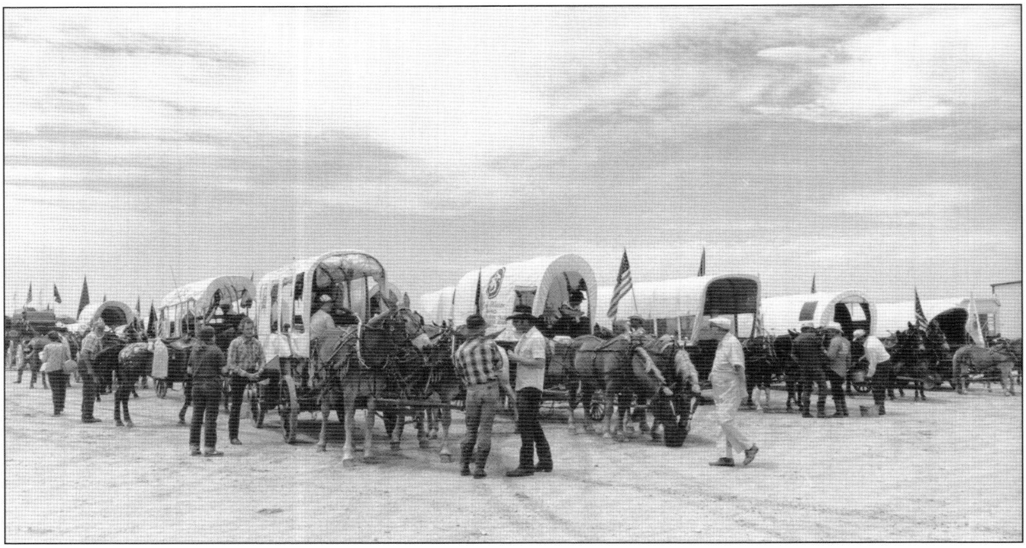

Wagons are lining up ready to pull out from Windthorst to travel to Wichita Falls on the morning of Sunday, June 15. An old church sits on a rise in the landscape in Windthorst, and its tower can be seen for many miles. Drivers in the train most surely watched it as they drew closer to the town. Windthorst was settled in 1891 by German Catholics and was named for Ludwig Windthorst, a German statesman. Teamster Dale "Apache" Barrett, driver of "Big Pop's" Wagon, and his wife, Vickie, are from Windthorst. Vickie's family, the Vitenheimers, were original settlers of Windthorst.

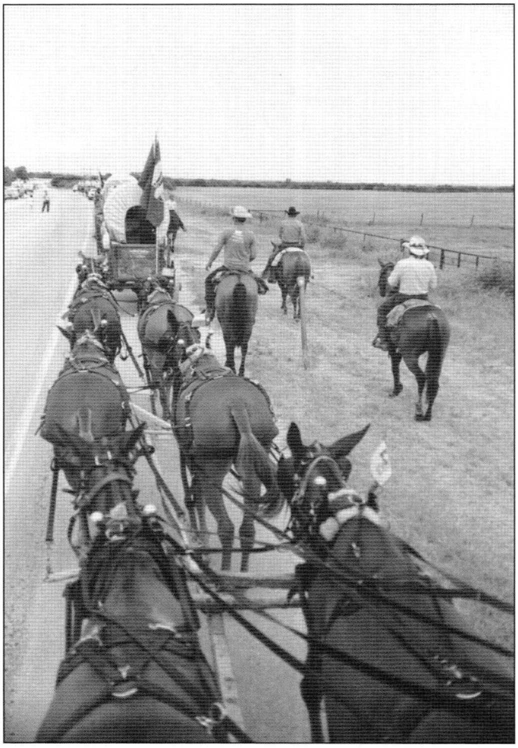

Here, the train has left the high country of far West Texas and is on the flat plains once again. A little less than three weeks remain on the journey as the train is traveling from Windthorst to Wichita Falls. Policemen met the wagon train in each town to help direct traffic and try to prevent trouble. If someone took a notion to honk his horn at the train, inexperienced animals whose owners had just joined the train might bolt. Back in 1983, before any plans for the train were set in stone, Jan France met with the Texas Highway Department, Texas Highway Patrol, and Texas Rangers to make sure the wagon train would have their cooperation.

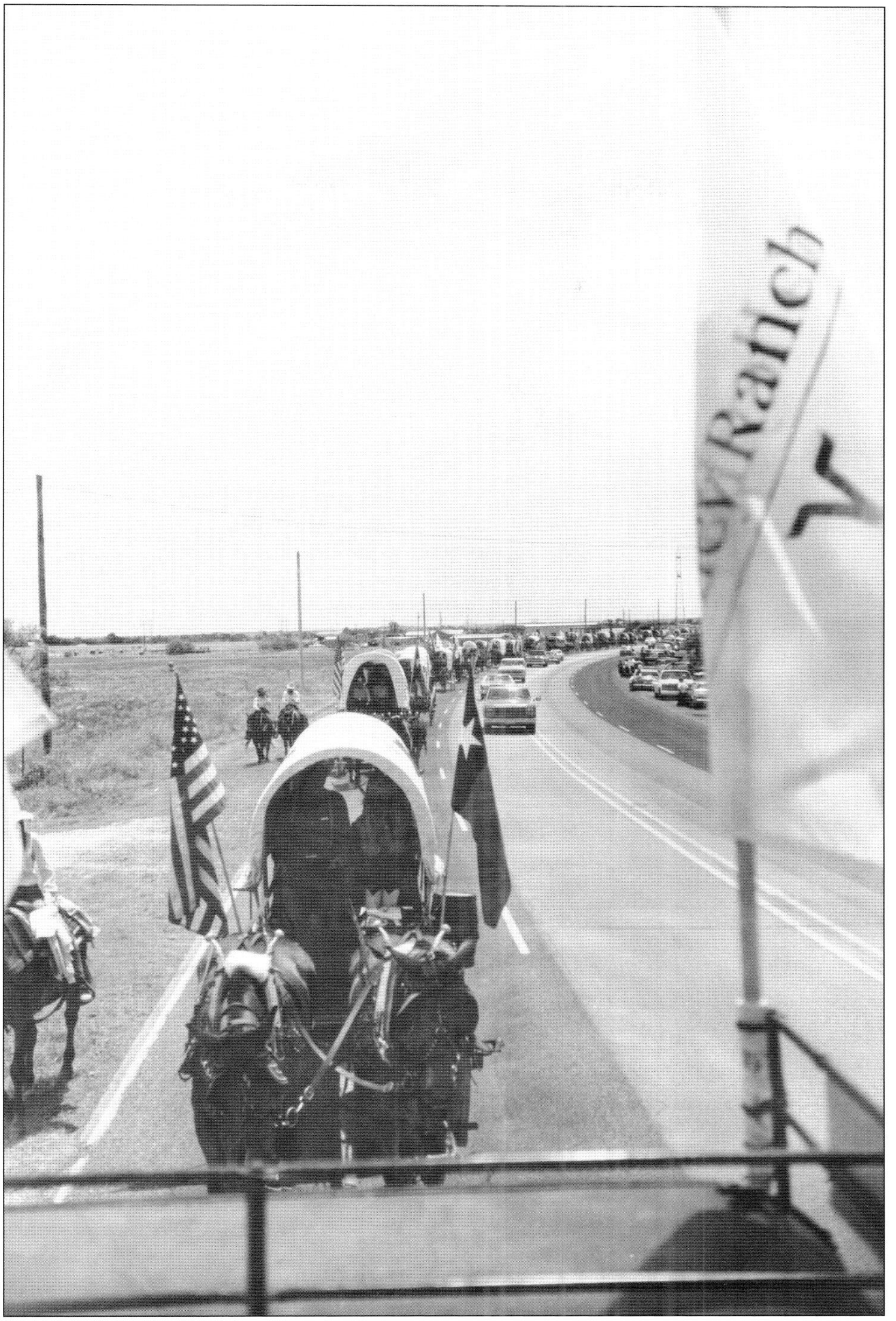

Photographer Dominick J. Cirincione rode in the stagecoach between Windthorst and Wichita Falls and took many photographs of the train behind him. Cars traveling on US Highway 281 north toward Wichita Falls slowed down as they passed the train. A lot of rubbernecking occurred.

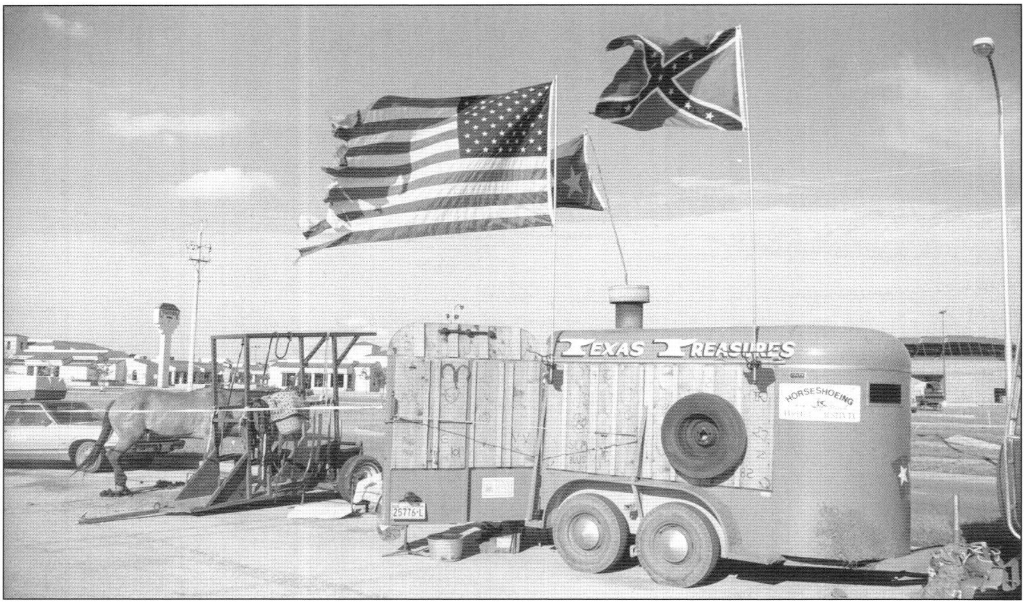

Portable horseshoeing equipment followed the wagon train. This was a definite necessary service with the distances traveled and the number of mules and horses pulling the wagons. Also a part of the train was the official veterinarian, who had the final word on whether an animal was healthy enough to continue. His word was absolute. Dr. Ken Carlson served as the veterinarian for the train. Weather, obviously, could affect the animals. The hottest day was 104 in February in West Texas, when participants still had their winter coats, and the coldest was a wind chill of nine degrees in May in Amarillo with snow.

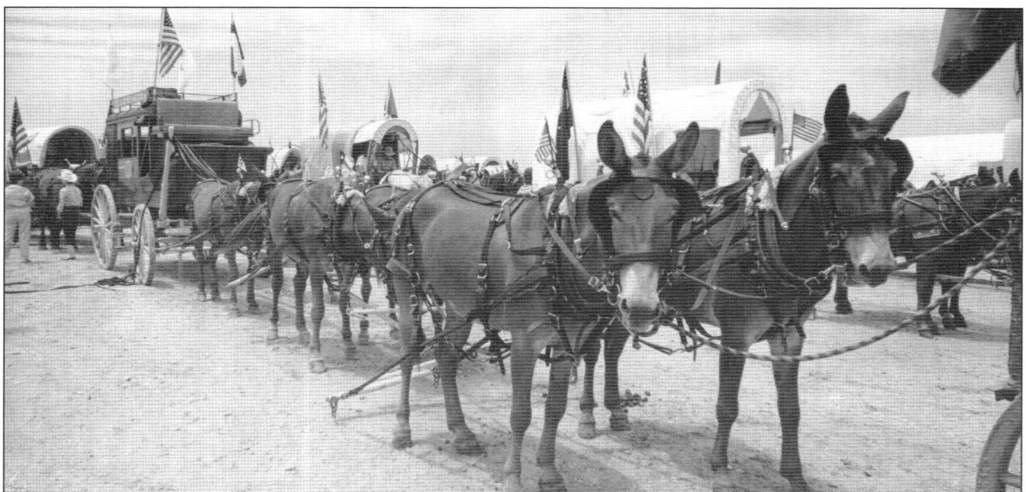

Readers may remember the 20 Mule Team Borax advertisements on television from years ago (the product is still manufactured today). The drivers of teams of mules pulling wagons of freight across the West helped form a union now known as the International Brotherhood of Teamsters, of which drivers of 18-wheeler trucks are members. The only stagecoach in the train, driven by Rudy Nelson, apparently needed three teams of mules. Here, they wait patiently either to get going in the morning or to end their day.

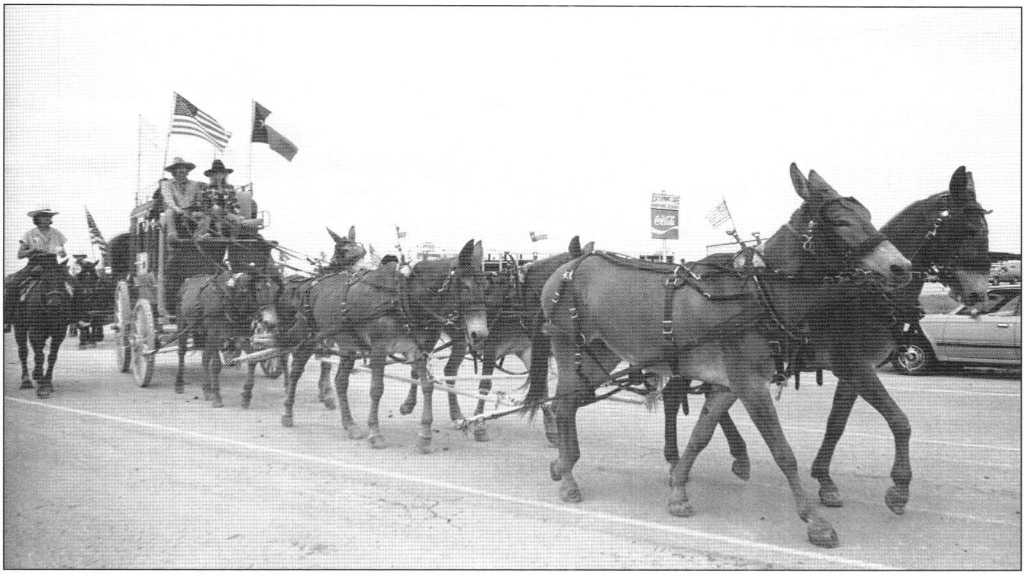

Photographer Cirincione, while riding beside driver Rudy Nelson, learned that Nelson used the leather reins as well as a collection of pebbles, which he bounced accurately off the mule's rear if it got out of line, to handle the six mules. Other seasoned drivers used the same trick as well, because just a light tap on the rump attracted the attention of their animals.

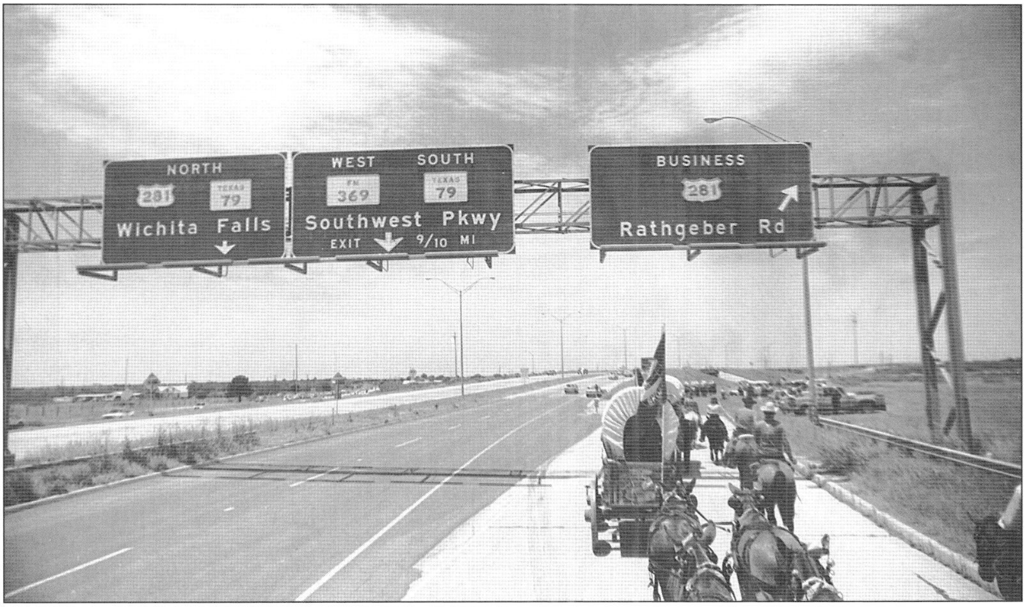

Riders of the wagons or horses felt like they were in a parade each time they entered a town or city. Folks gathered in great numbers on both sides of the street to greet them. Sometimes wagon train business manager Quentin McGown would arrive ahead of the train, meet city fathers, and, with a microphone, introduce each wagon as it traveled past the reviewing stand. McGown also acted as master of ceremonies for talent shows in camp. The entire journey was like one long parade; not a mile was traveled without someone stopping to cheer the wagons on—even in far West Texas.

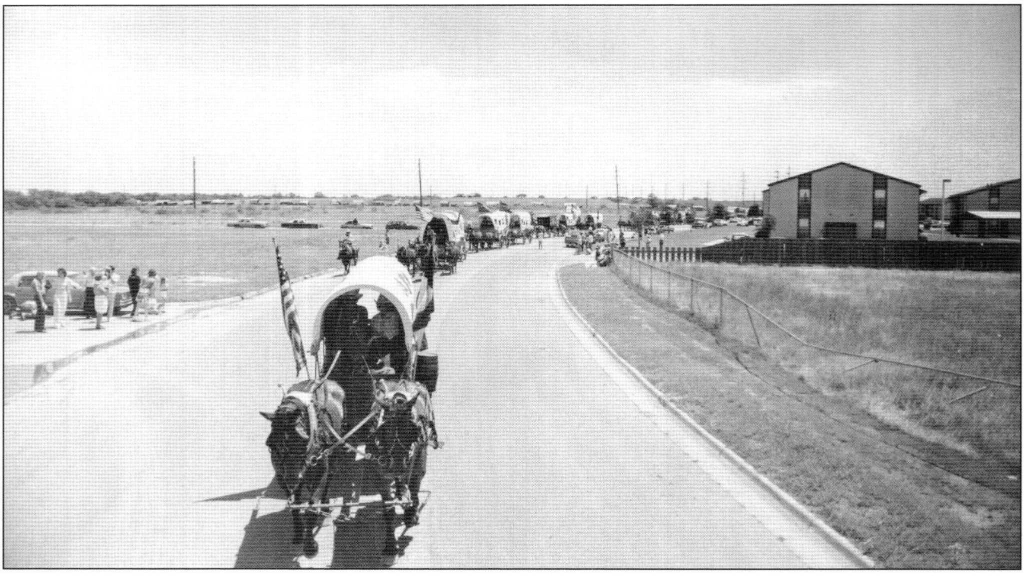

The train arrived in Wichita Falls on June 15. The city of over 100,000 was named for the Wichita Indians, who camped near waterfalls on what is now the Wichita River. The railroad's arrival and an oil boom helped the community to grow. Spectators began gathering on the highway as the train headed for its two-night stop.

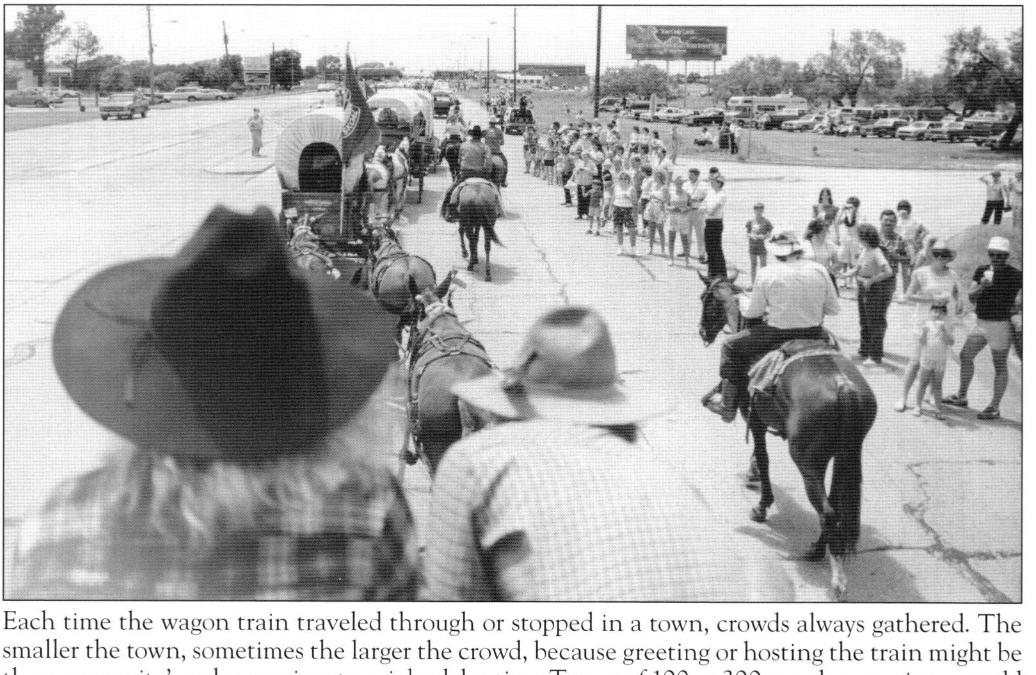

Each time the wagon train traveled through or stopped in a town, crowds always gathered. The smaller the town, sometimes the larger the crowd, because greeting or hosting the train might be the community's only sesquicentennial celebration. Towns of 100 to 300 people sometimes would have a crowd of 1,000 enthusiasts appear from surrounding areas. The tiny town of Eola had a population of only 200, but 4,000–5,000 people greeted the train there. Mentone, the smallest town in Texas in 1986 with a population of 12, had over 1,000 people present when the train arrived. Mentone is in Loving County, the smallest county (by population) in the United States.

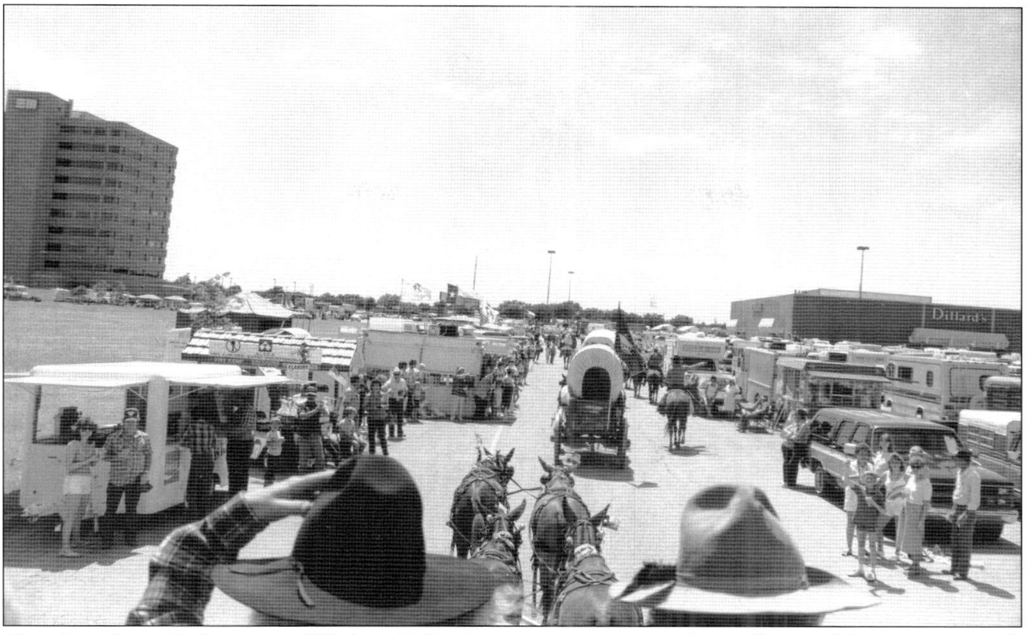

Traveling through downtown Wichita Falls, the wagon train created a traffic jam. Visitors increased, as did wagons joining the train the closer it got to Fort Worth. Wichita Falls would be about a two-hour drive in a car to Fort Worth, but after two nights there, 16 more camps remained before the train reached Fort Worth and the end of the journey.

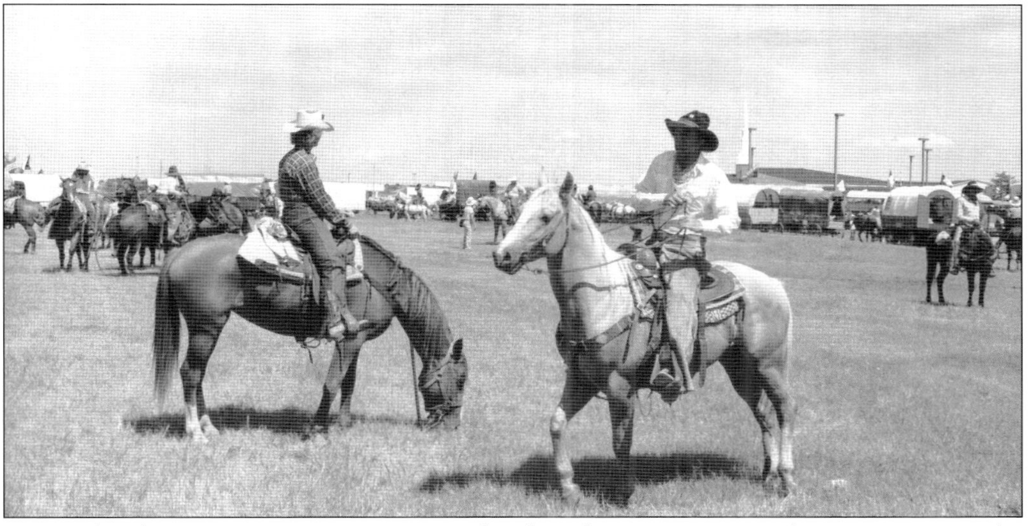

During the planning stage, Jan France visited with each committee in each stopover town to let them know what to expect, whether morning water break, afternoon break, as well as overnight camps. An area of at least 100 acres was needed to accommodate all the wagons, RVs, campers, support personnel, and visitors from the town to the campsite. France drove and met with everyone at least three times before the actual wagon train journey. Her daughters, Sunday Steward and Misty Steward, assisted her at different times. A crew of about 45, including nurse, blacksmith, veterinarian, teachers, camp jacks, wagon masters, outriders, security guards, vehicle drivers, and office staff, became a well-disciplined crew that got the train down the road safely.

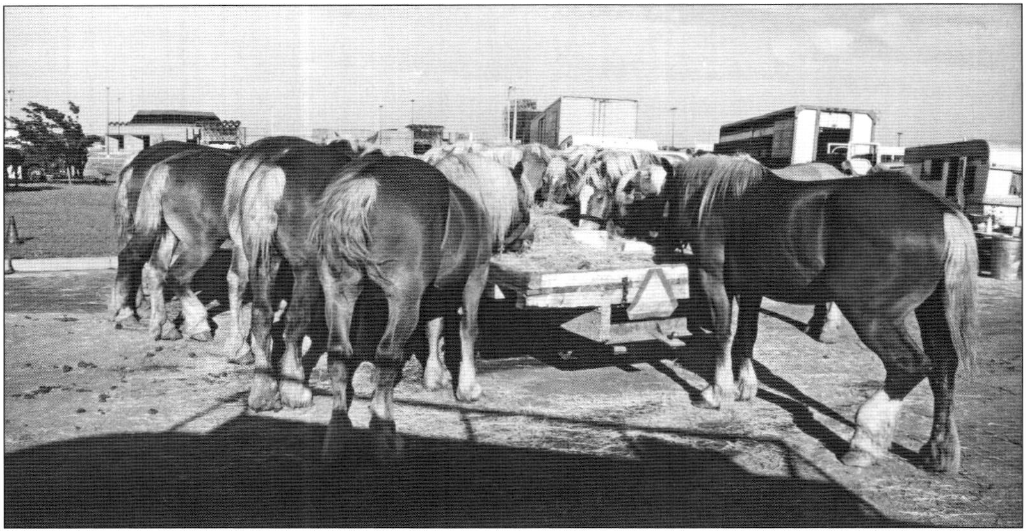

Feeding and watering one's animals required regular attention morning and evening. It was one of the chores that equated exactly the tasks that the pioneers tackled 150 years earlier when they arrived in Texas. Shown here are the draft horses from the McCrosson Boys Ranch in South Dakota. Boys from the ranch rotated in and out of the wagon train over the six-month trip. Craig R. "Rusty" Hebel, official South Dakota representative, drove the McCrosson Belgian mares the entire trip. He used 30 Belgian mares over the six months and was in charge of their health. He had been a teenager during the 1976 bicentennial wagon train. Hebel, a rancher from Glen, Montana, passed away October 23, 2010.

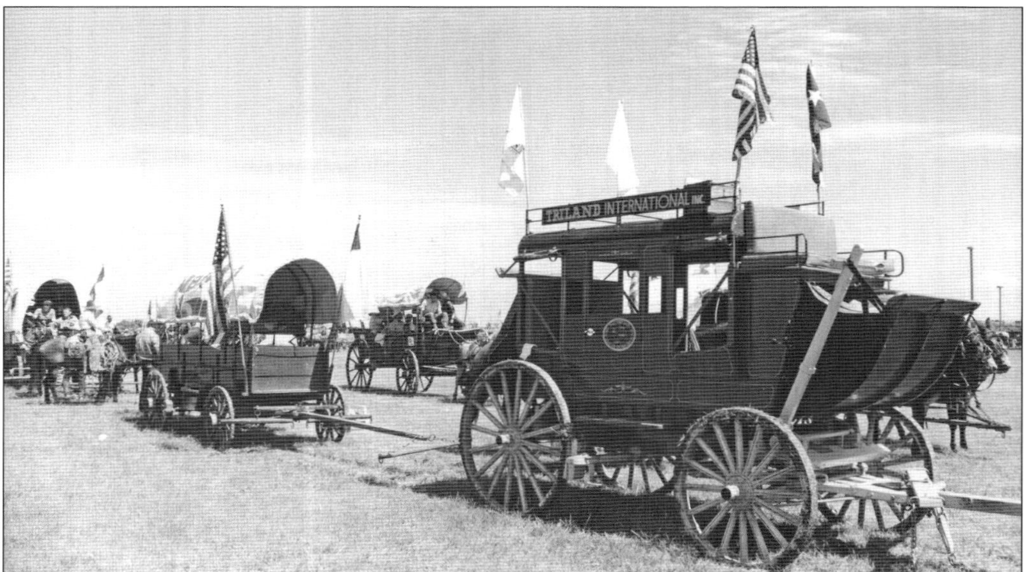

The train spent two days in Wichita Falls. After reaching camp and taking care of their animals, the drivers and riders could sit around and take part in the fun and entertainment that the townspeople usually provided. If they did not furnish food, the train association had a large 40-foot semitrailer kitchen truck available to sell it. Andy Anderson and his wife, Helen, also ran a food concession wagon.

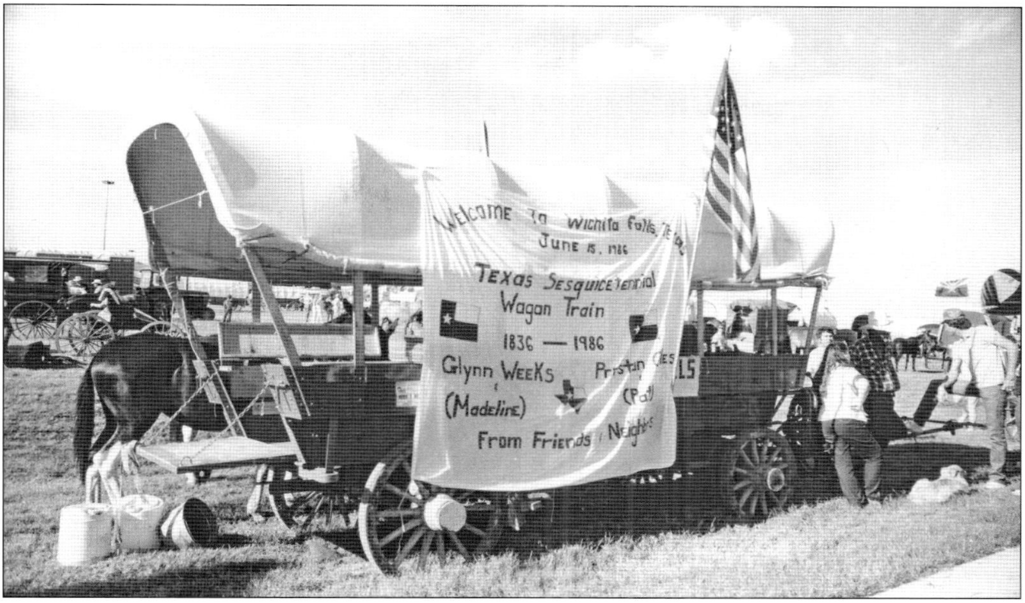

This homemade sign welcomed the wagon train to Wichita Falls. Its final message is "From Friends and Neighbors." Local communities often furnished meals for the riders in the train. What is more appropriate and Western than barbecue and beans? Unfortunately, most towns served that same meal, and the folks on the train got tired of it. However, some towns also served chicken, buffalo burgers, chicken-fried steak, and chili, especially on cold days.

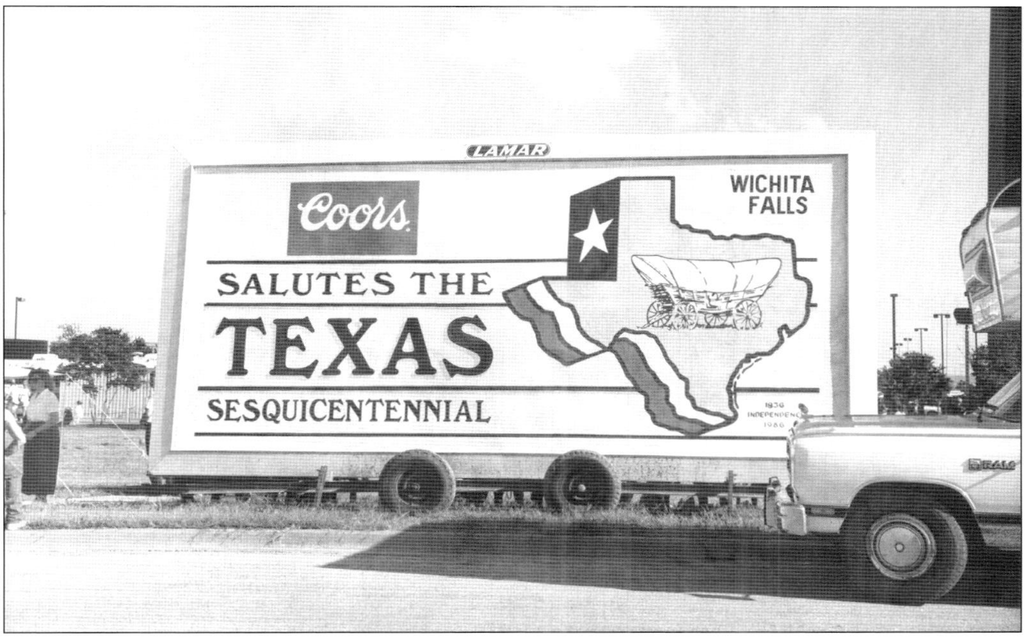

This official and very professional sesquicentennial sign welcomed the train to Wichita Falls. Indeed, the wagon train was well received and welcomed by all the towns and cities visited. It became one of the most visible and publicized aspects of the celebration of Texas's 150th birthday. After leaving Wichita Falls, the train stopped in Henrietta, Nocona, Muenster, and Gainesville.

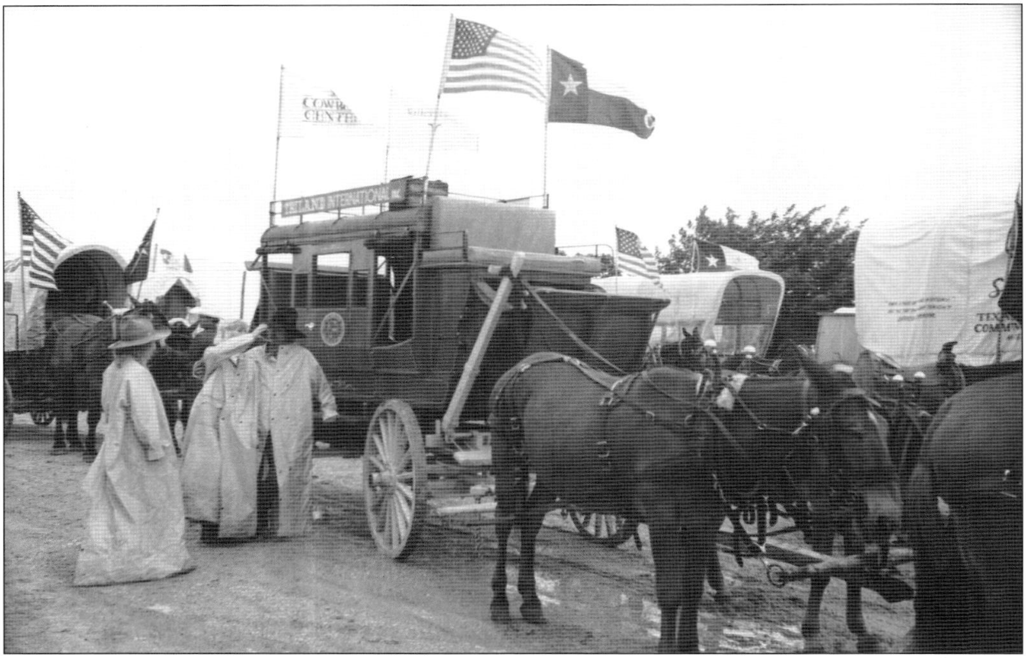

"Keep moving, rain or shine" became the motto. While waiting in mud and water, mules to pull the only stagecoach in the train are hitched and ready to go. Riders have their slickers and hats on to protect against the dreary, drippy day. This is when participants really began feeling that "pioneer spirit"—or was it an appreciation for that warm RV at camp? Some of them, however, roughed it like their ancestors did.

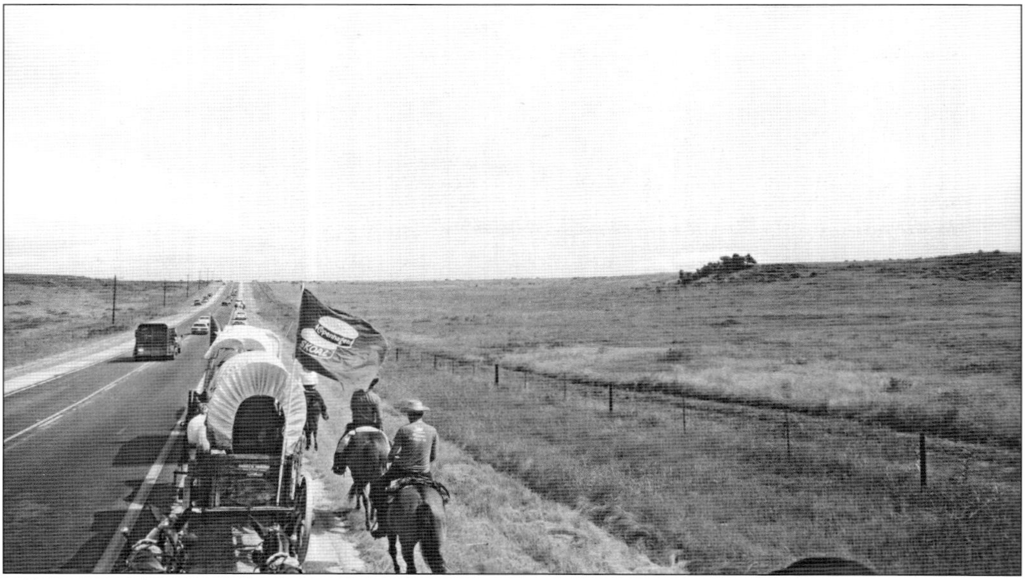

All was not always quiet and peaceful while plodding along each day. There were runaway horses. Sometimes a wagon would get too far off the road and would tip over. The tongue might break, and the horses bolt. Axles sometimes snapped, and a tractor was available to tow disabled wagons to camp. Each camp was only 20 miles or so from the previous one.

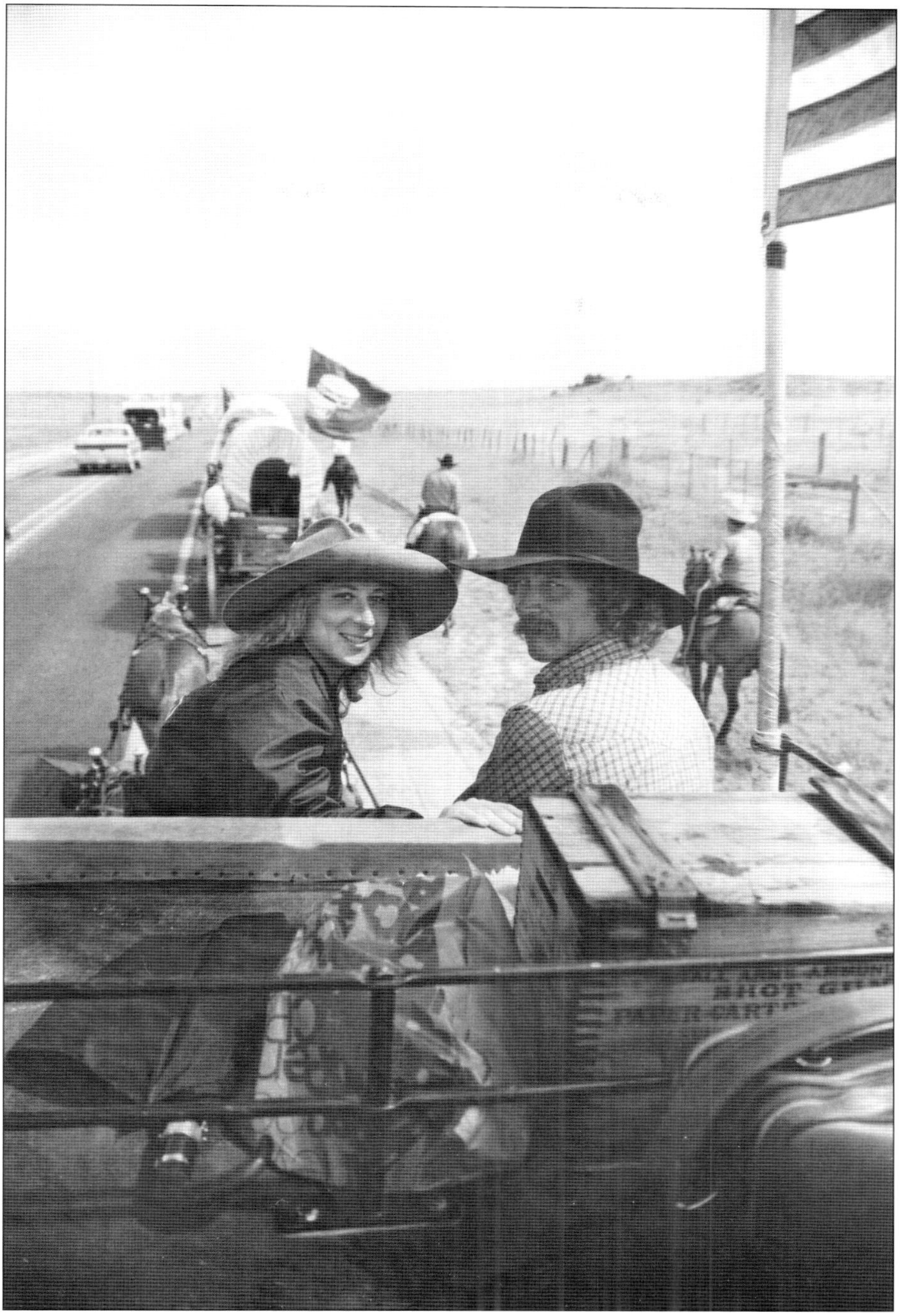

Jana Miranti and Rudy Nelson provided romance to the train. Meeting Miranti on May 19 at a stop in Amarillo, Nelson offered her and her six-year-old son a ride on the stagecoach he drove. She met the train the next week and stayed with it. The couple married at Valley Ranch in Irving at the end of the journey with their wagon train friends as well-wishers. Country-and-western singer Charley Pride turned out to be the entertainment for that stop, so they can tell their grandchildren he sang at their wedding. Actually, several couples married during the course of the trip.

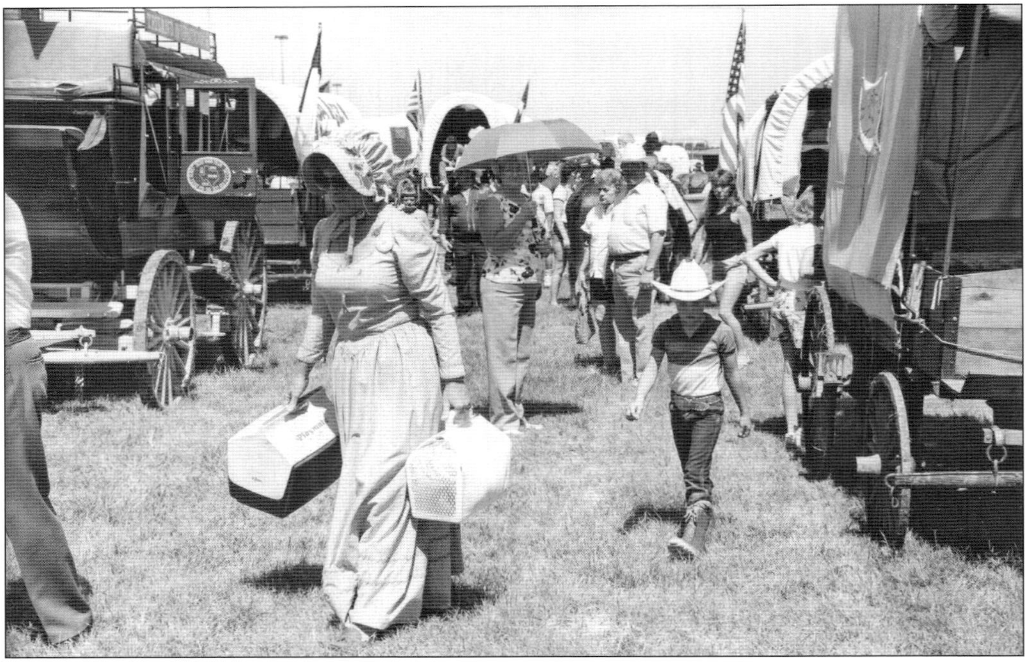

While in camp, modern fashions and convenience mixed with pioneer garb, such as this lady in her long dress and bonnet carrying her Playmate ice chest. Tourists from each town or city mingled. Not everyone traveled on the train for the entire route of 3,228 miles during its six-month trek. People could join the train for a day or for a week or two, but they had to ride all day from campsite to campsite. In all, 10,000 different riders or drivers from 27 states took part.

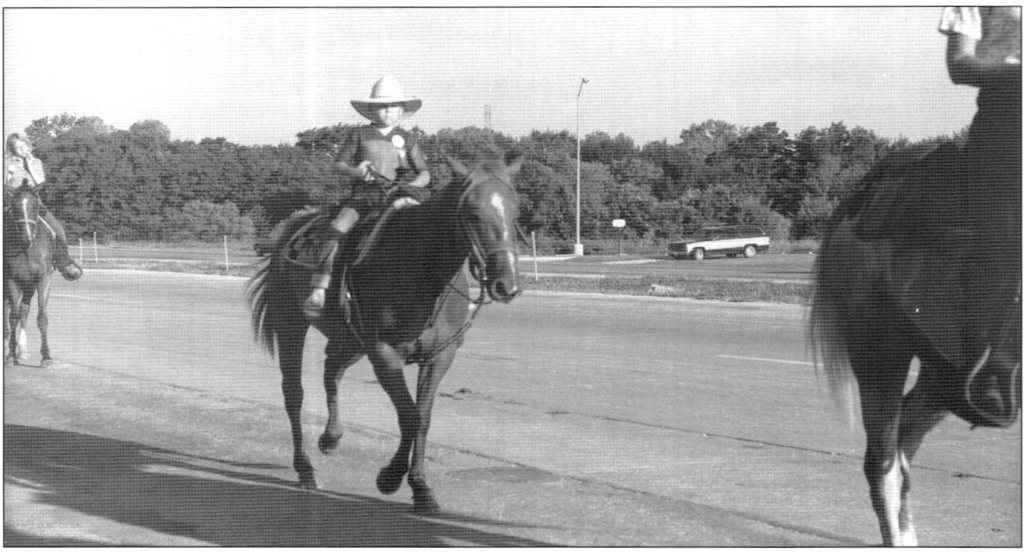

The 27 youngsters who completed the entire trip with their parents attended the Wagon Train School, which was fully affiliated and certified with the State of Texas. They studied in a schoolhouse that traveled on an 18-wheeler. The children had some time to ride horses, too. One student, Lori Warner, 17, of Longview, even graduated from high school in a special commencement ceremony at the conclusion of the trip.

This is a photograph of Hazel Bowen as she looked in 1976 when she rode in the bicentennial celebration for the United States. She drove the same Texas wagon for the Texas wagon train trip. See her as she looked in 1986 on page 25. (Courtesy Jem Publishers.)

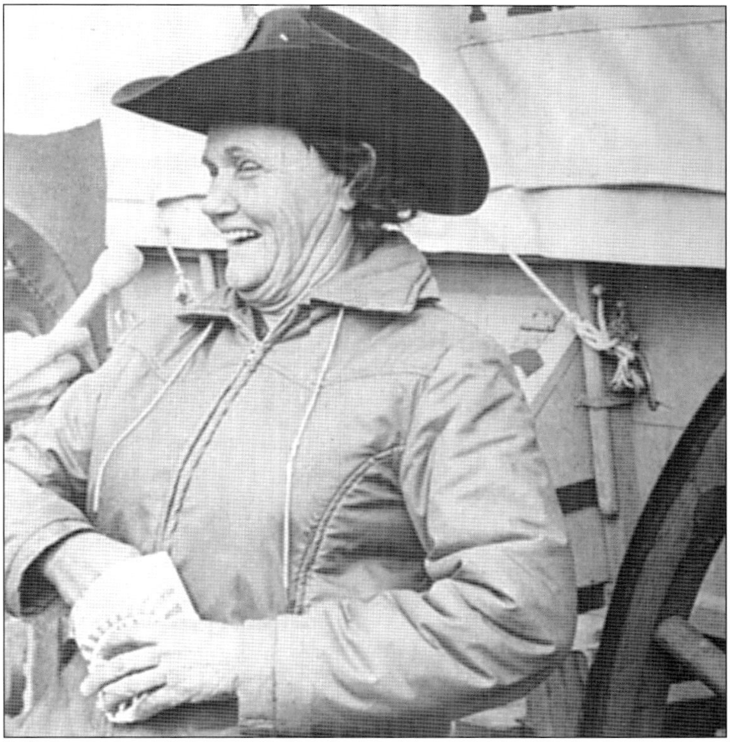

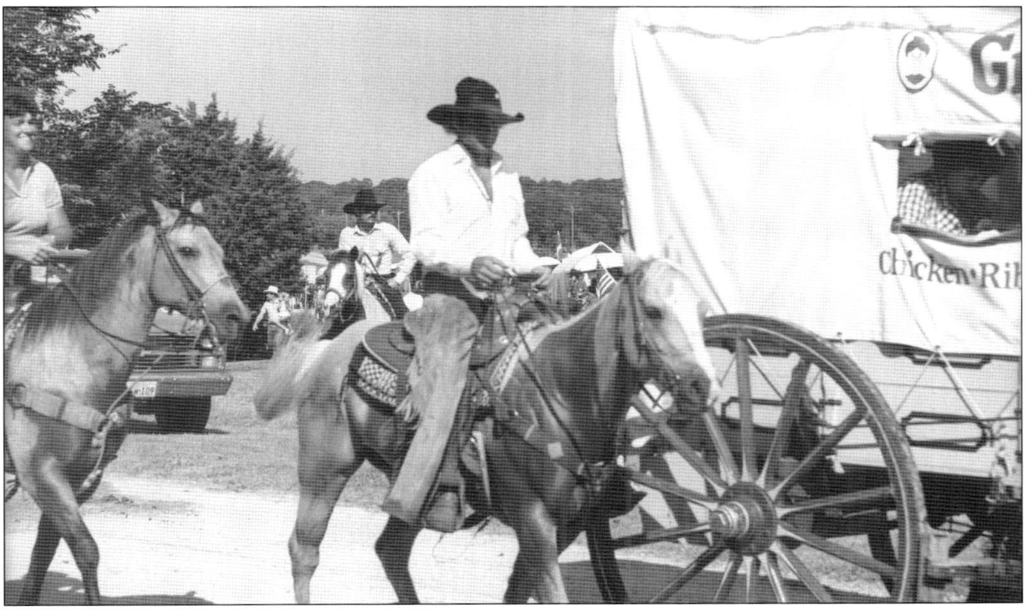

Grandy's, Inc. was one of the official sponsors of the train, so the word "chicken" showing on the white canvas wagon cover was permissible. Outriders like the one shown here, if a part of the wagon train staff, performed a valuable service. Viola Cook was the head outrider and could tame unruly horses and their riders before trouble developed. Unfortunately, many inexperienced riders, who joined the train for only a day or two, sometimes got into trouble before help could arrive.

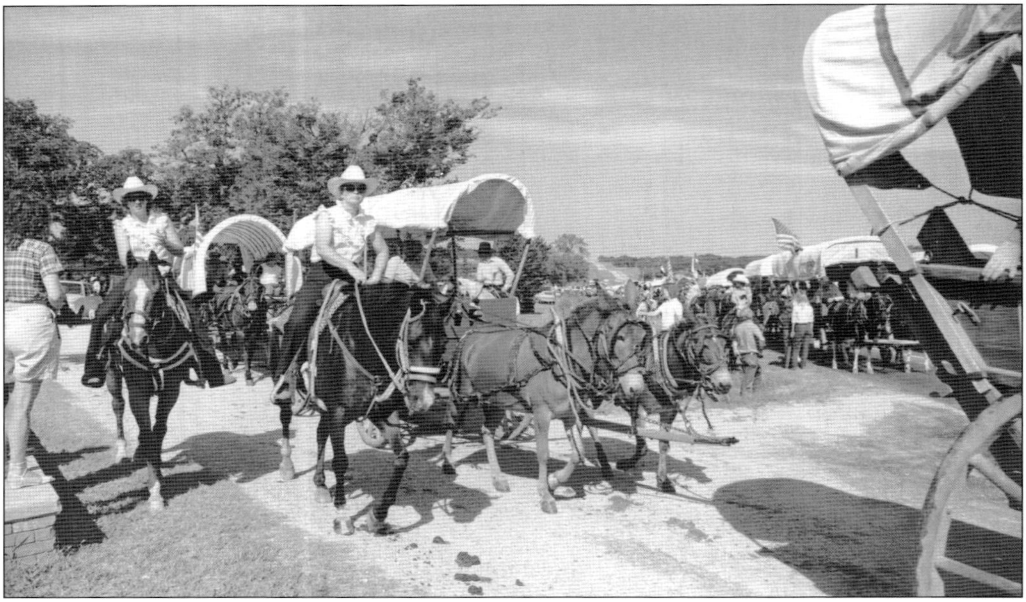

Two unidentified young ladies are coming into this camp in Gainesville on their horses. Tourists and townsfolk always enjoyed visiting the camp after it arrived and set up. For their convenience, the official Texas Sesquicentennial Wagon Train tourist souvenir trailer opened up for business each evening. For the participants, treasured memories became their best souvenirs. Riding clubs from many communities joined the train for a day.

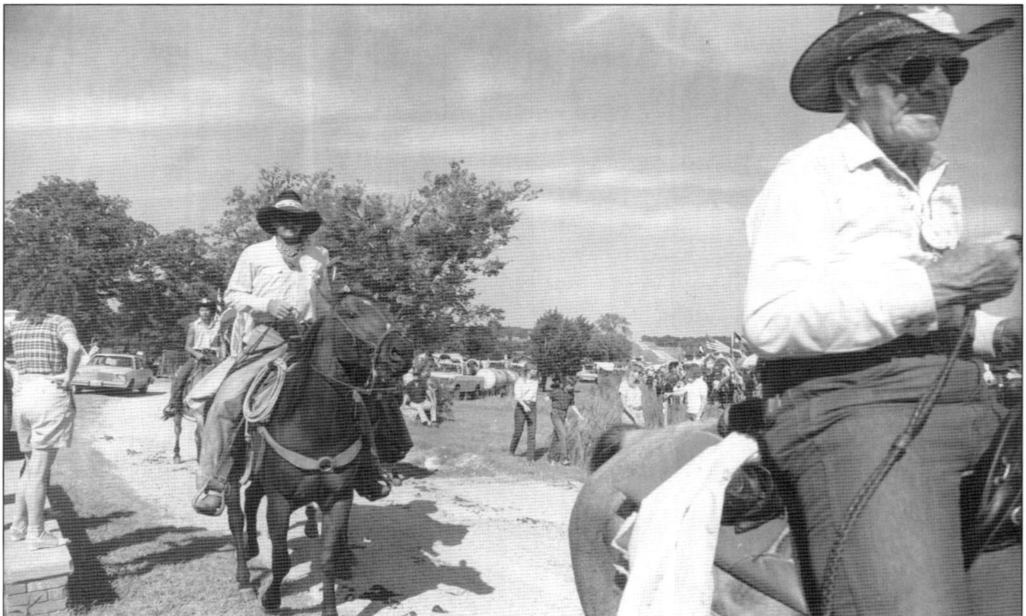

Gainesville, a town of 15,000, welcomed the train for a two-day stop on June 20–21. One of only 12 Texas travel information centers in the state is located at Gainesville as visitors enter Texas on I-35 coming south from Oklahoma. The train is enjoying a rest stop as many tourists also do when they arrive in Texas.

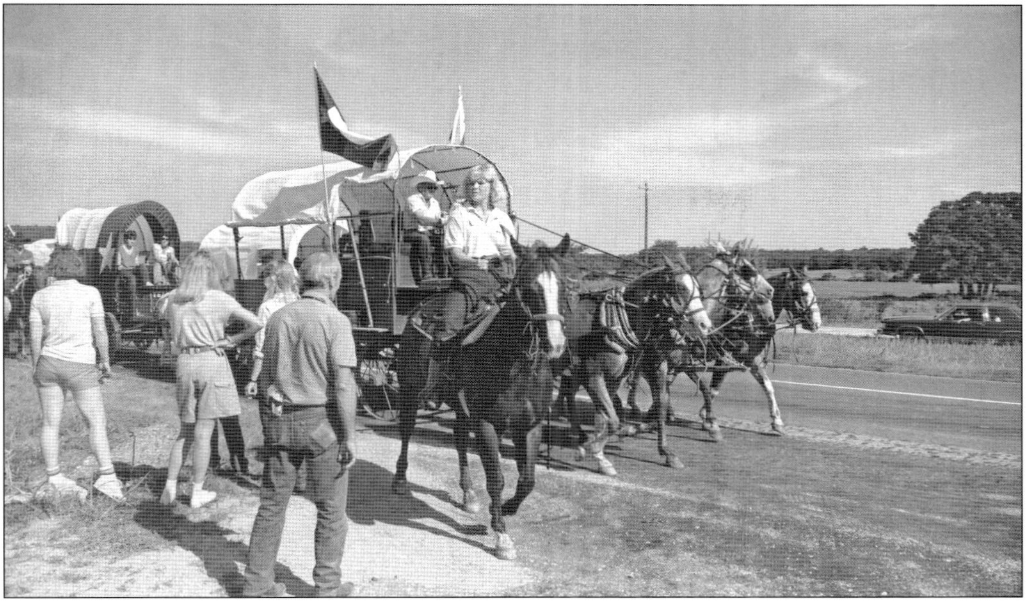

This wagon setup is a bit unusual because the driver is handling three horses lined up side by side. The young lady on the horse in front makes it difficult to see. Notice the spectators in their shorts, who have arrived to see the train close up. Tourists could enjoy lighter clothing to be more comfortable during the hot Texas summer, but many of the riders still have their typical jeans and long-sleeved shirts to keep from getting sunburned.

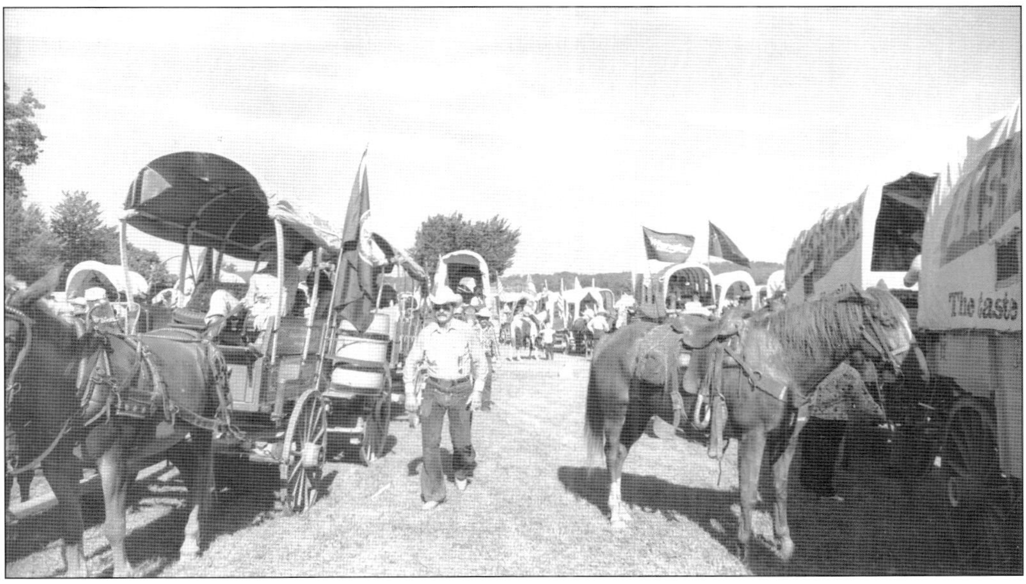

The man in the center of this photograph in the white shirt and white hat is Quentin McGown, the business manager of the train who made things work behind the scenes. He had a small office inside an 18-wheeler that also served as a tool house and dressing room and could be transformed into a stage for performances. McGown, a lawyer by profession, worked on the wagon train project beginning in May 1985. Before that, he served as a part of the Texas Sesquicentennial Commission.

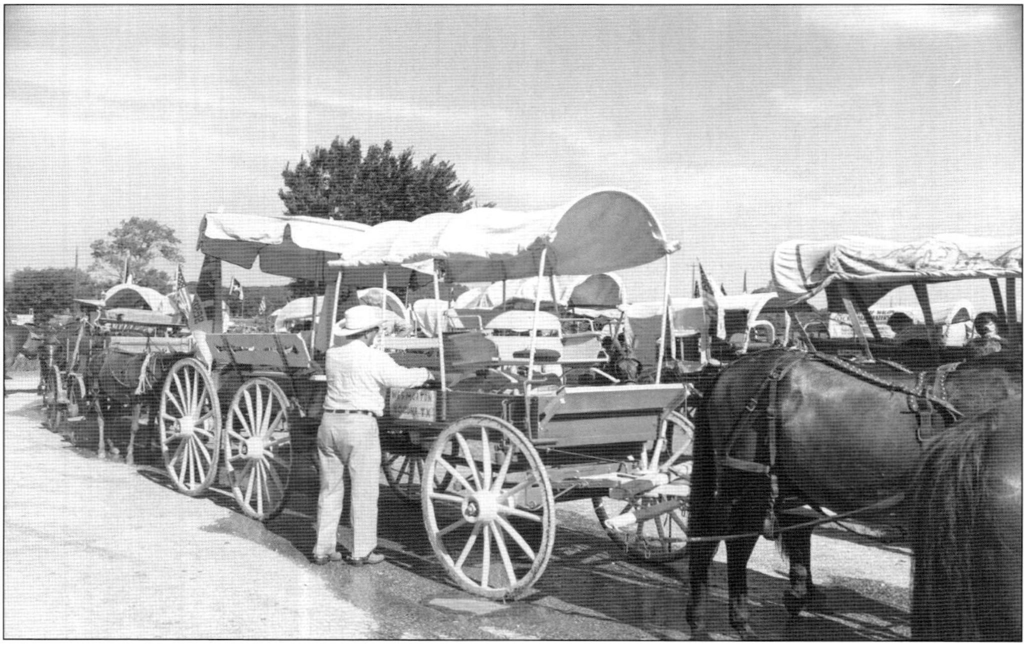

This unusual wagon with double wheels on the rear belonged to Wes Morton of Nocona. He also planned it to be naturally air-conditioned by rolling up the canvas sides. The double rear wheels may have been for the purpose of providing for a heavy load in a previous usage of the wagon. The train stopped in Nocona on June 18. Justin Boots had its beginning in Nocona in 1879.

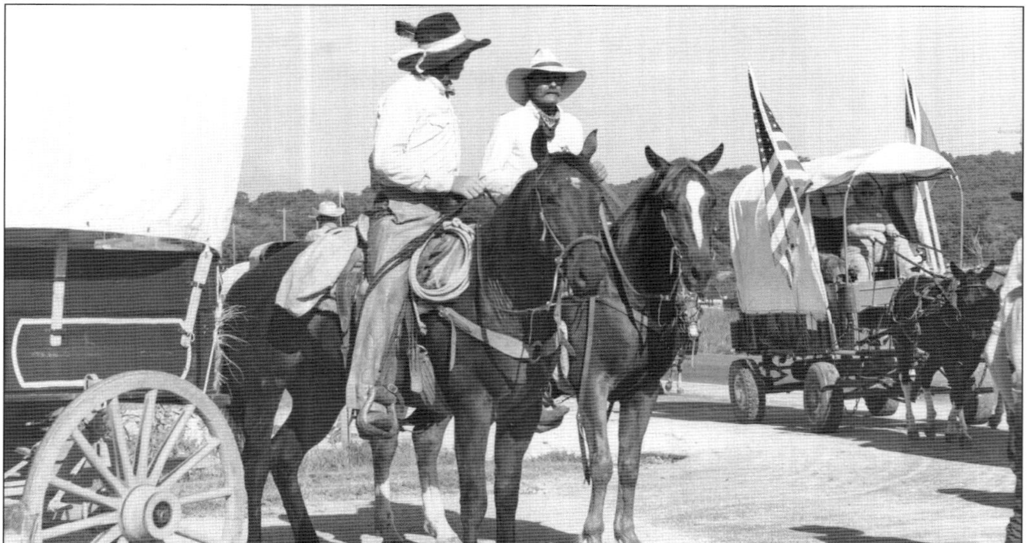

The horseback rider in the white hat is Vern Renz, assistant wagon master and pacesetter. The wagon on the right is not exactly authentic because it has small rubber wheels. Its driver, however, probably enjoyed a smoother ride than those who drove a more historically accurate wagon with hard, wooden wheels. Some of the 1986 "pioneers" insisted upon as much accuracy as possible, while others accepted some comforts. Folks in 1836 did not have that choice. The wagon train kept its most authentic wagons toward the front so that townspeople would see historical ones first.

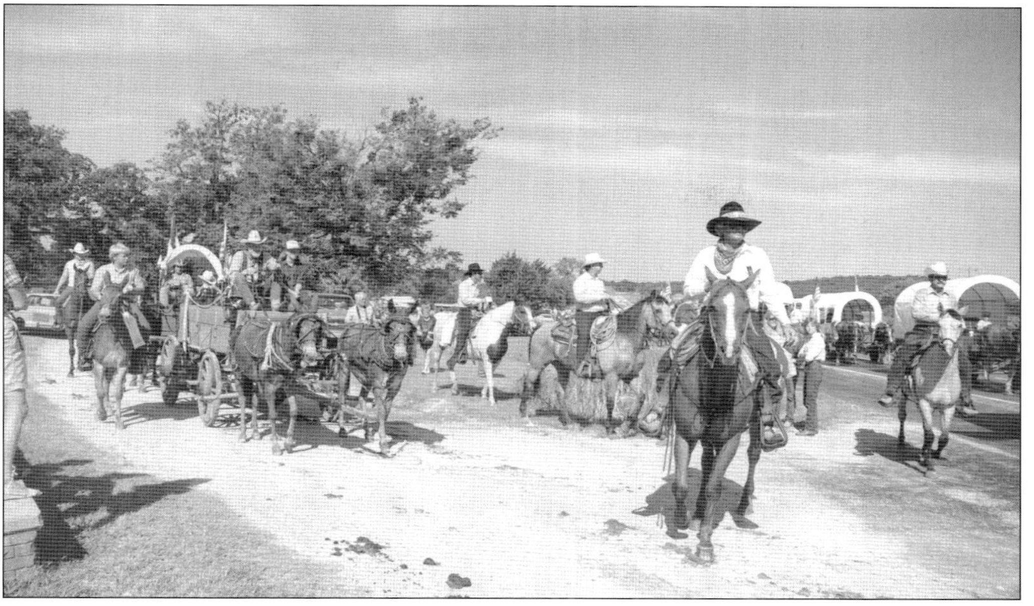

Wagon master Garry France apparently has just shouted "Wagons, ho!" in this photograph and is leading the train out to continue its journey for another day. Because France was the wagon master, and because his wife, Jan, was executive director of the Texas Wagon Train Association (and had the idea for it in the first place), she drove the first wagon and helped host dignitaries in each town.

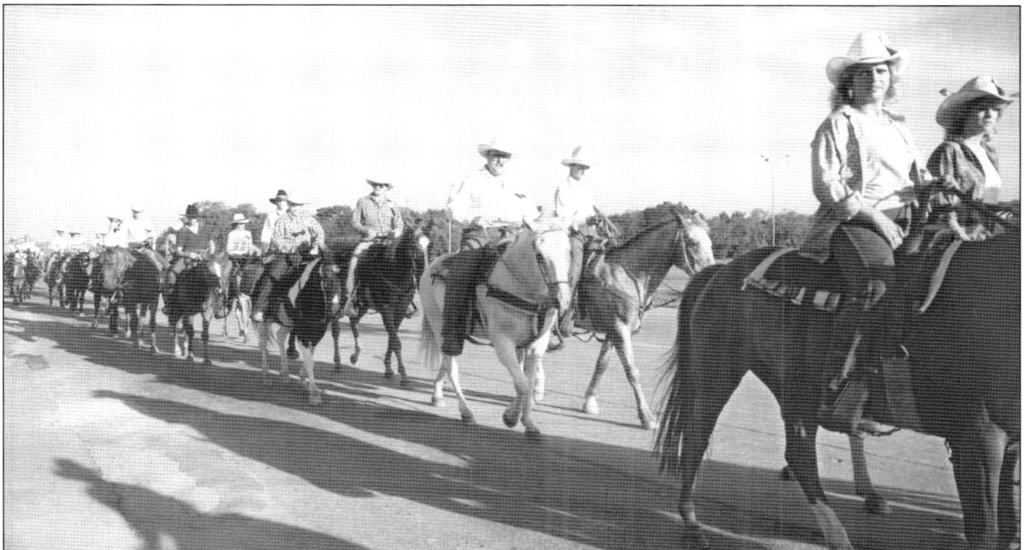

The number of outriders increased as the train came closer to Fort Worth. These have just left the Gainesville area on June 21 and are headed toward Whitesboro. A town of less than 4,000, Whitesboro was established in 1848 when Ambrose B. White built an inn, which became a stagecoach station on the Butterfield Overland Mail route. That sounds appropriate for the train to be heading there for its next stop. Highway 82 is in most part the Butterfield route, which is why it was selected as part of the journey.

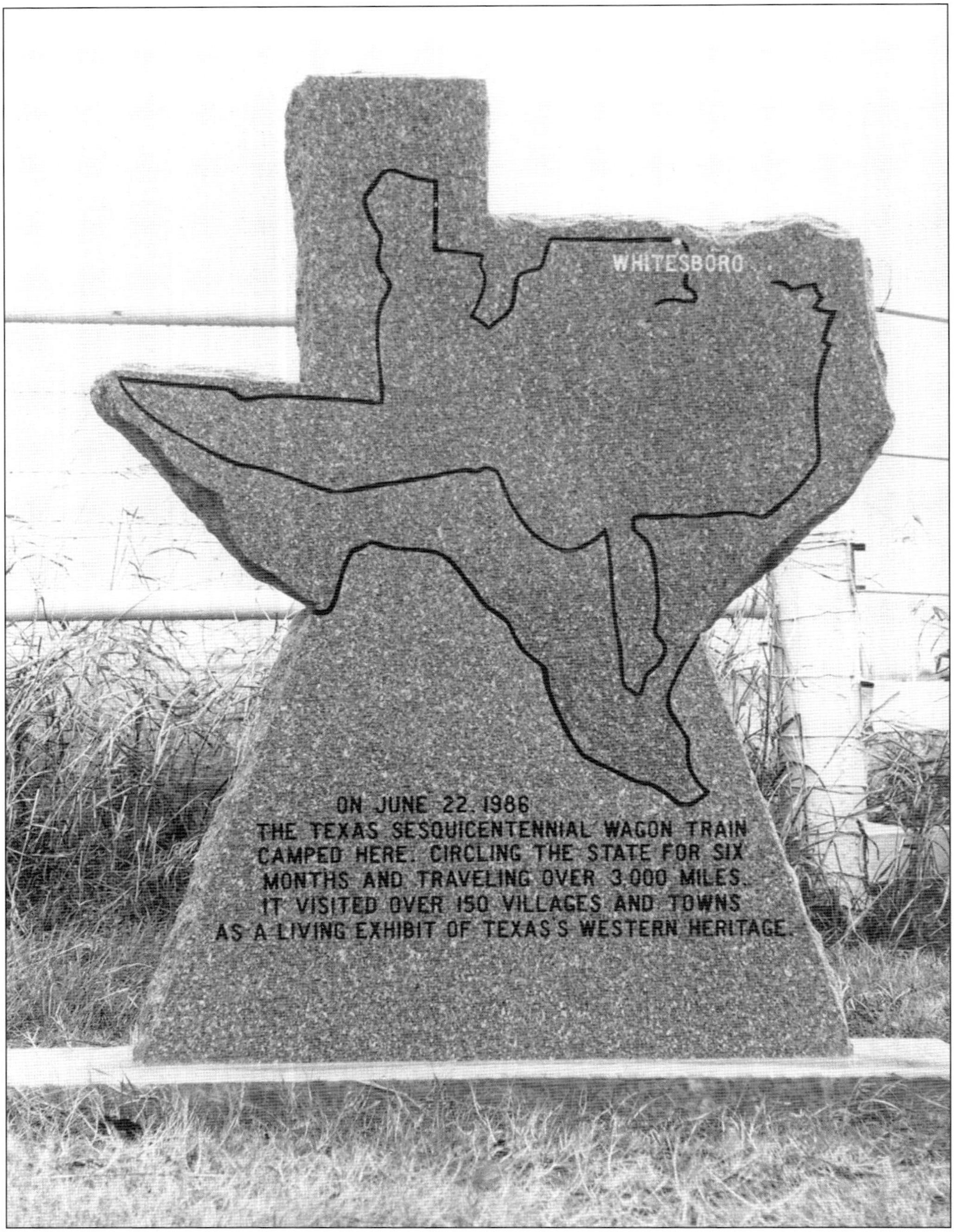

The train arrived in Whitesboro on June 22. Because citizens of Whitesboro realized that 3,000 miles would be reached in their city, they created this marble marker with the approximate route on it. The inscription states, "On June 22, 1986, the Texas Sesquicentennial Wagon Train camped here. Circling the state for six months and traveling over 3,000 miles, it visited over 150 villages and towns as a living exhibit of Texas's Western heritage." Markers can be found at many of the stops made around the state; a nice one exists in Sulphur Springs as well.

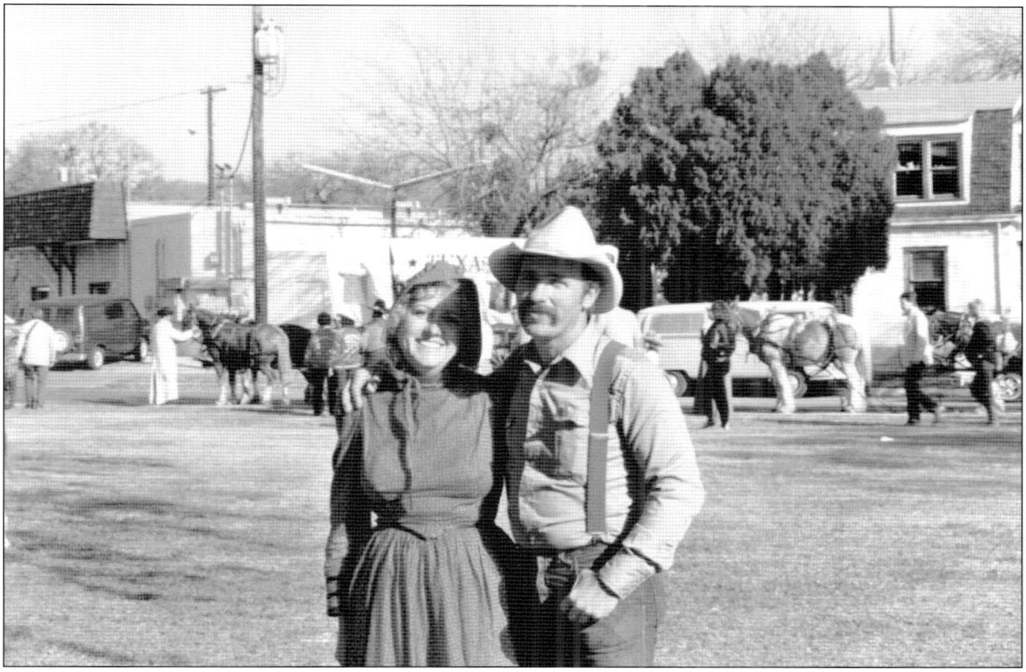

In her pioneer dress and bonnet is Betty McGaha, who drove a wagon and finished the entire six-month trip. To her right is J.R. Newton, assistant camp jack, in his jeans and suspenders. Once, after a particularly long day on the road, Betty read off her shopping list to purchase at the town where they camped: nails, two-by-fours, glue, and Jack Daniels. (Courtesy Quentin McGown.)

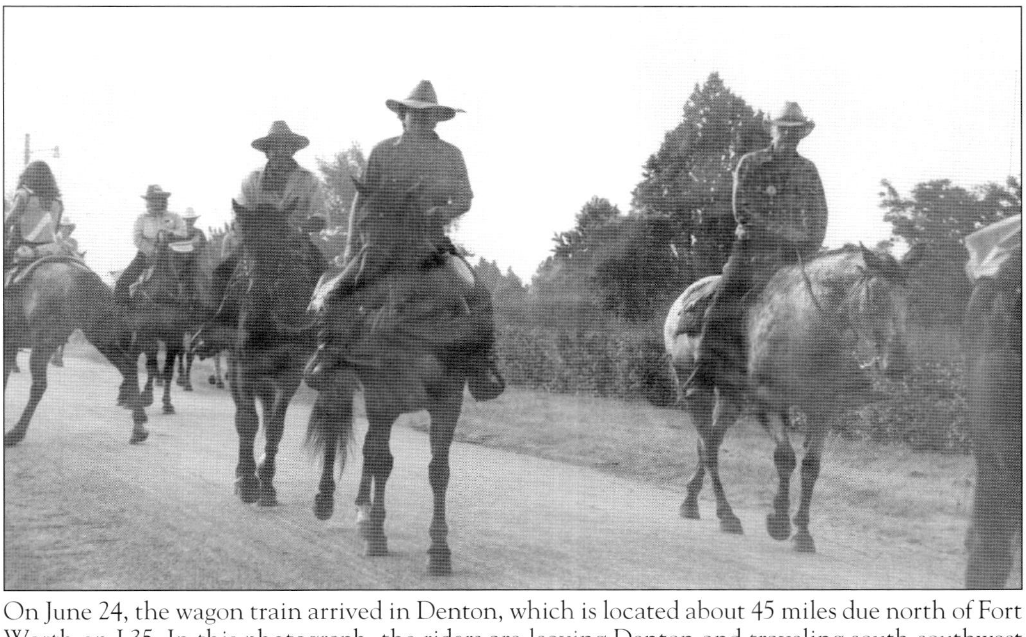

On June 24, the wagon train arrived in Denton, which is located about 45 miles due north of Fort Worth on I-35. In this photograph, the riders are leaving Denton and traveling south-southwest to Ponder. The communities of Argyle, Lewisville, Irving, Grapevine, Colleyville, and North Richland Hills in the Fort Worth area were next.

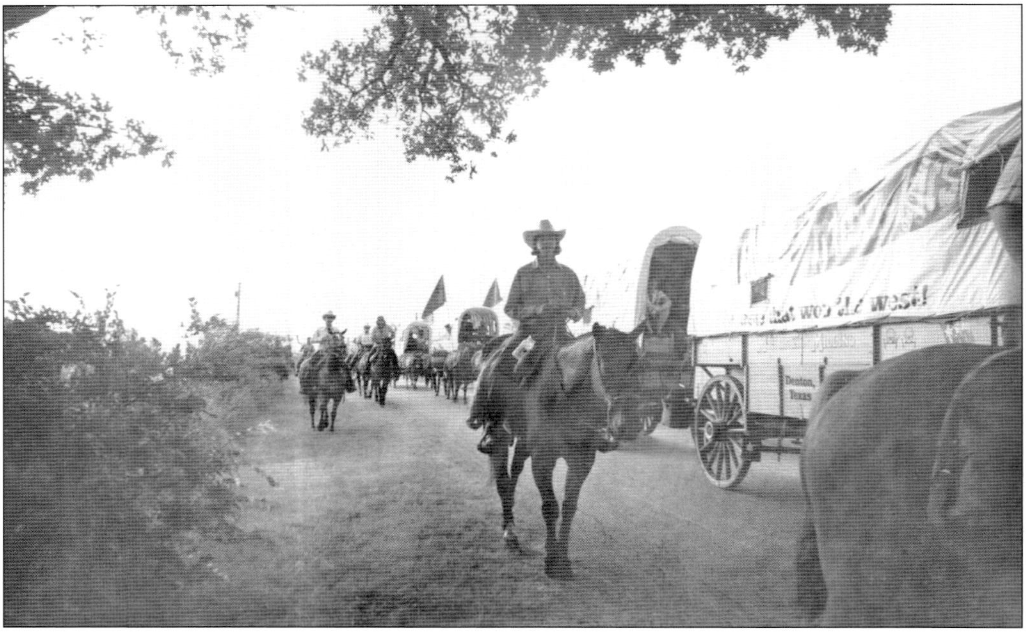

Denton, the university town at the apex of the Golden Triangle of Dallas to the east and Fort Worth to the west, hosted the wagon train as it neared the metroplex. Both the University of North Texas and Texas Woman's University call Denton home. Outriders enjoyed the cool of shade trees on a country road that connected with Denton.

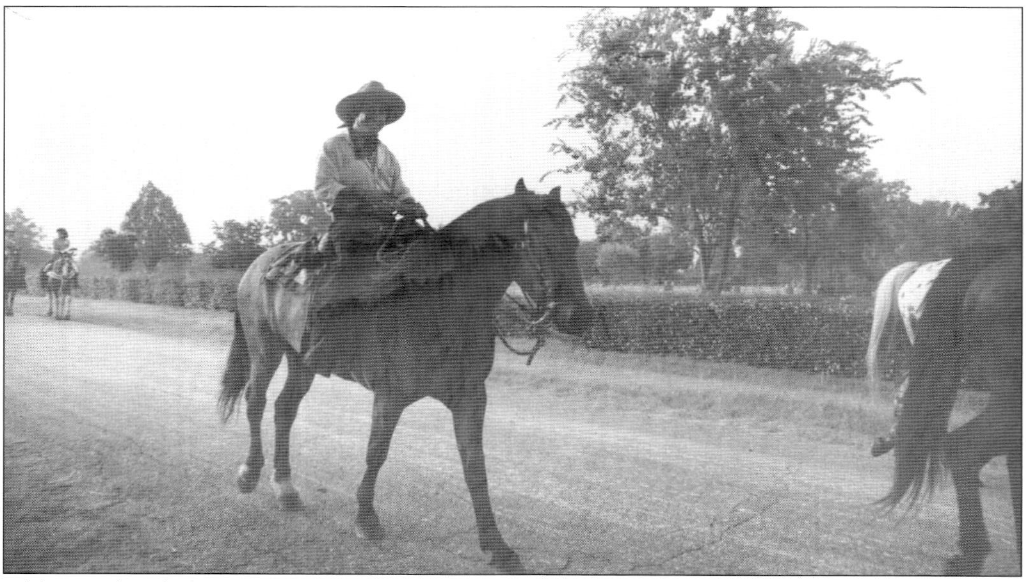

Eddie Sandoval, an associate professor of psychology at the Northeast Campus of Tarrant County Junior College, began his association with the wagon train early, when he served on the Texas Historical Commission that sought ideas for celebrating the sesquicentennial of Texas independence. Sandoval helped Dominick J. Cirincione obtain sanctioning as an official part of the Fort Worth sesquicentennial celebration because of his photography. Sandoval traveled on the train during the summer months as soon as school was out.

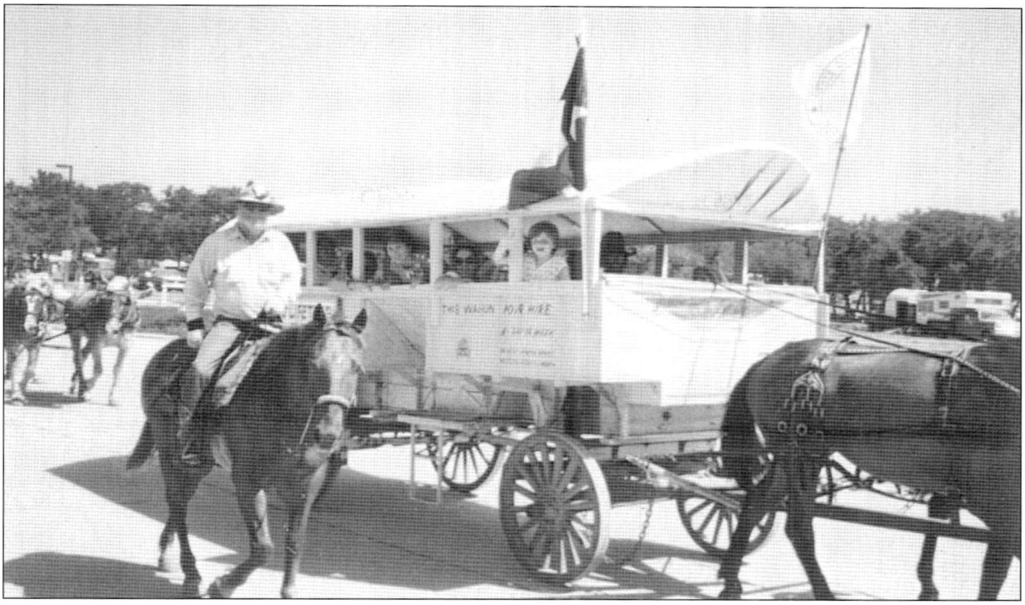

On June 28, the Phillip and Victoria Williams family decided to take advantage of an offer to ride in a wagon for a day. The wagon and its owner both were called "Big Pop." In this photograph, Victoria (left, middle of wagon) and her daughter Rebecca are watching the rider next to the wagon. The owner of the wagon for hire, T.B. Logston, was the stepfather of Garry France. (Courtesy Phillip and Victoria Williams.)

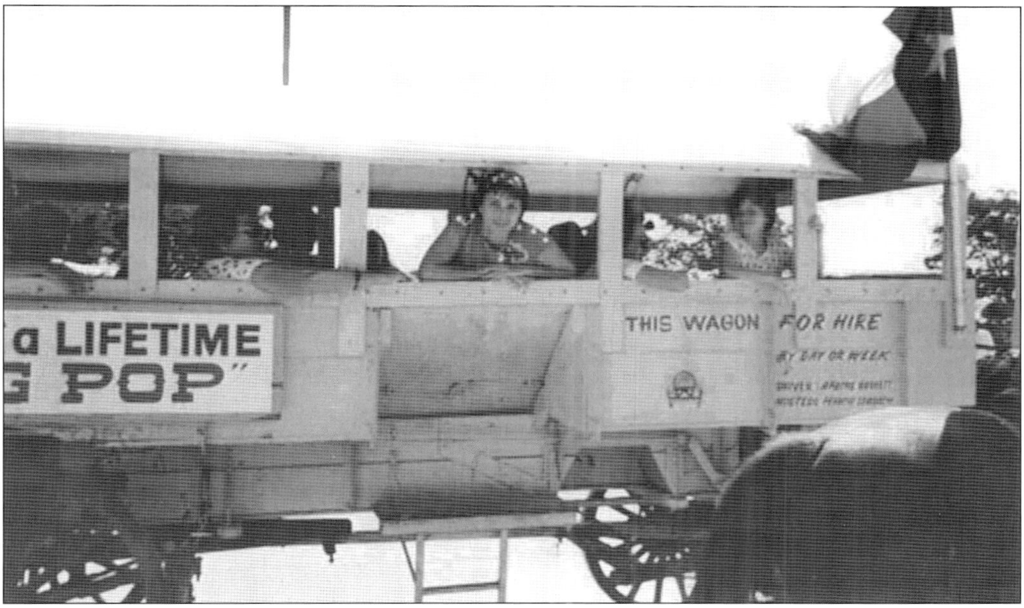

Note in the close-up of the wagon that Big Pop and his wagon had traveled 1,000 miles on the train. The insignia of a wagon representing that milestone is branded directly under the words *this wagon* and the window framing a smiling Rebecca Williams. Victoria, her mother, is to the left. She is not in the photograph, but Frances Limboch helped Big Pop out by taking money and reservations. (Courtesy Phillip and Victoria Williams.)

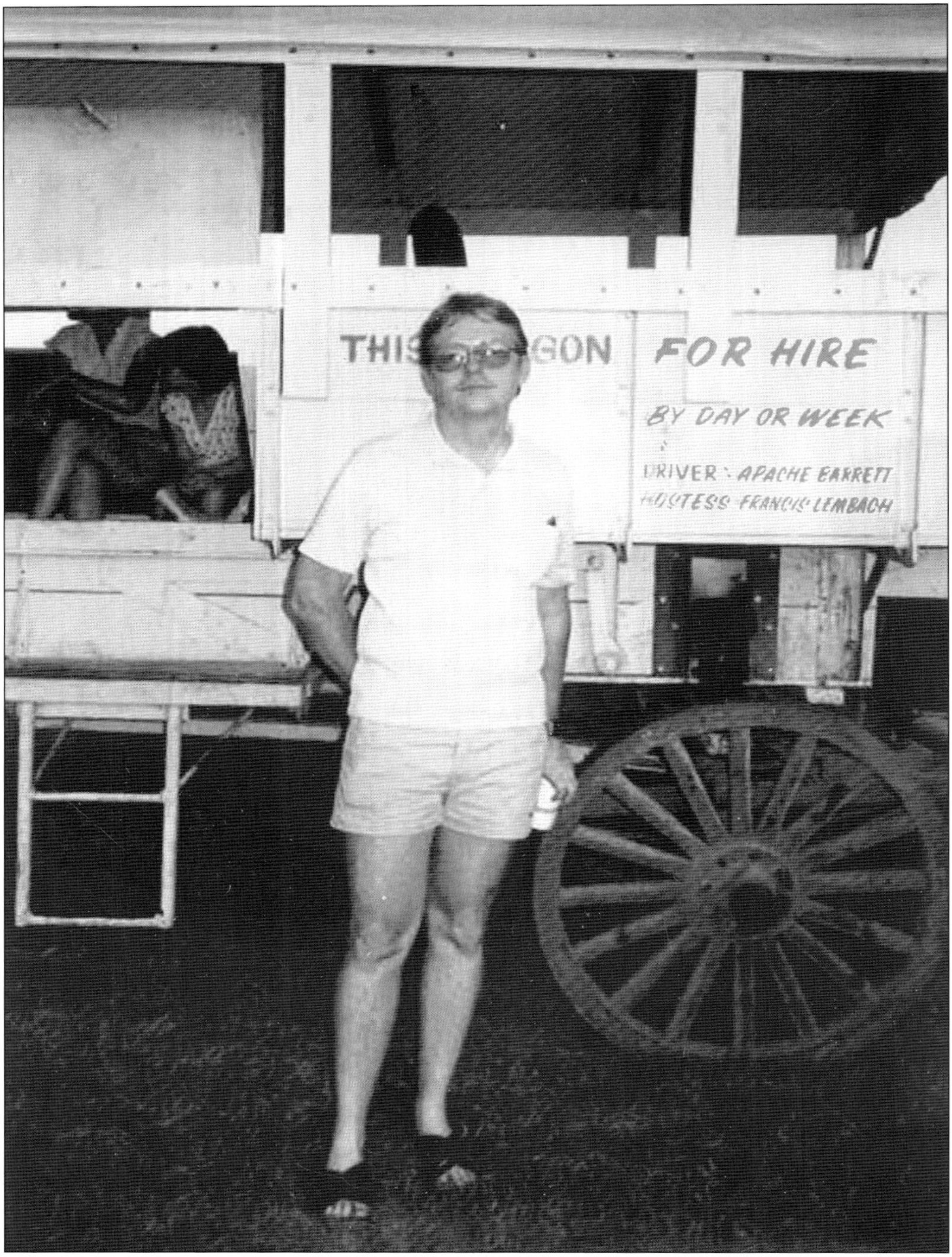

Phillip Williams chose the more comfortable clothing of a tourist out for a lark than the more serious would-be wrangler attire of boots and jeans that some who rode for a day favored. Williams did not ride Big Pop's wagon, but he picked his family up at the next campsite. Otherwise, all would have had to ride a shuttle back to the previous stop to pick up their car. (Courtesy Phillip and Victoria Williams.)

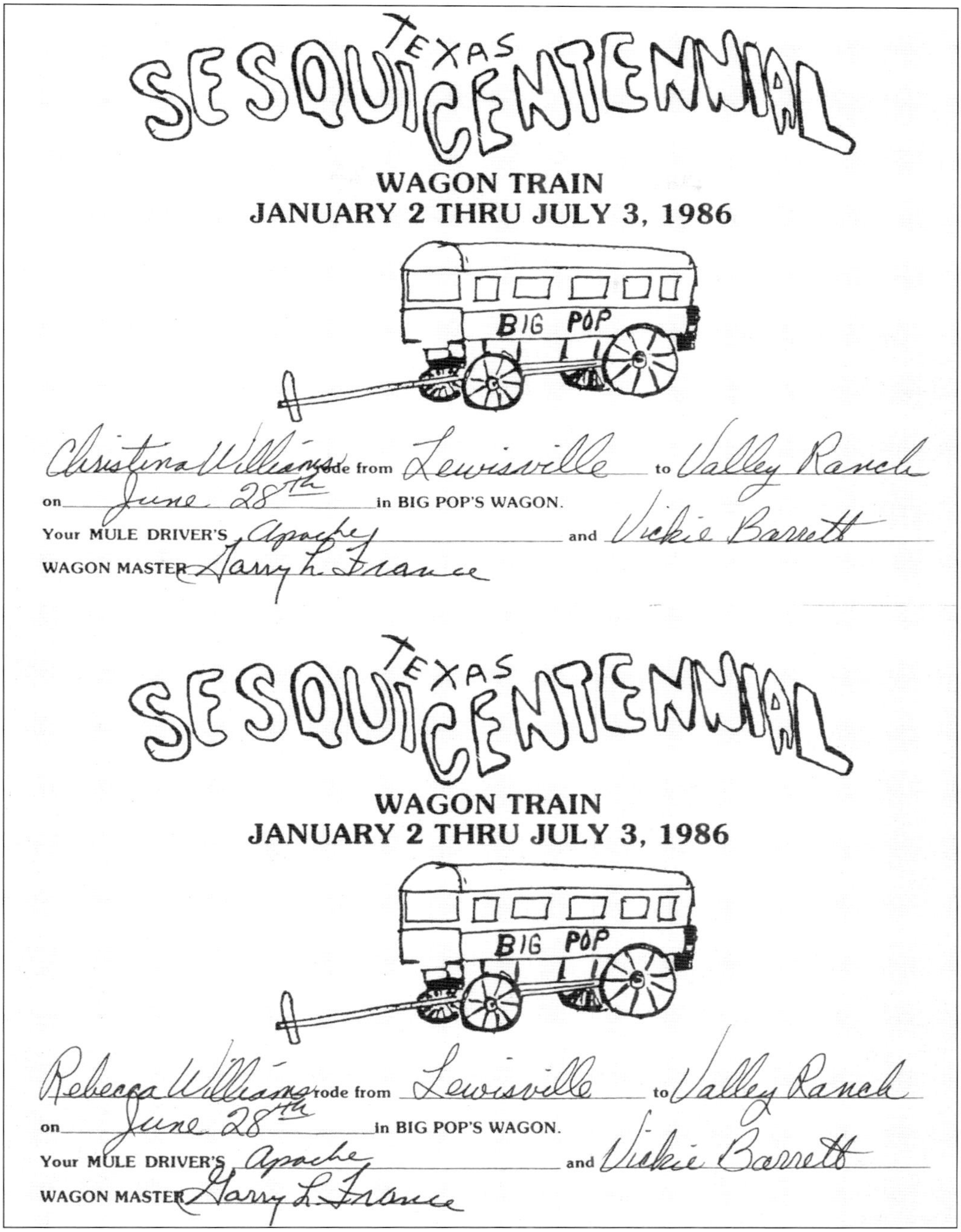

TEXAS SESQUICENTENNIAL

WAGON TRAIN
JANUARY 2 THRU JULY 3, 1986

BIG POP

Christina Williams rode from Lewisville to Valley Ranch
on June 28th in BIG POP'S WAGON.
Your MULE DRIVER'S Apache and Vickie Barrett
WAGON MASTER Garry L. France

TEXAS SESQUICENTENNIAL

WAGON TRAIN
JANUARY 2 THRU JULY 3, 1986

BIG POP

Rebecca Williams rode from Lewisville to Valley Ranch
on June 28th in BIG POP'S WAGON.
Your MULE DRIVER'S Apache and Vickie Barrett
WAGON MASTER Garry L. France

Big Pop issued certificates to each rider of his wagon to commemorate the ride with him. The mule drivers on this day were Vickie and Dale "Apache" Barrett. Wagon master Garry France signed the certificate as well. In ceremonies at the end of the journey, riders in the train received certificates from the Texas Wagon Train Association. (Courtesy Phillip and Victoria Williams.)

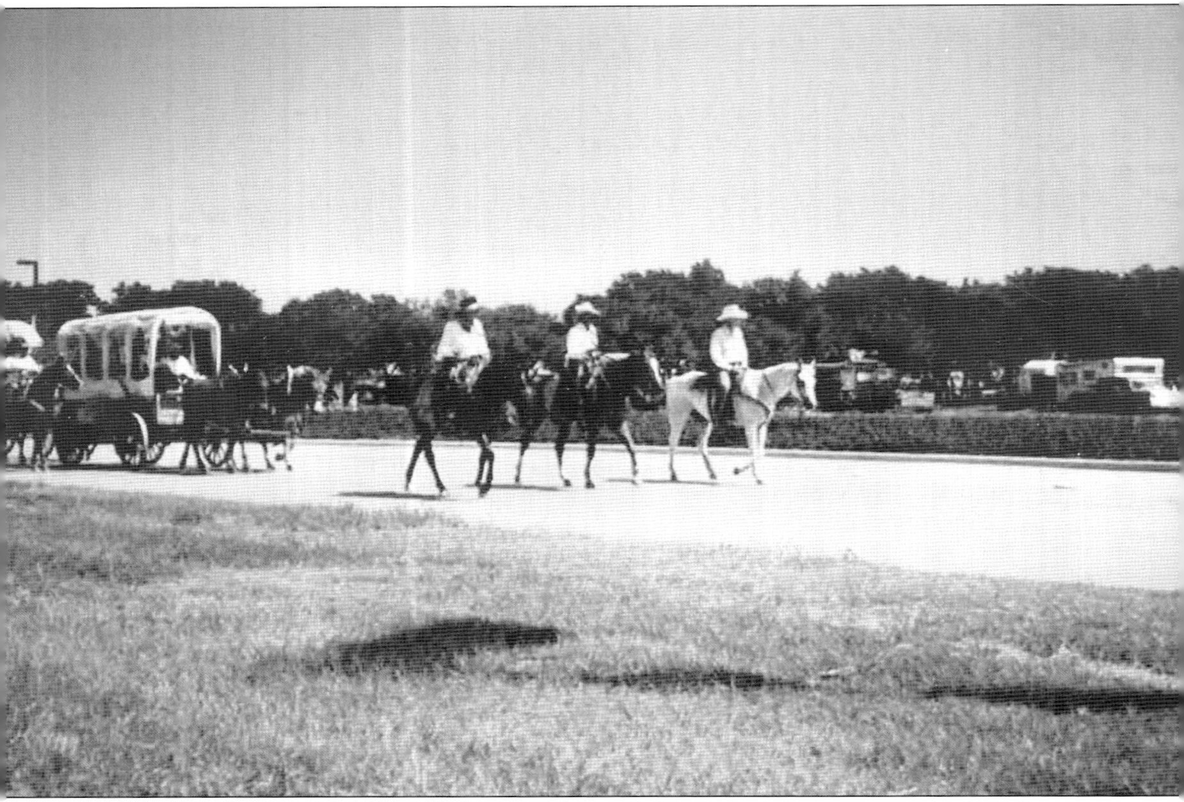

Wagon master Garry France (left) rides alongside his two assistants on June 28 as the wagons come within five days of arriving in Fort Worth—the final stage of the journey. With him are Vern Renz and West Pearce, head camp jack. Pearce most likely had just joined them to lead the train into that evening's campsite at Valley Ranch, which he had recently scouted for the best place to park the wagons. New folks kept joining the train every day. Some had ridden earlier and came back. (Courtesy Phillip and Victoria Williams.)

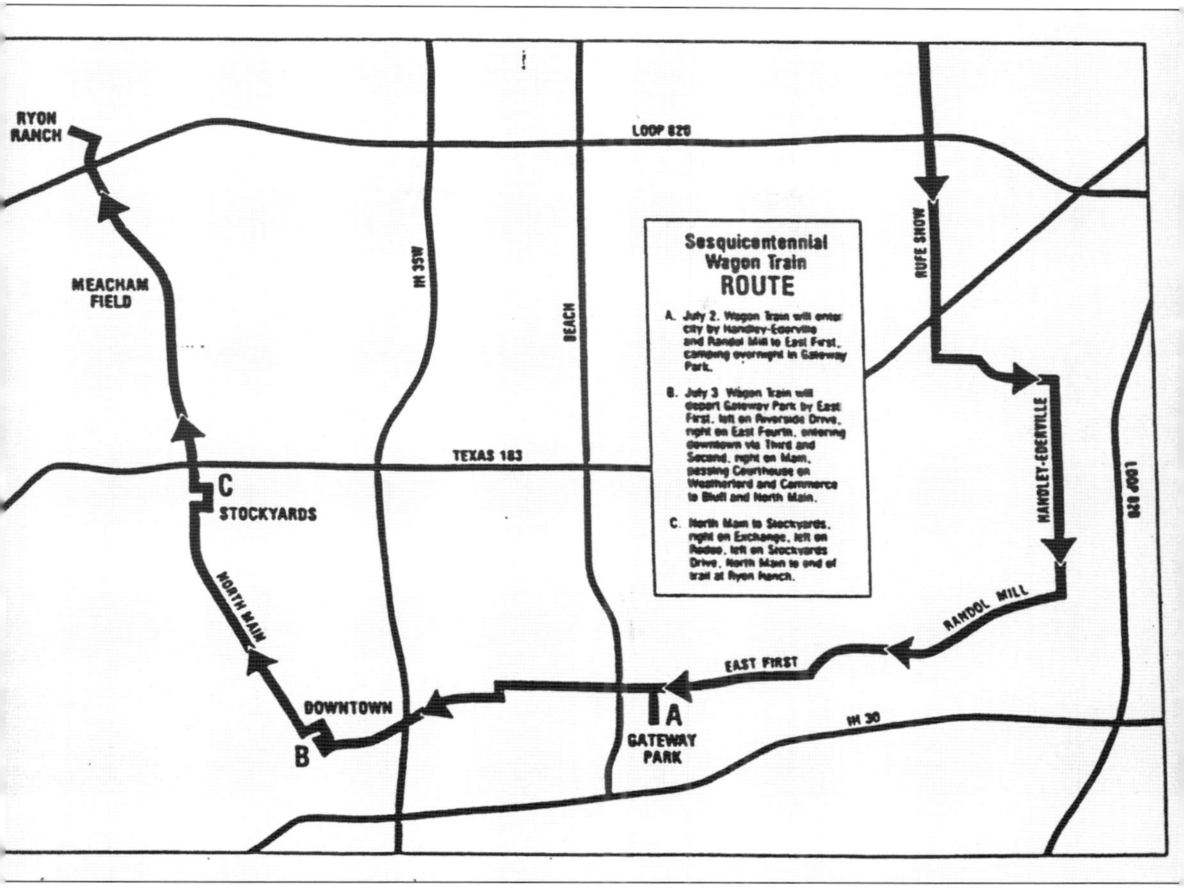

This is the route that the wagon train took after reaching Fort Worth. The information in the box reads: "A. July 2 Wagon Train will enter city by Handley-Ederville and Randol Mill to East First, camping overnight in Gateway Park. B. July 3 Wagon Train will depart Gateway Park by East First, left on Riverside Drive, right on East Fourth, entering downtown via Third and Second, right on Main, passing Courthouse on Weatherford and Commerce to Bluff and North Main. C. North Main to Stockyards, right on Exchange, left on Rodeo, left on Stockyards Drive, North Main to end of trail at Ryon Ranch."

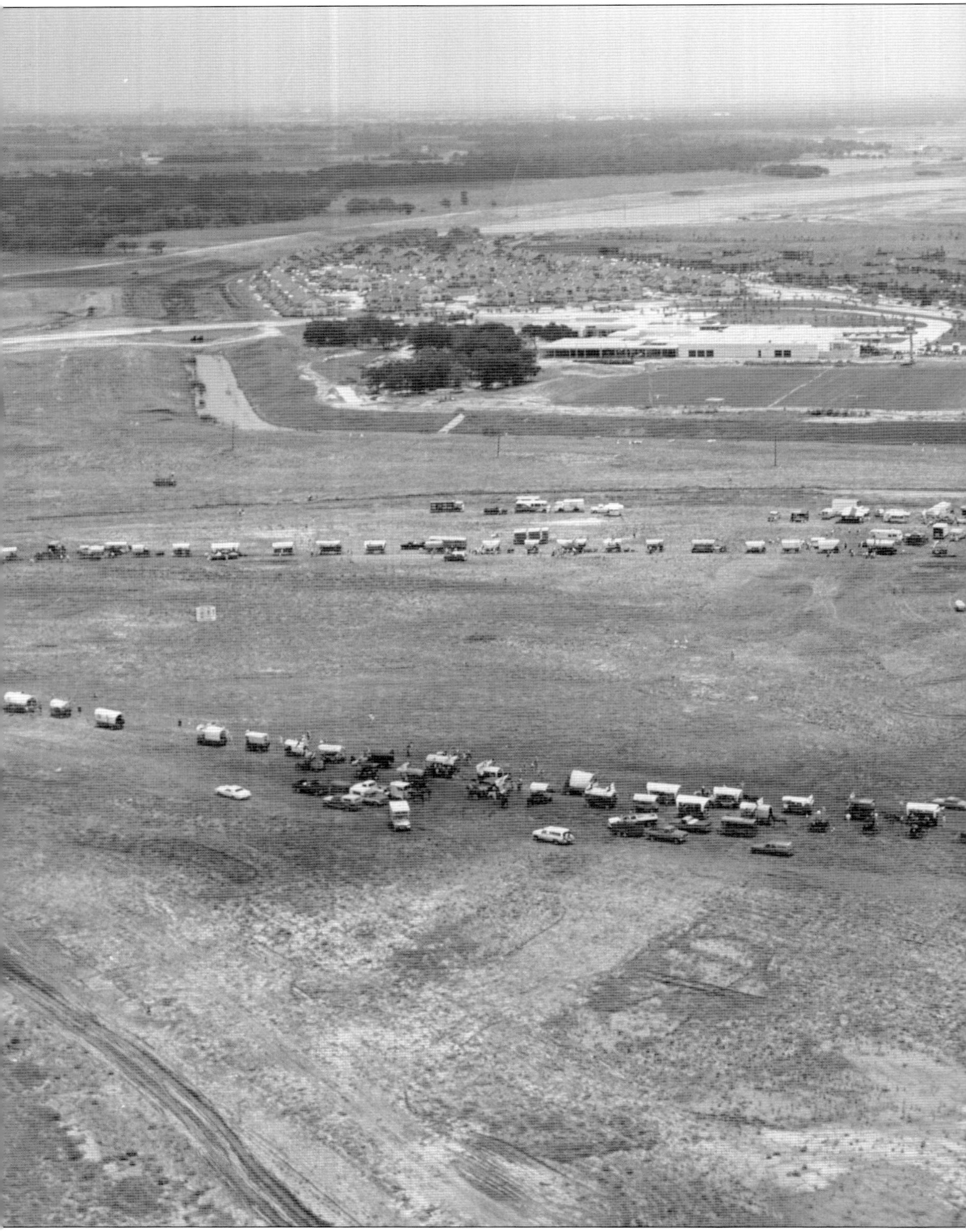

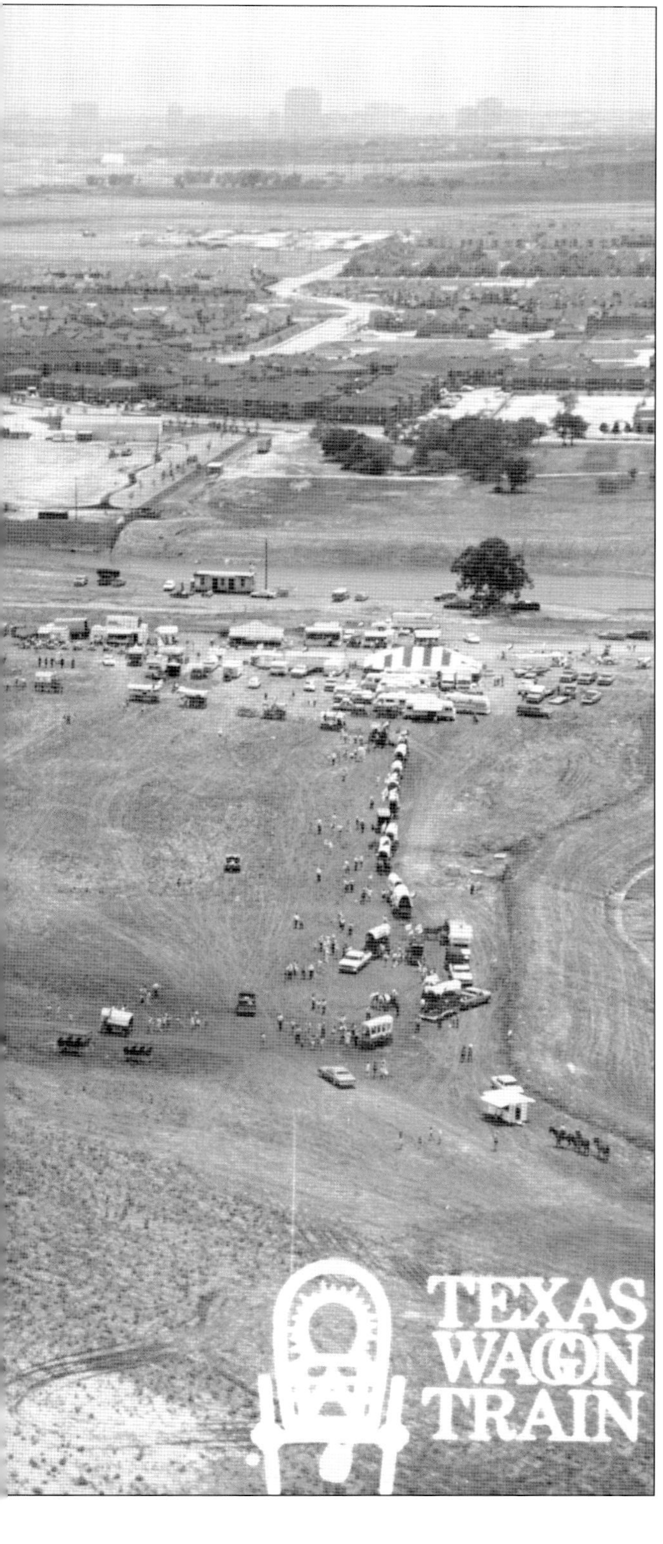

Circling the wagons was always the practice of Western pioneers, so the 1986 Texas wagon train did so as well. These wagons are already in the metroplex, with downtown Fort Worth in the far right background. (Courtesy Texas Wagon Train Collection, North Fort Worth Historical Society.)

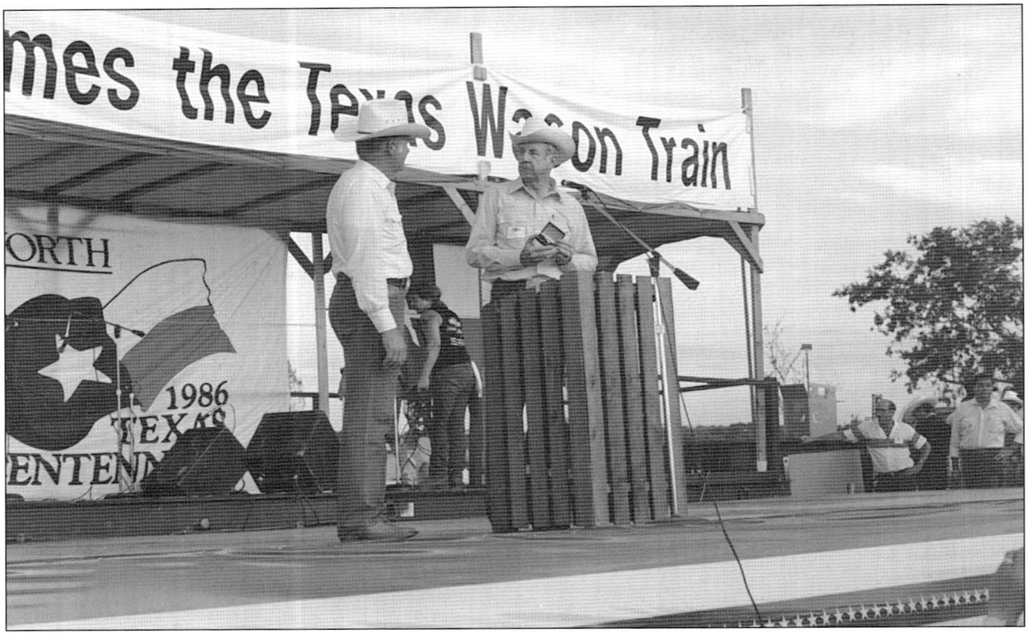

Charles Oliver (left), president of the wagon train association, and Bob Bolen, mayor of Fort Worth, appear together on the stage in Gateway Park as the wagon train arrived in Fort Worth on July 2, 1986, on the last leg of its six-month journey. Mayor Bolen is presenting a key to the city to Oliver. (Courtesy Quentin McGown.)

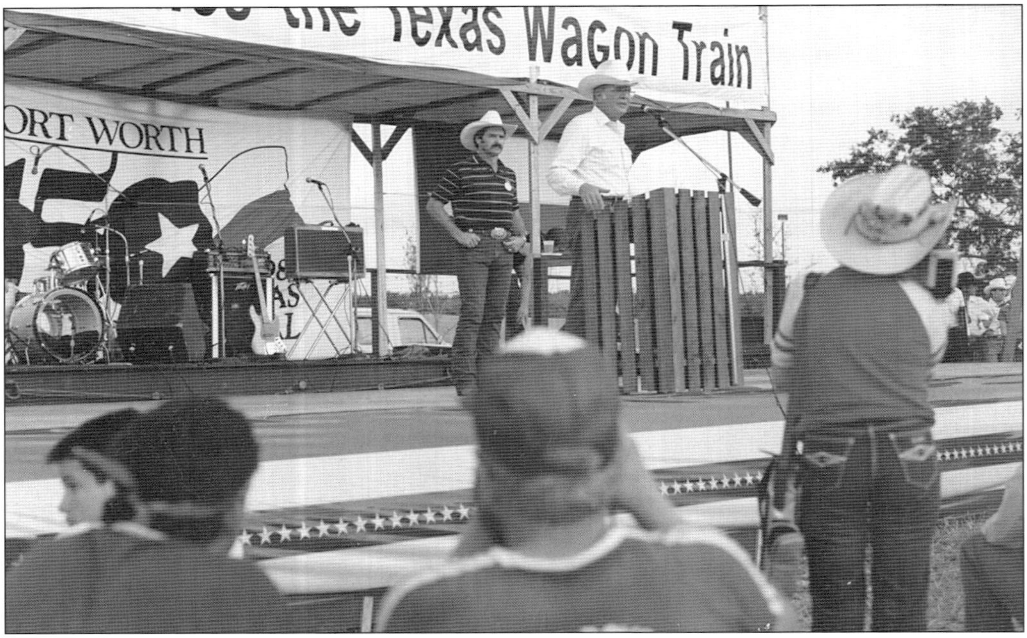

Wagon train president Charles Oliver addresses the crowd on July 2, 1986, at Gateway Park in Fort Worth as the city welcomed the train. The man with the white hat behind Oliver is Walt Garrison, a Dallas Cowboys football star, who served as the honorary wagon master of the train. (Courtesy Quentin McGown.)

Everyone who took part in the wagon train in any capacity received an official certificate of appreciation from officials of the train. Charles Oliver signed it as association president, as did Jan France, executive director of promotions. Quentin McGown, business manager, signed similar certificates as well. (Courtesy Texas Wagon Train Collection, North Fort Worth Historical Society.)

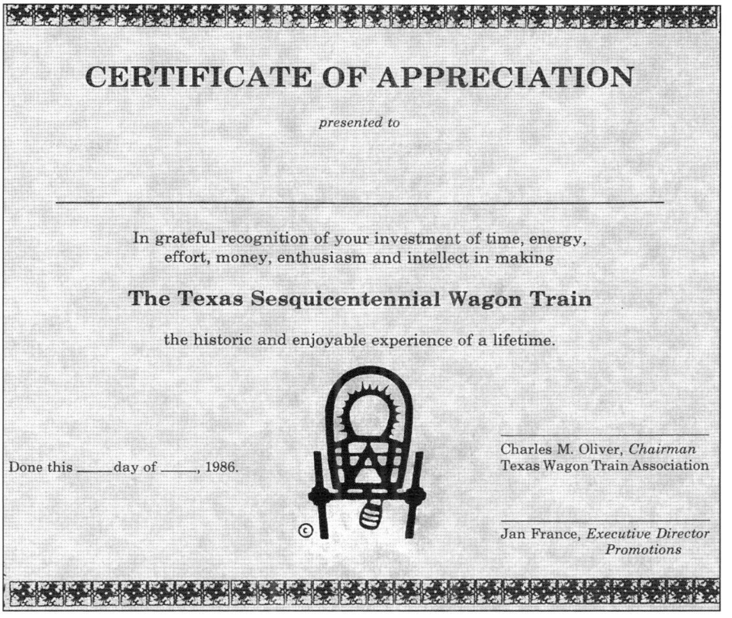

CERTIFICATE OF APPRECIATION

presented to

In grateful recognition of your investment of time, energy, effort, money, enthusiasm and intellect in making

The Texas Sesquicentennial Wagon Train

the historic and enjoyable experience of a lifetime.

Done this ____ day of ____, 1986.

©

Charles M. Oliver, *Chairman*
Texas Wagon Train Association

Jan France, *Executive Director Promotions*

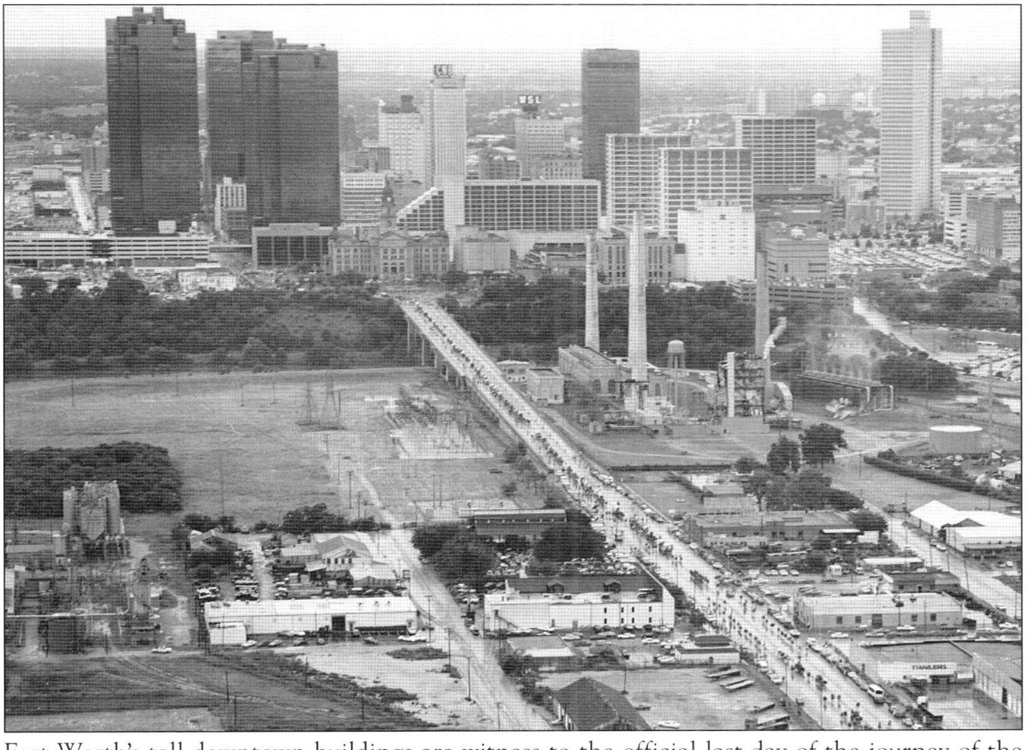

Fort Worth's tall downtown buildings are witness to the official last day of the journey of the wagon train. After circling the Tarrant County Courthouse on the bluff overlooking the Trinity River, the wagons head north across the Paddock Viaduct on their way up North Main Street to Exchange Avenue and the Fort Worth Stockyards for the final ceremonies. (Courtesy Texas Wagon Train Collection, North Fort Worth Historical Society.)

15

THE STOCKYARDS
FORT WORTH, TEXAS ™

CALENDAR OF EVENTS

July 3

Noon - 2:30 pm	WAGON TRAIN PARADE
2:30 - 3:00 pm	Final Shoeing—GOLD HORSESHOE & SILVER NAIL
3:00 - 4:00 pm	Goddess of Liberty Celebration
3:00 - 1:30 am	Wagon Train Street Dance The Pridesmen Breaking Point
10 pm	Wagon Train Appreciation Presentation - Billy Bob's Texas
11:00 pm	John Schneider in Billy Bob's

July 4

11:00 am - 5:00 pm	Wagon Train Auction - Cowtown Coliseum
3:00 pm - 1:30 am	Street Dance Tamara Comstock Sargeant Fury&the Valient All Stars
8:00 pm	PRCA Rodeo - Cowtown Coliseum
11:00 pm	Sawyer Brown in Billy Bob's Texas

July 5

8:30 pm	PRCA Rodeo - Cowtown Coliseum
9:00 pm - 1:30 am	Street Dance Treasure Island
11:00 pm	John Conlee in Billy Bob's

Final festivities for the Texas Sesquicentennial Wagon Train covered three days in the Fort Worth Stockyards, as this calendar of events shows. About 20 wagons then drove to Ryon's arena in Saginaw, only about three miles to the northwest of the stockyards, to camp that night. Thirteen wagons, including the one driven by Jan France, and 45 horseback riders made it full circle back to Sulphur Springs. They wanted to circle Texas completely, and they did.

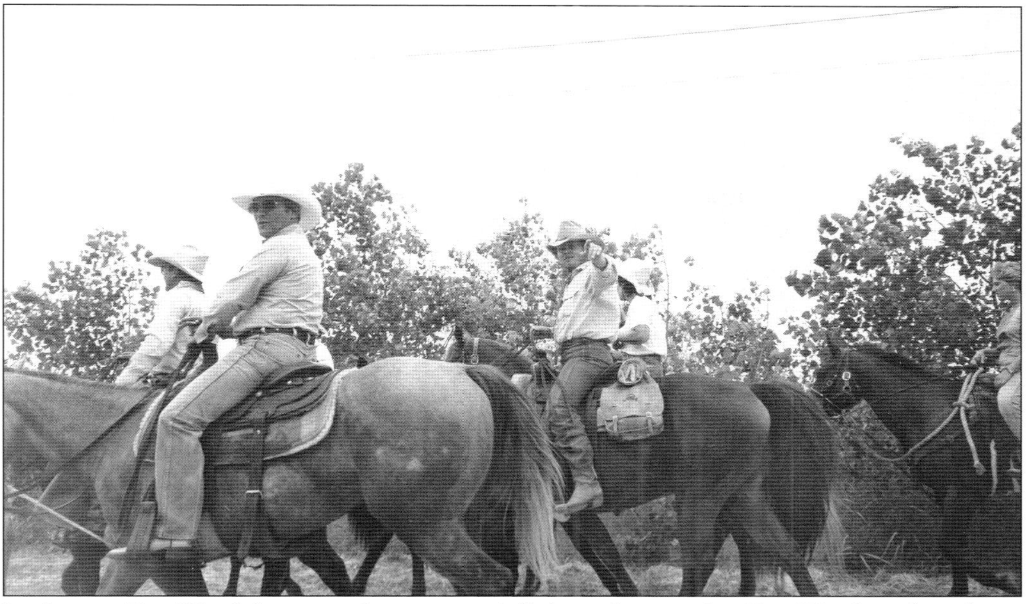

Jim Lane, a Fort Worth lawyer and supporter of all things historical in Fort Worth, is the rider in the center pointing toward the camera. The men on horseback following the train have arrived in Fort Worth. Near the end of the trail in Fort Worth's Gateway Park, a ceremony was held honoring those who completed the entire trip without missing over five days. Twenty-one people received certificates. (Courtesy Mary Ann Greene.)

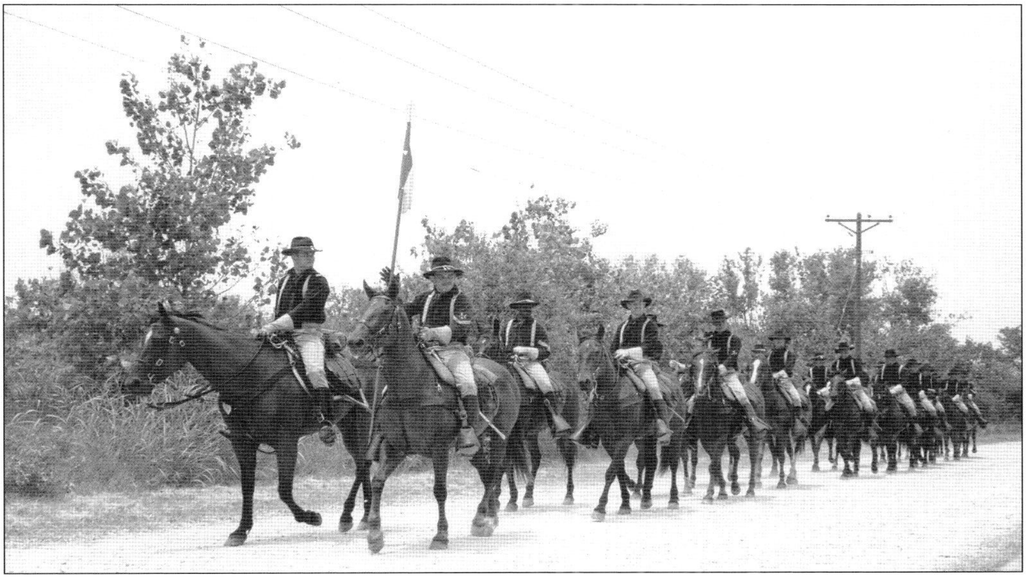

The 1st Cavalry Division Horse Platoon from Fort Hood, Texas rides with the train as it approaches Fort Worth. The general rule was that no dogs were allowed on the trip. However, on the days that the 1st Cavalry Division rode, its mascot, Missy, was permitted. The train circled the courthouse in downtown Fort Worth. Jan France rode with the 1st Cavalry Division Horse Platoon from Fort Hood in the Bicentennial Wagon Train in 1976 and through that contact was able to secure the platoon's participation in 1986 for Texas. (Courtesy Mary Ann Greene.)

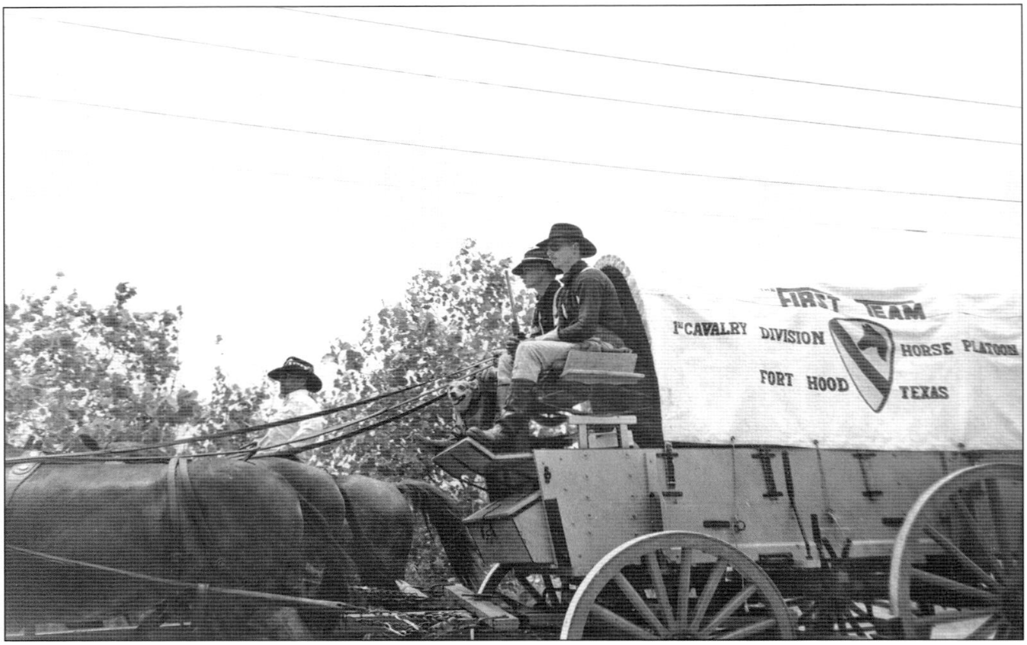

The First Team of the 1st Cavalry Division Horse Platoon from Fort Hood enjoyed being a part of the train temporarily. Fort Hood, covering 108,000 acres in central Texas northwest of Austin, is home to 41,000 Infantry Division (mechanized) personnel. It is the largest active-duty armored post in the US armed services. The 1st Cavalry Division rode with the train at the beginning in Sulphur Springs, at the end in Fort Worth, and at important points in between, including the Alamo and around the capitol building in Austin. (Courtesy Mary Ann Greene.)

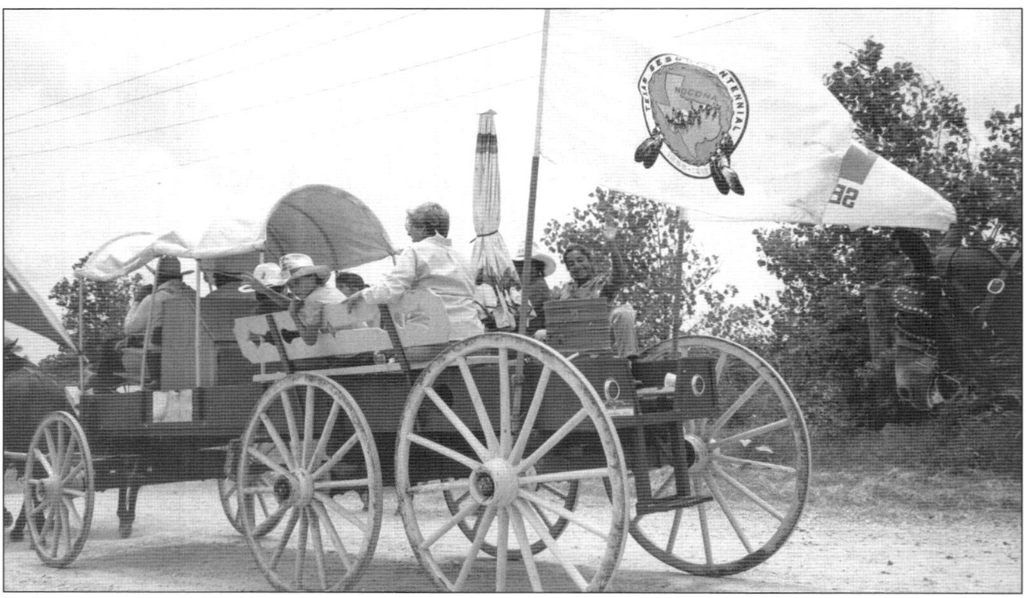

When it is July 3 with the temperature soaring, an open-air "convertible" wagon is appealing. Besides, the train is heading to the stockyards, so everyone is on parade. Notice the unusual wagon with double wheels at the back end for heavy loads. (Courtesy Mary Ann Greene.)

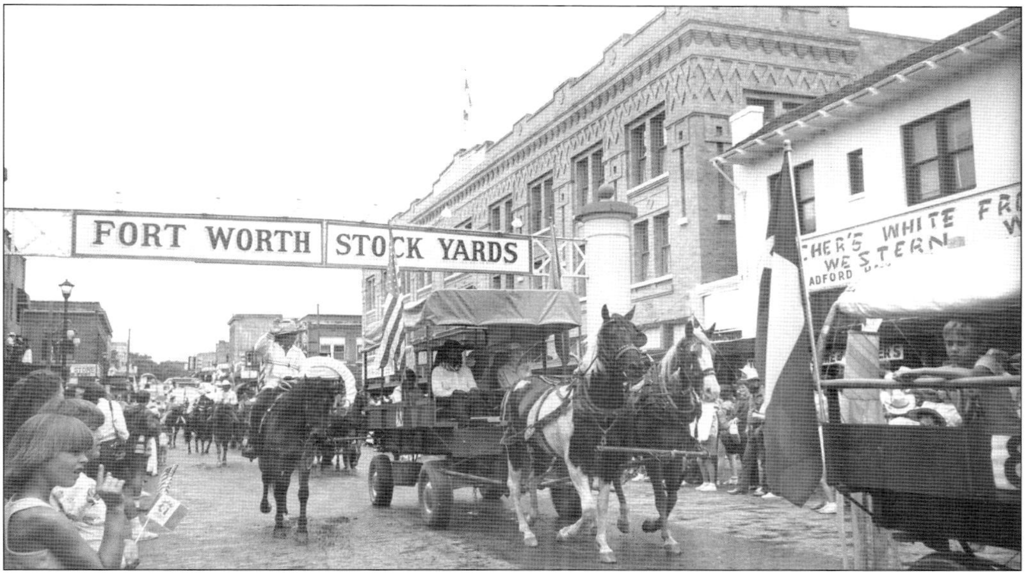

Crowds gathered along East Exchange Avenue on July 3, 1986, to welcome the Texas Sesquicentennial Wagon Train to the last stop in the long six-month journey. Festivities that day included a parade, a giant western fandango, fireworks, and a greeting from Texas governor Mark White. White was on hand for the beginning day of the wagon train and returned to be present at the conclusion as well. The waving rider on horseback is Eddie Sandoval, whose sister took the picture. (Courtesy Mary Ann Greene.)

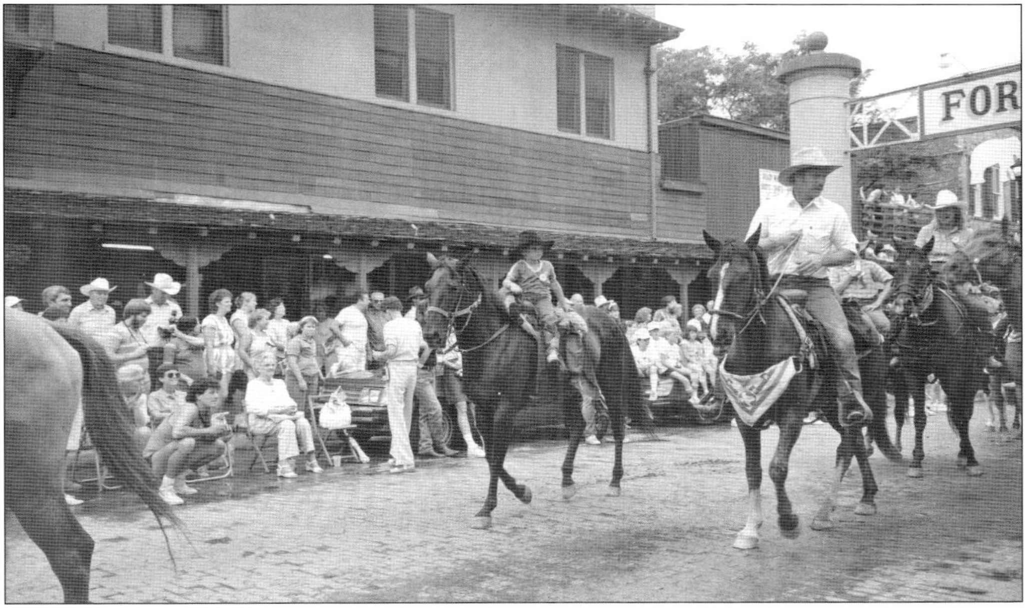

Welcome home. The six-month journey around Texas ended in the Fort Worth Stockyards. All ages rode in the wagon train, especially on that last day. Note the little boy on the horse in the center of the photograph. An auction would take place at the Cowtown Coliseum in the Fort Worth Stockyards the following day, July 4. Some participants sold off their wagons and horses. (Courtesy Mary Ann Greene.)

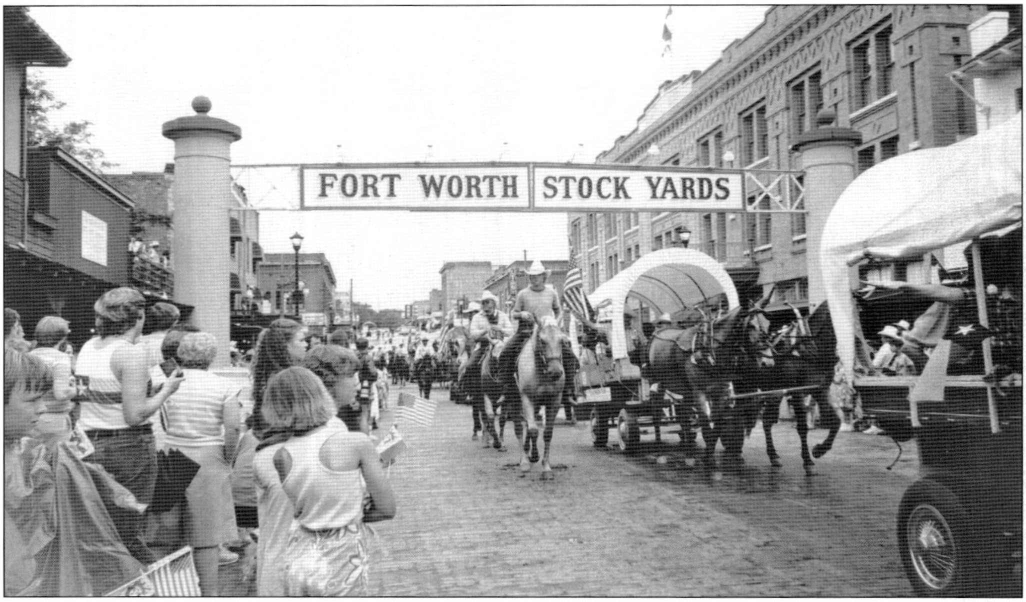

On July 3, crowds awaited the wagon train for hours at the Fort Worth Stockyards to witness the conclusion of a journey that had begun six months earlier on January 2. While 104 wagons started the trip, and the number dwindled to 30 at the lowest, 159 wagons with four or five guests in each arrived in the stockyards on the last day. The wagon train was 4.5 miles long. Texans say it was the longest ever and had the most participants. (Courtesy Mary Ann Greene.)

TEXAS WAGON TRAIN

Billy Bob's Texas and the Stockyards would like to honor the Texas Wagon Train for their historical contribution to the Texas Sesquicentennial.

Just present your Wagon Train Badge at Billy Bob's Thursday & Friday for FREE ADMISSION

A very special award will be presented to the person you feel contributed most to the Wagon Train. At 10:00 pm John Schneider will present this award in Billy Bob's.

Please cast your secret ballot below

NAME (Please print)

THE STOCKYARDS FORT WORTH TEXAS

Billy Bob's TEXAS Fort Worth Stockyards TM

PLACE BALLOTS IN DESIGNATED BOXES

Billy Bob's, the largest honky-tonk in Texas, offered free admission to wagon train participants with presentation of their badges. Each rider of wagon or horse had worn a badge each day to simplify the process of keeping actual members of the wagon train separate from visitors in the towns and in camp. The authors have not been able to determine who won the award described here.

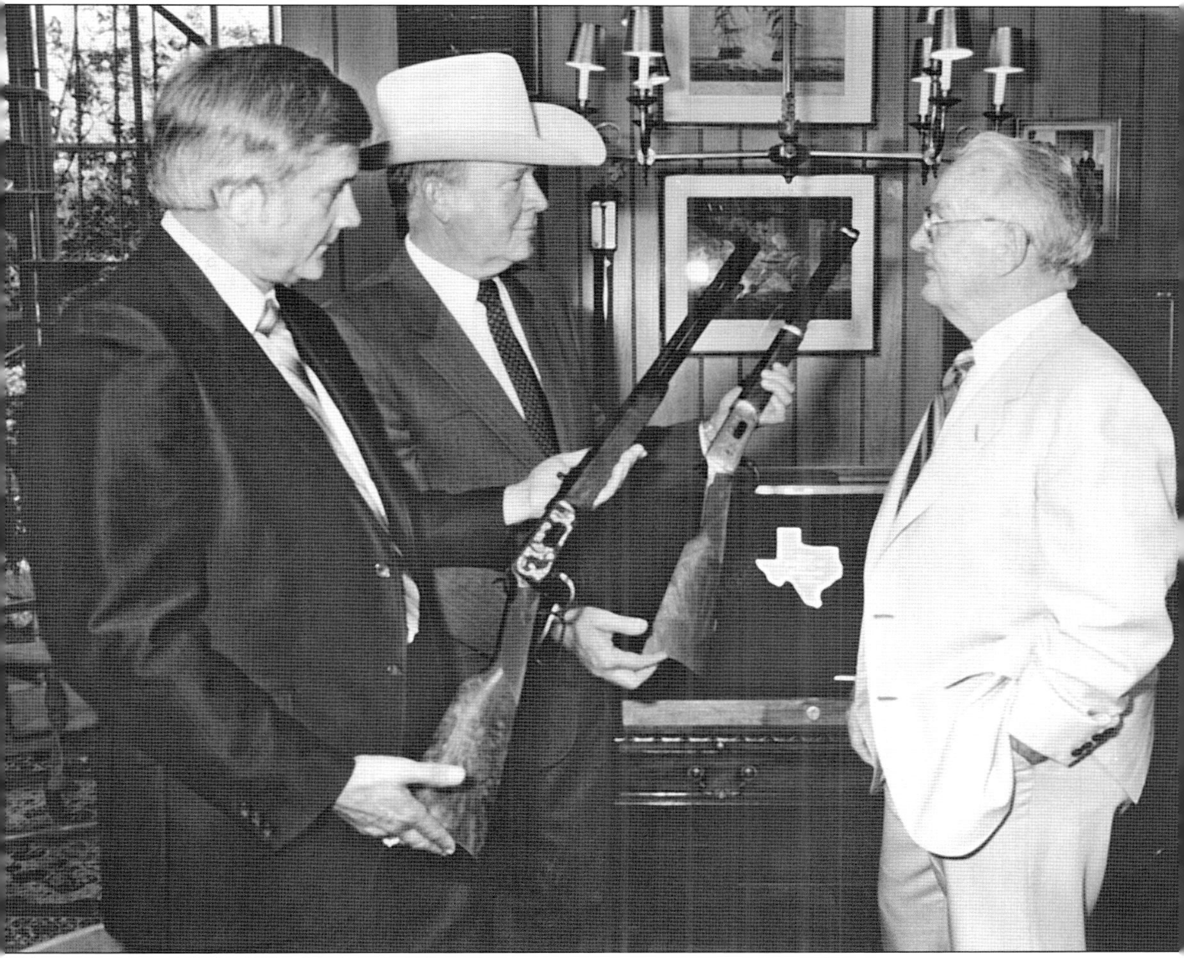

Glen Courson (left) volunteered space for an office for the wagon train, and Charles Oliver (center) was president and chairman of the wagon train association. The pair presents former governor William Clements with a Winchester commemorative rifle that Courson persuaded the Winchester company to offer to honor the Texas Sesquicentennial Wagon Train. (Courtesy Texas Wagon Train Collection, North Fort Worth Historical Society.)

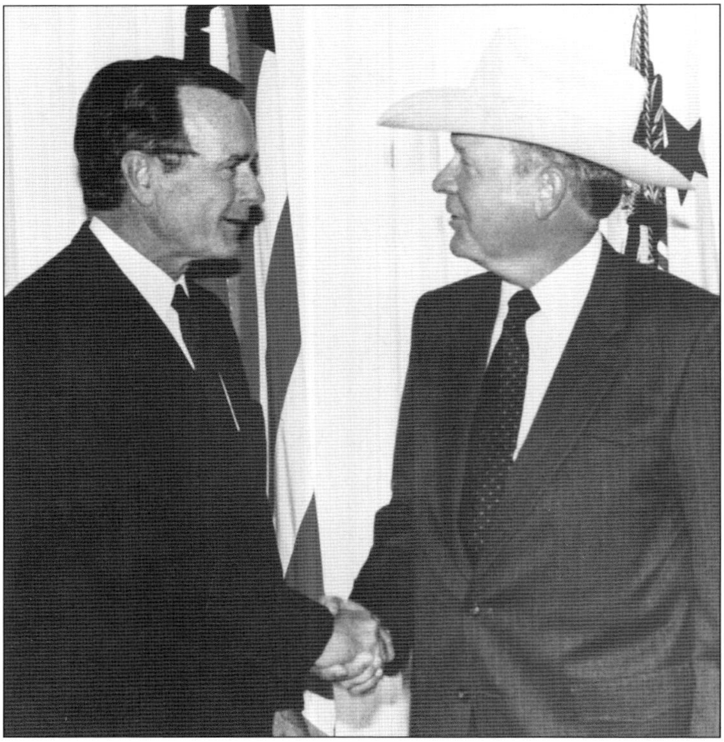

George H.W. Bush (left), later 41st president of the United States, was serving as vice president in the Ronald Reagan administration in 1986. Here, he thanks Charles Oliver for the Winchester commemorative rifle that Oliver had just presented to him. Bush was one of four Texans who have served as president. These were Dwight D. Eisenhower, born in Denison, Lyndon Baines Johnson from Johnson City, and the Bushes, father and son, who came to Texas as soon as they could. (Courtesy Texas Wagon Train Association, North Fort Worth Historical Society.)

VICE PRESIDENT OF THE UNITED STATES

July 24, 1986

Dear Charles:

I wanted to take this moment to thank you for the beautiful Winchester Sesquicentennial Rifle. It's been a special privilege for Barbara and me to participate in many of the Sesquicentennial events. This Rifle commemorates not only this year of celebration, but Texas' proud and rich heritage, as well.

Thanks, again, for your thoughtful gift.

Warm best wishes,

This note, affixed with the official seal of the vice president of the United States, is addressed to Charles Oliver. It is signed by Vice Pres. George Bush, who received a commemorative Winchester rifle from Oliver. (Courtesy Texas Wagon Train Association, North Fort Worth Historical Society.)

Three

A Home for the Wagon Train Artifacts

Many Texans today may not realize that all of the keys to the city, plaques, and other gifts from cities and towns to the Texas Wagon Train Association have been preserved together in one place. The many artifacts now are housed in the North Fort Worth Historical Society Museum in the Fort Worth Stockyards National Historic District. These are displayed permanently on the walls and in glass cases for all to see. Tourists come from all over the world to visit the stockyards, and they have an opportunity to learn about the Texas sesquicentennial experience for the first time, or if they already knew about the wagon train, to reminisce about what they saw or experienced in 1986. In fact, the museum refurbished and rearranged the wagon train exhibit in 2011 during its 25th anniversary year. The Texas Wagon Train Association planned a reunion that October.

Items in the exhibit include one of the whips the riders used in driving the wagons, paintings, and letters proclaiming a special day for a town when the wagon train came through. Keys to the city in various styles, plaques, plates, mugs, and special Texas postage issues indicating the wagon train comprise more of the exhibit, which covers two walls of the north end of the museum.

At the conclusion of the wagon train's trip around Texas in 1986, the State Fair of Texas in Dallas displayed the artifacts and photographs in a large exhibit in its Hall of State. Outside on the fairgrounds, visitors could see several of the wagons that had participated in the trip around Texas. An observer who experienced quite a number of days with the actual moving train and then saw the exhibit appreciated it but felt that the static nature of the wagons in no way expressed the excitement the participants enjoyed each day on the actual moving, breathing Texas wagon train. The state fair exhibit and the items housed in the museum in the Fort Worth Stockyards remind viewers that the once-in-a-lifetime experience for those who took part had receded into history. They never want it to be forgotten. Therefore, in this 25th anniversary year, it is a pleasure to commemorate the wagon train's accomplishments with this book of photographs of the train and its legacy of museum artifacts.

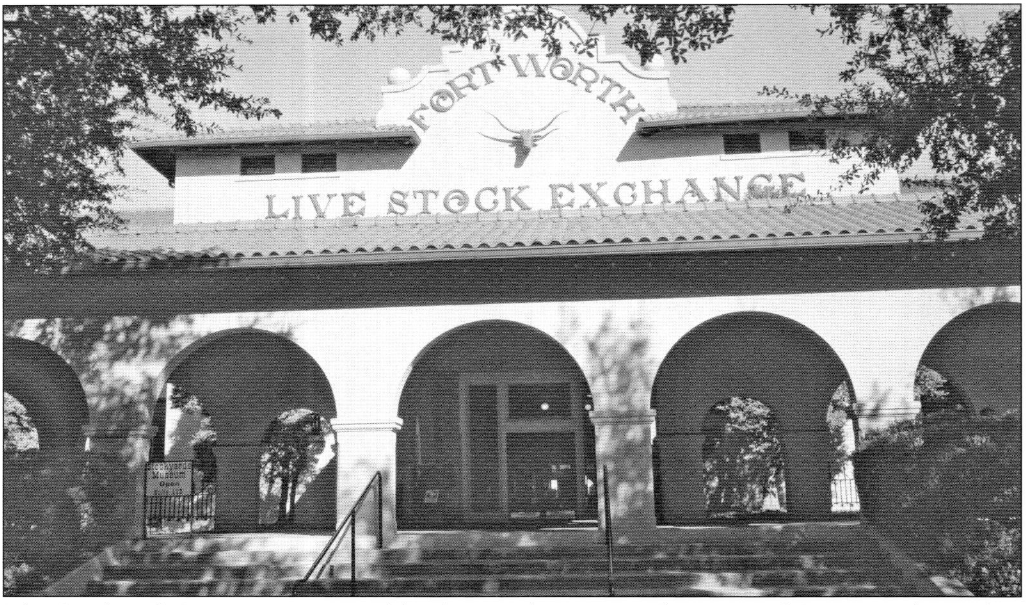

The Stockyards Museum, sponsored by the North Fort Worth Historical Society, is located in Room 131 on the first floor of the Livestock Exchange Building. This structure was built in 1903 by the Fort Worth Stockyards Company to contain its offices and those of private commission companies. The museum houses the artifacts given to the wagon train as well as a huge collection of livestock and stockyards memorabilia.

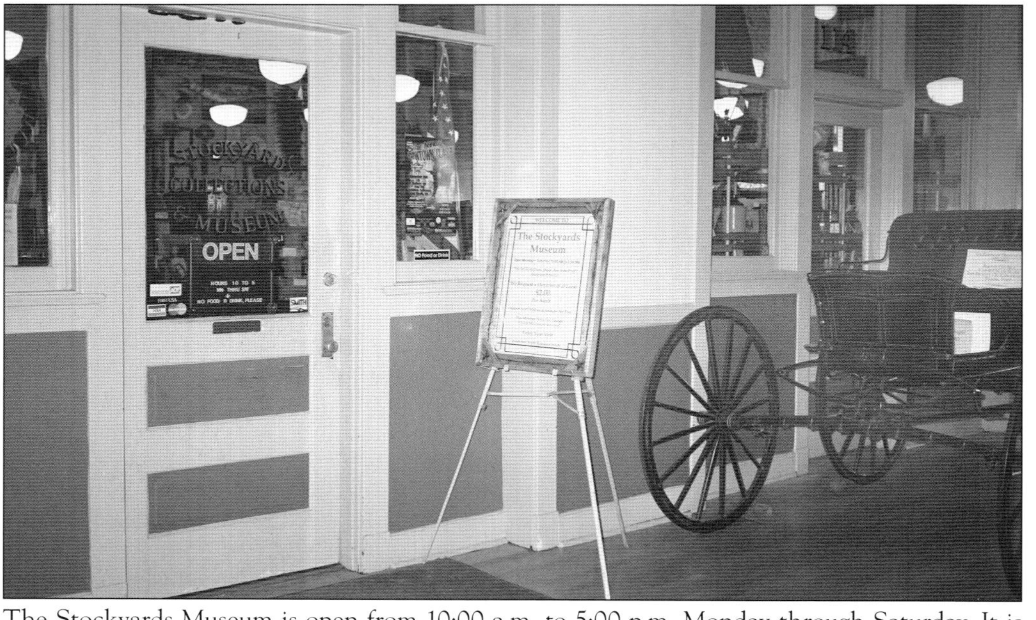

The Stockyards Museum is open from 10:00 a.m. to 5:00 p.m. Monday through Saturday. It is closed Sundays, except during the summer, when the hours are 12:00 p.m. to 5:00 p.m. Visitors from all over the world have entered this door to see the livestock items on display and are able to view the wagon train artifacts as well. The memory of the accomplishment of the Texas wagon train is kept alive.

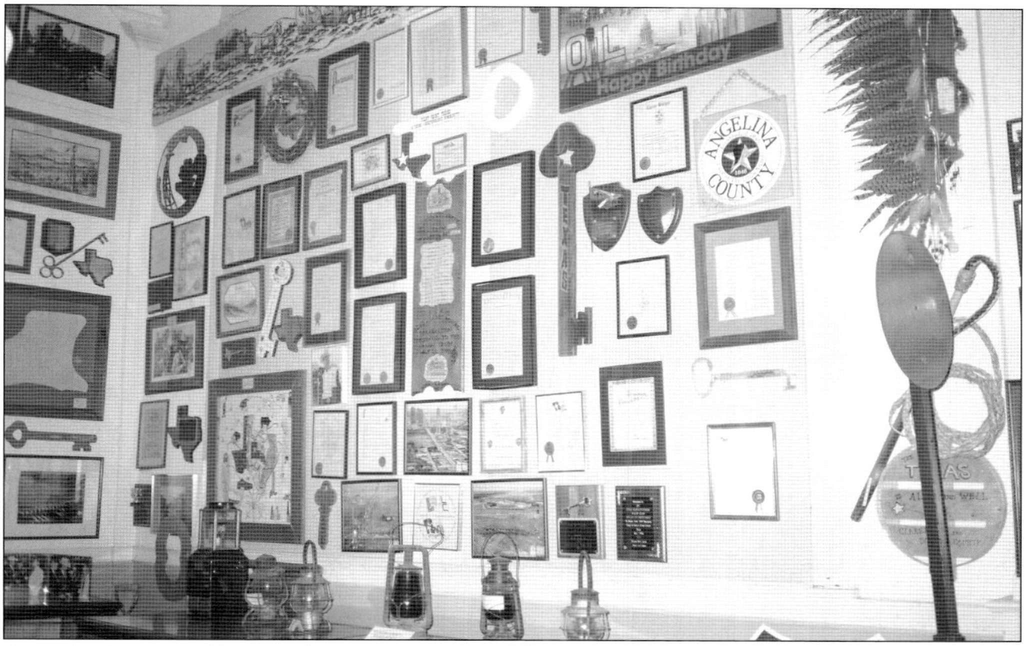

Over 50 plaques and keys to the city cover part of the west wall of the North Fort Worth Historical Society (NFWHS) Museum. This is only a brief glimpse of the artifacts. Because the wagon train ended its six-month journey in the Fort Worth Stockyards and the museum is located in the Livestock Exchange Building, it was appropriate to donate the items there.

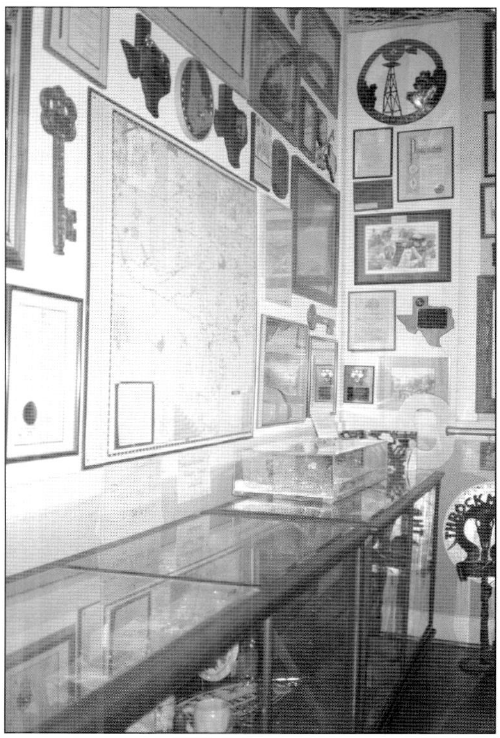

Wagon train artifacts cover another partial wall at the NFWHS Museum. Several items are made of wood, including the two plaques shaped like Texas. The large map of Texas in the center of the picture shows every visitor to the museum the route of the wagon train. It truly covered Texas.

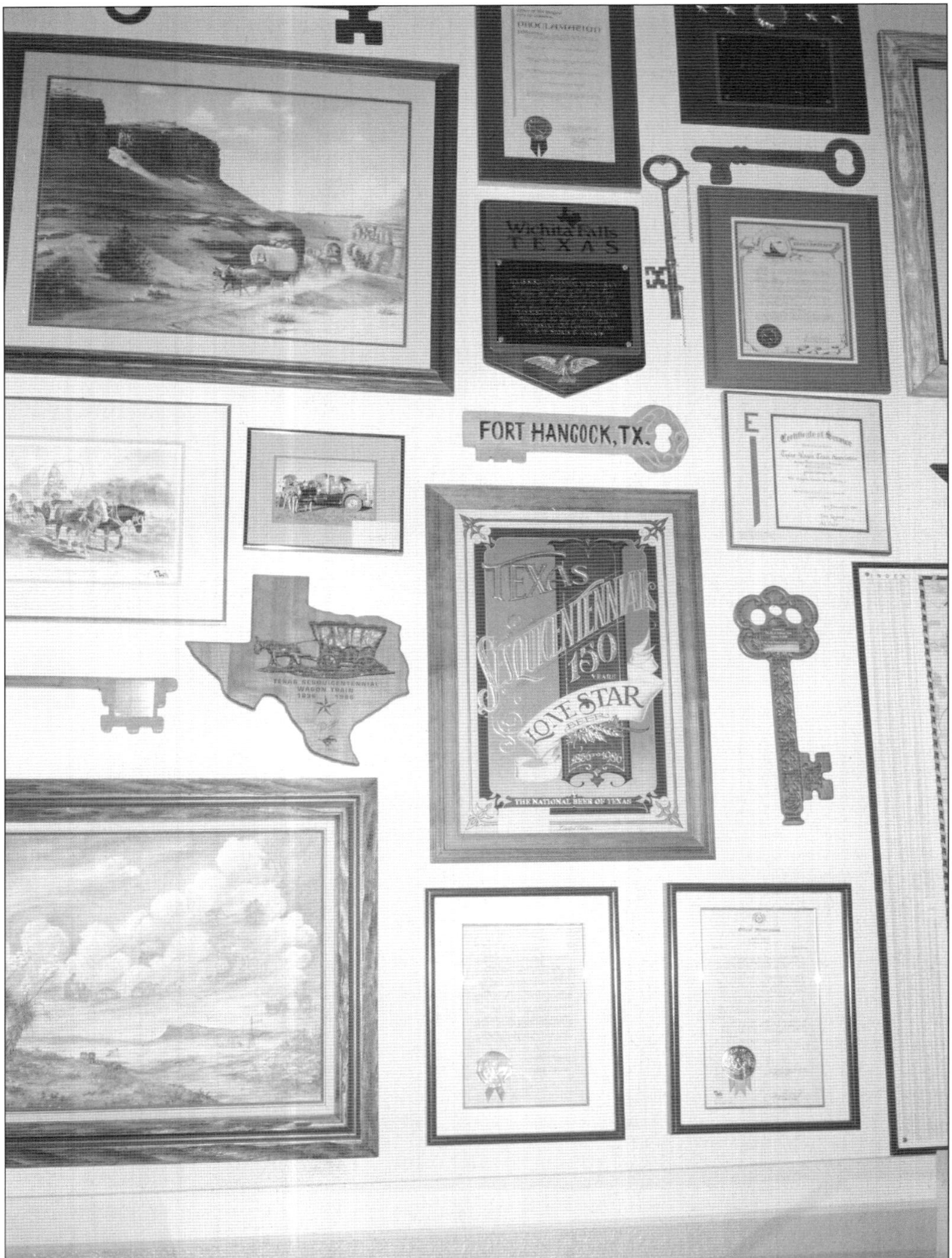

In a close-up of the larger wall of items, one can see the numerous keys, proclamations, and paintings that various towns and cities presented to the wagon train in official ceremonies. Towns on the route planned festivals and rodeos when the train arrived. Many times, they planned their own sesquicentennial celebrations around the arrival of the train.

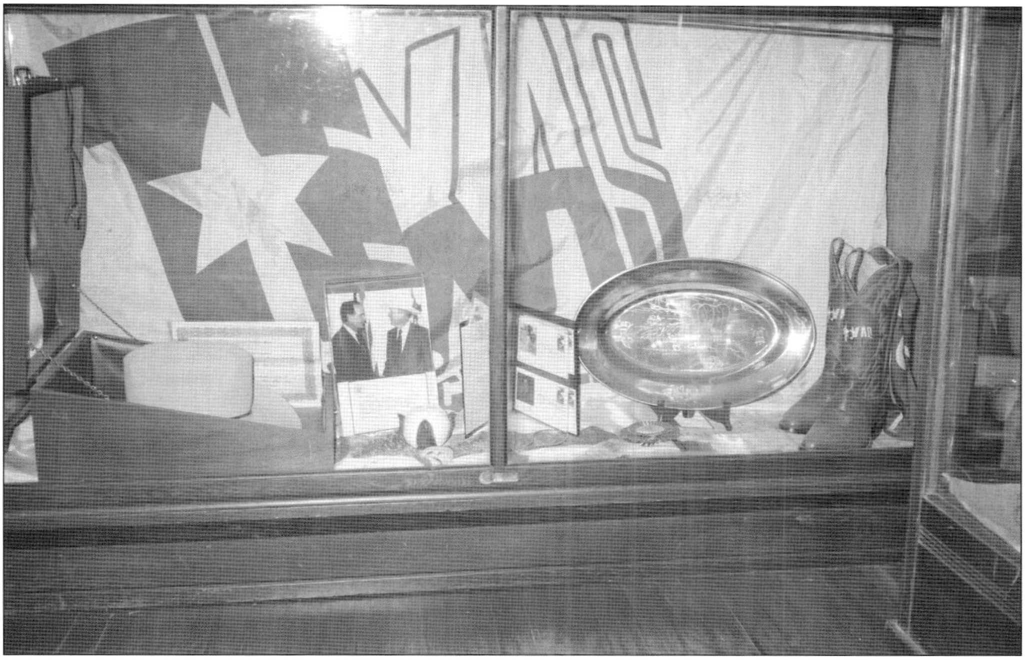

Boots, a silver tray, and a Texas sesquicentennial flag signed by the wagon train participants are preserved in this showcase. They are treasured remembrances of the Texas wagon train, happily presented to the train from each town in special ceremonies.

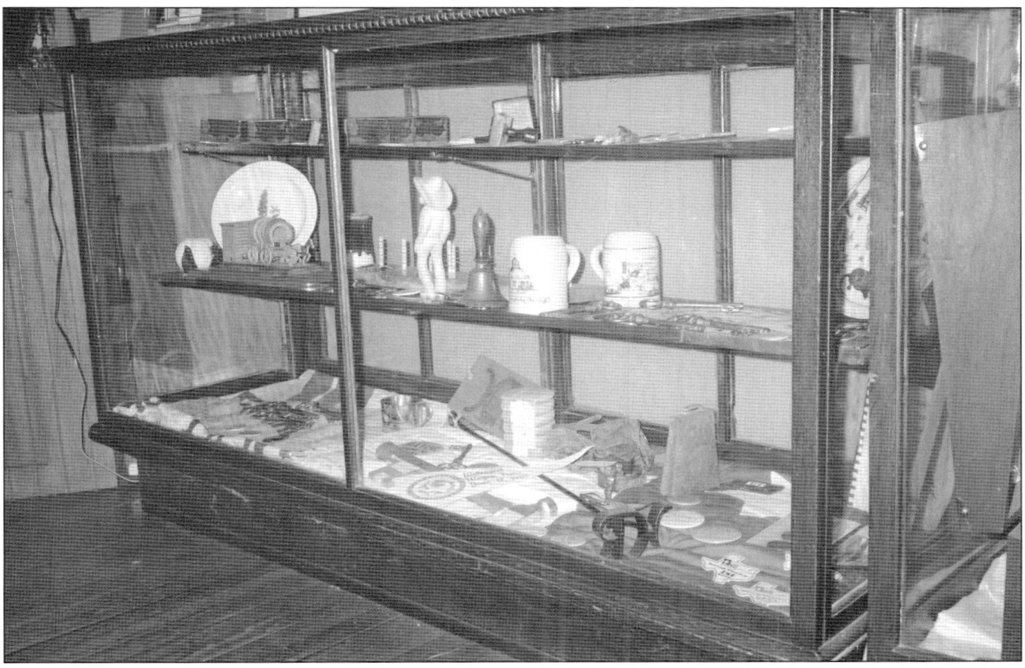

This case shows a branding iron, beer steins, a small ceramic cowboy, a school bell, and other artifacts donated to the wagon train by the various towns it visited. Some towns held ceremonies as the wagon train passed through but did not stop for the night. Other towns enjoyed festivities at camp.

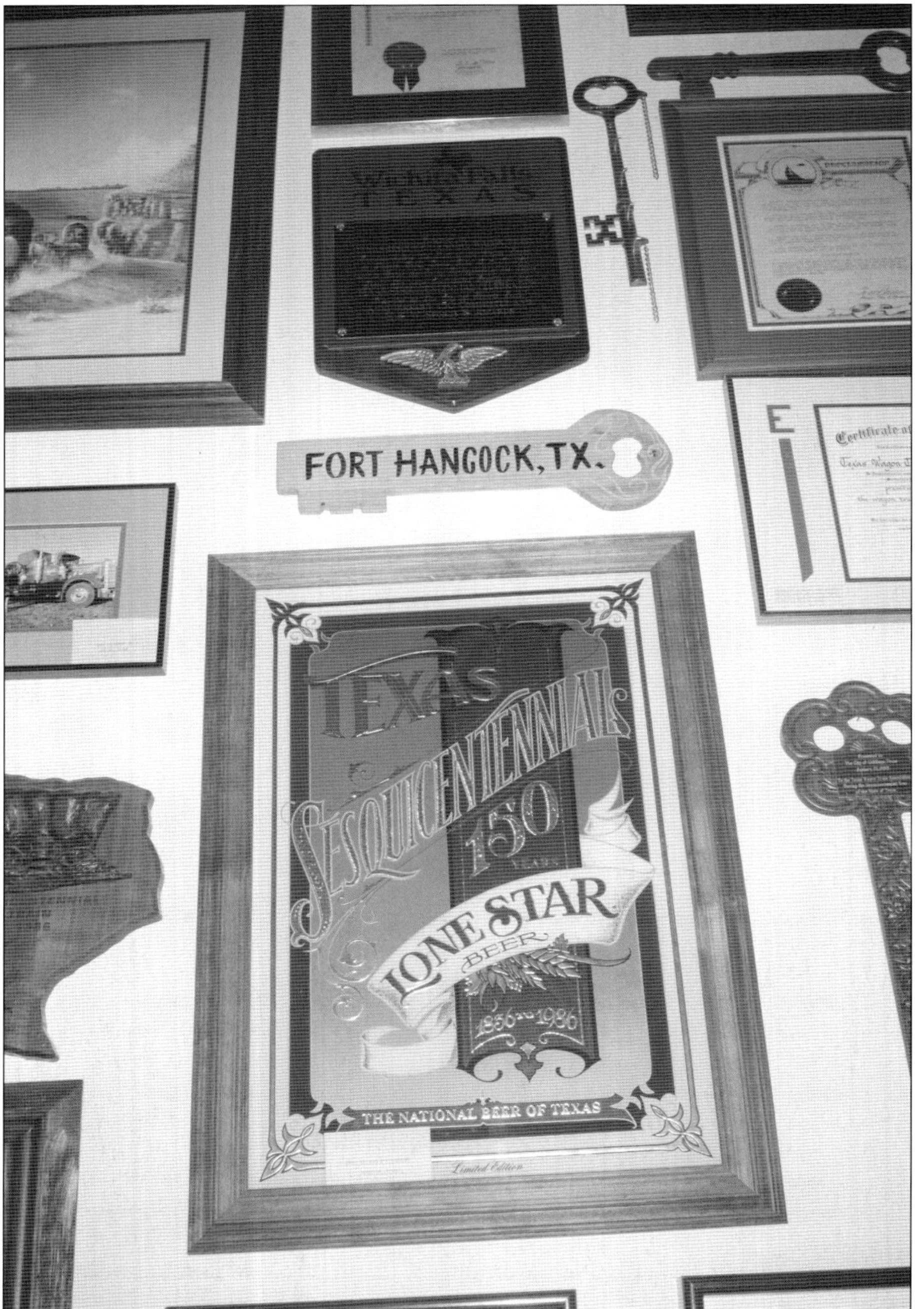

Lone Star, the "National Beer of Texas," donated this picture to the train in honor of Texas's first 150 years of existence. Texans sometimes claim that their state is the only one that was a separate republic before becoming a state. Actually, Hawaii had a brief republic, and California proclaimed the "Bear Flag Republic" but did not have an actual operating government. Texas certainly was the only state to have its own presidents, congress, and a working democracy with foreign diplomats for a full 10 years, from 1836 to 1845.

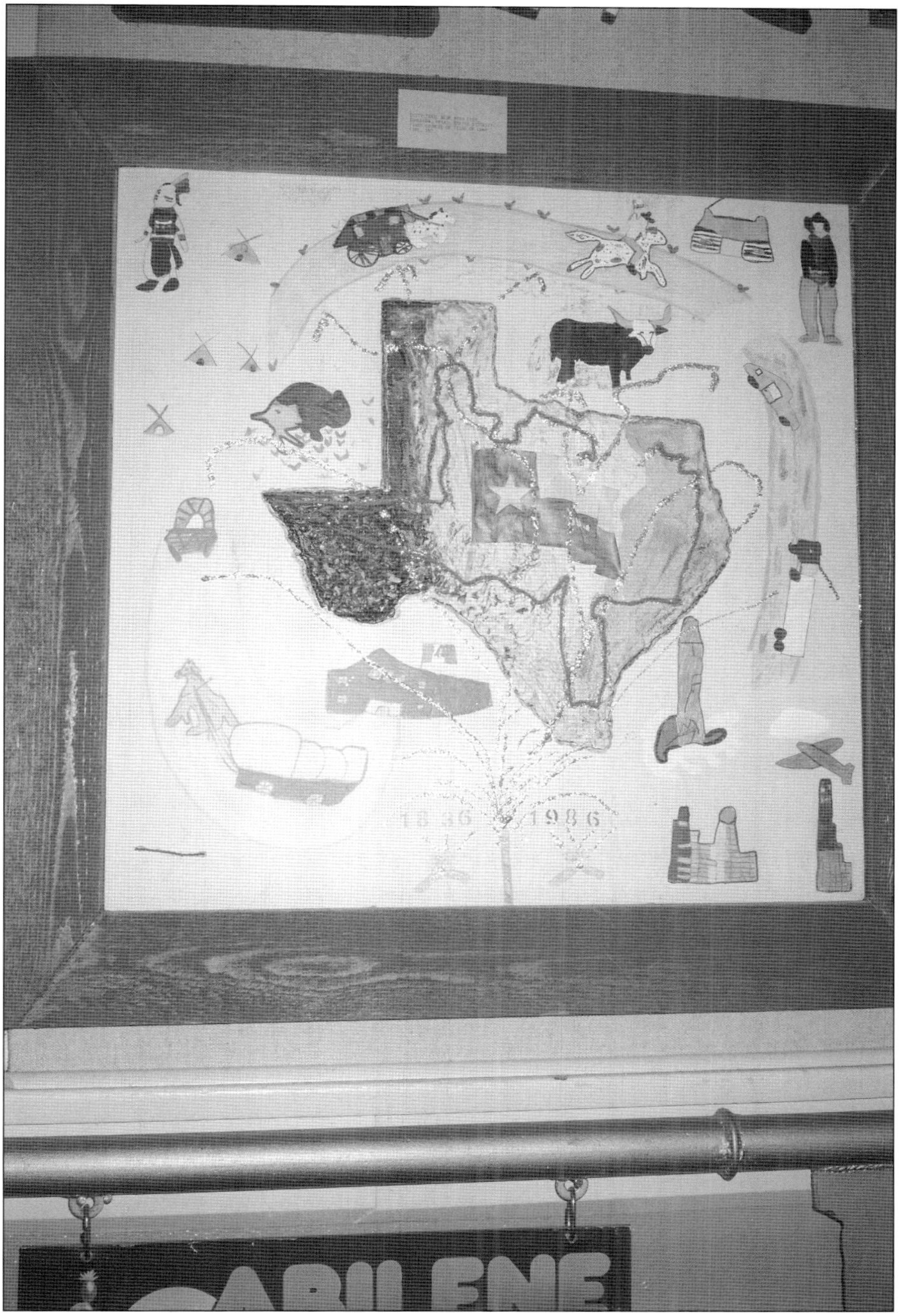

A schoolchild painted this large map of Texas and donated it to the wagon train. Students participated in the train in their own one-room school with wheels, where they kept up with the curriculum necessary for their grade levels. All across the state, visitors seemed to like the schoolhouse best. Throngs of schoolchildren let out for the day visited the school and thought that combining school with the wagon train was exciting. A special graduation ceremony was held in a real one-room school in Ponder, near Denton, for the one senior on the train, Lori Warner.

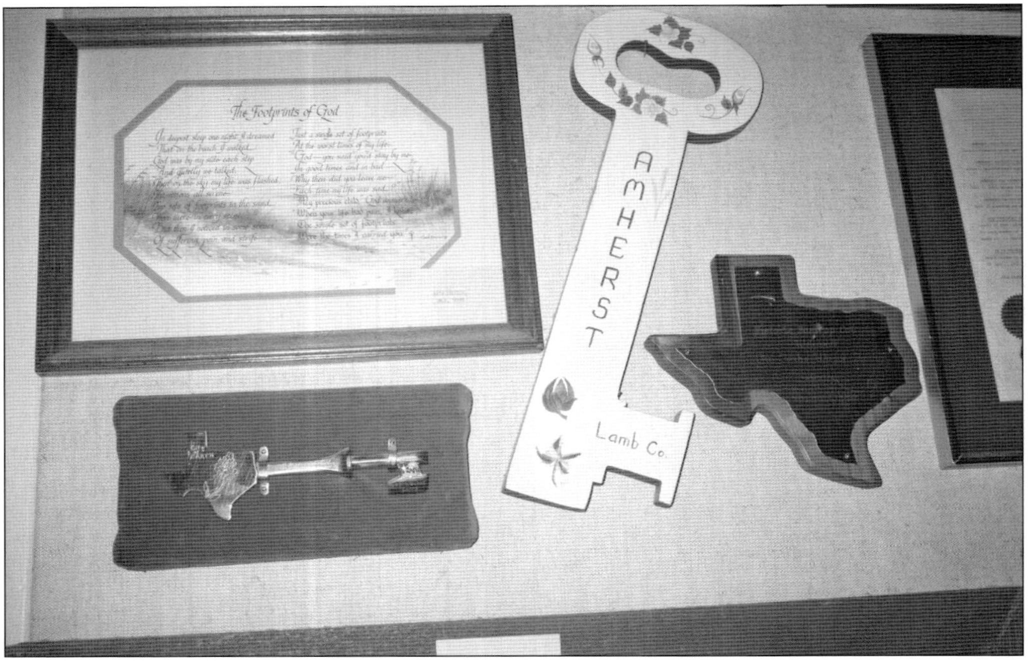

Amherst in Lamb County began as the station on the railroad for the Mashed O Ranch in 1913. The townsite was named for Amherst College. The town of Earth, also in Lamb County, donated the item that is located in the lower left.

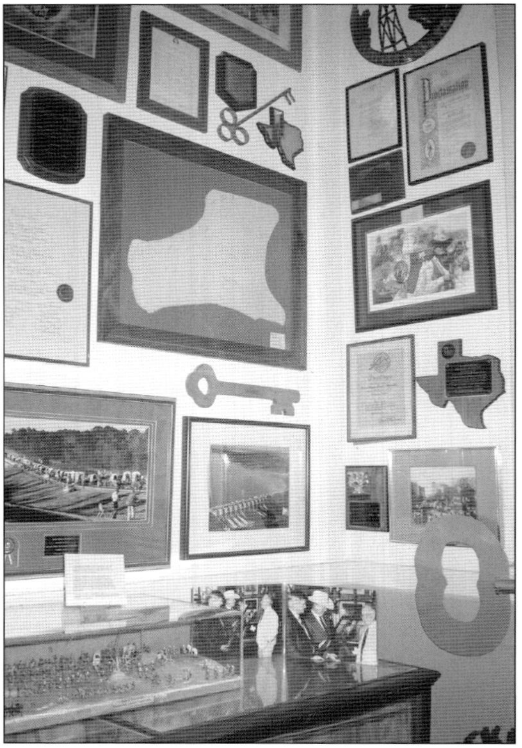

This corner display area of the Texas wagon train exhibit shows a couple of keys to the city, many plaques, proclamations, and pictures from the towns along the 3,000-mile route. The exhibit honors the wagon train that celebrated the 150th birthday of the state in 1986. However, folks also remembered the train's 25th anniversary at the stockyards in 2011, a quarter-century after it ended the trip there.

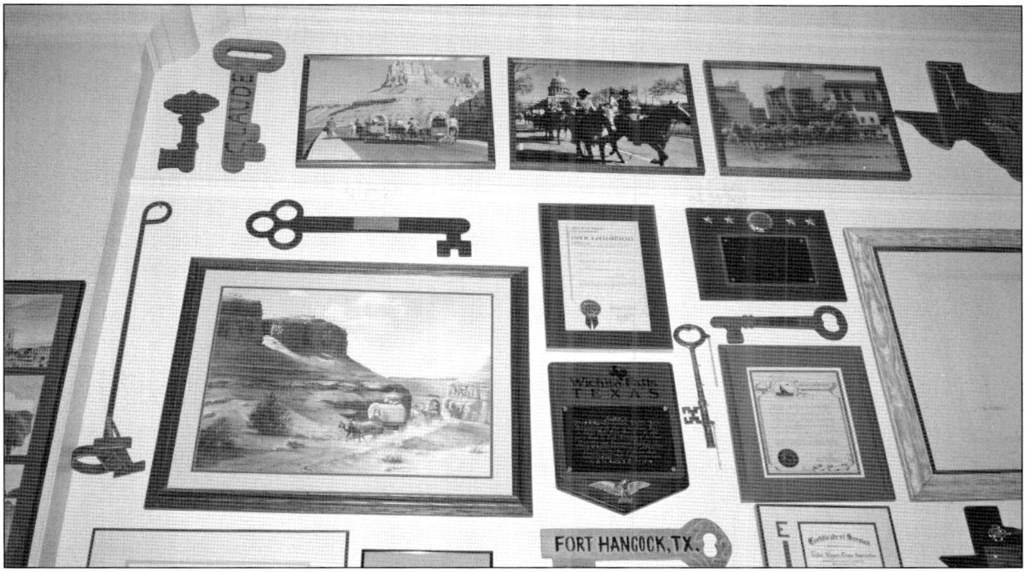

Six keys to the city are found in this wall display. Participants in the train at an auction on July 4 sold off many of the items they had used during their six-month trip, even horses and wagons. They kept together all the artifacts specifically given to the train and eventually donated them to the North Fort Worth Historical Society's Stockyards Museum. They are there on display and welcomed even more visitors to view them on the 25th anniversary of the wagon train in 2011.

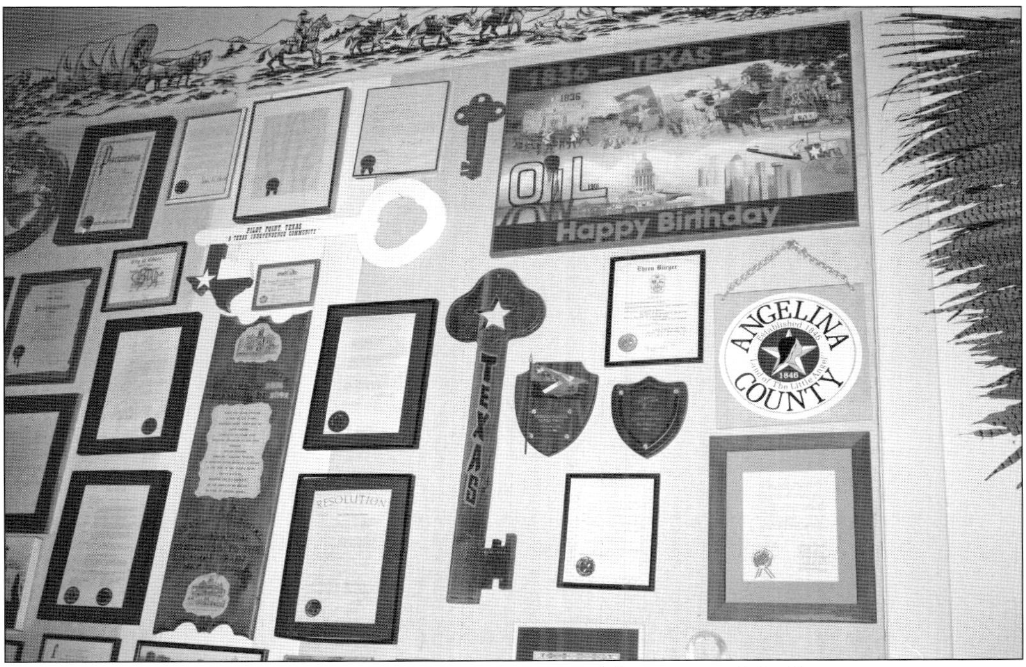

Angelina County, located in the extreme eastern part of the state with Lufkin as its county seat, made sure that folks would remember that the wagon train came through its way. The county was named for a legendary Indian maiden named Angelina. Caddo Indians lived in the area before Anglo settlers arrived in the 1820s.

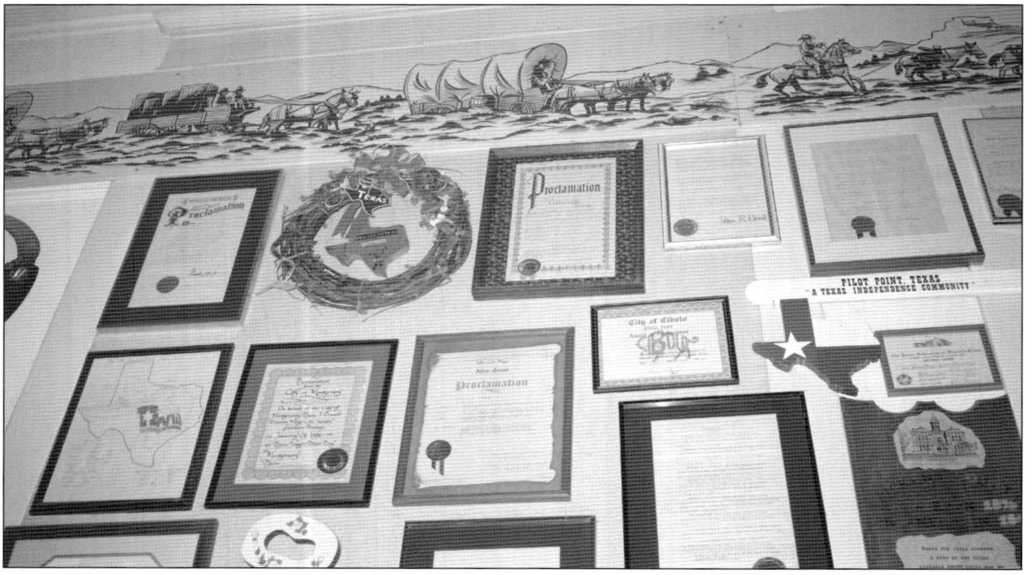

Notice the mural of a wagon train on the wall at the top of this display. An out-of-state or out-of-country tourist could learn a great deal about the names of Texas counties and cities after a careful perusal of all of the plaques and proclamations displayed here. Some of these cities' gifts to the wagon train required a great deal of effort and dedication to prepare.

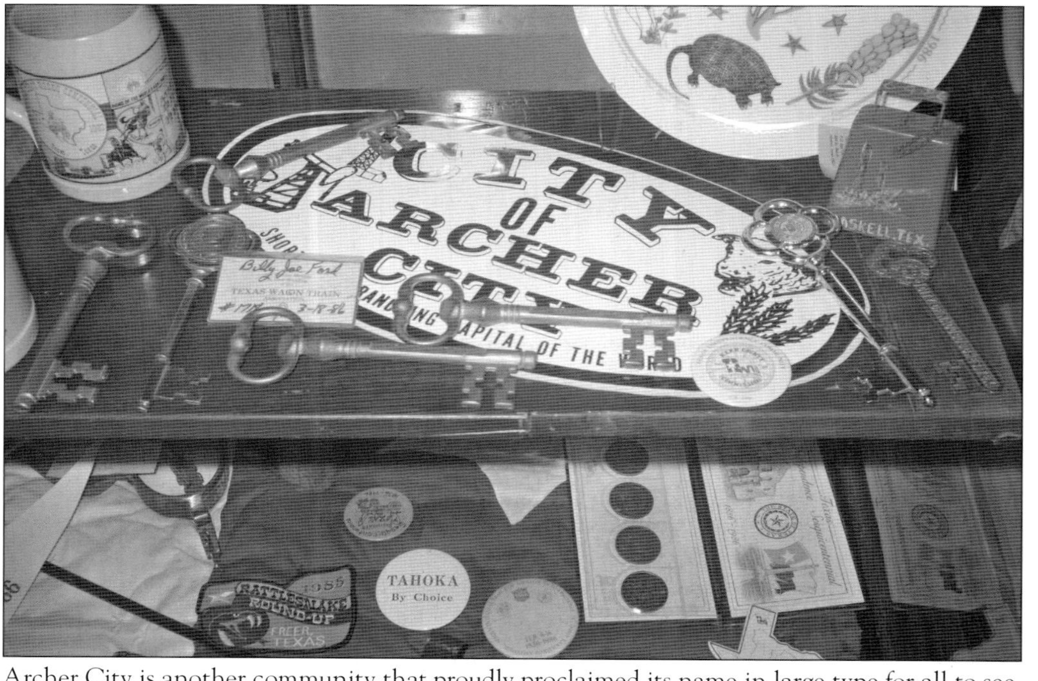

Archer City is another community that proudly proclaimed its name in large type for all to see. Located in far north Texas near the Red River and Oklahoma border, Archer County has about 10,000 people, while Archer City has about 2,000. The county and city were named after Dr. B.T. Archer, who was a commissioner to the United States when Texas was an independent republic. Hazel Bowen, driver of the state of Texas wagon lived in Archer County all of her life.

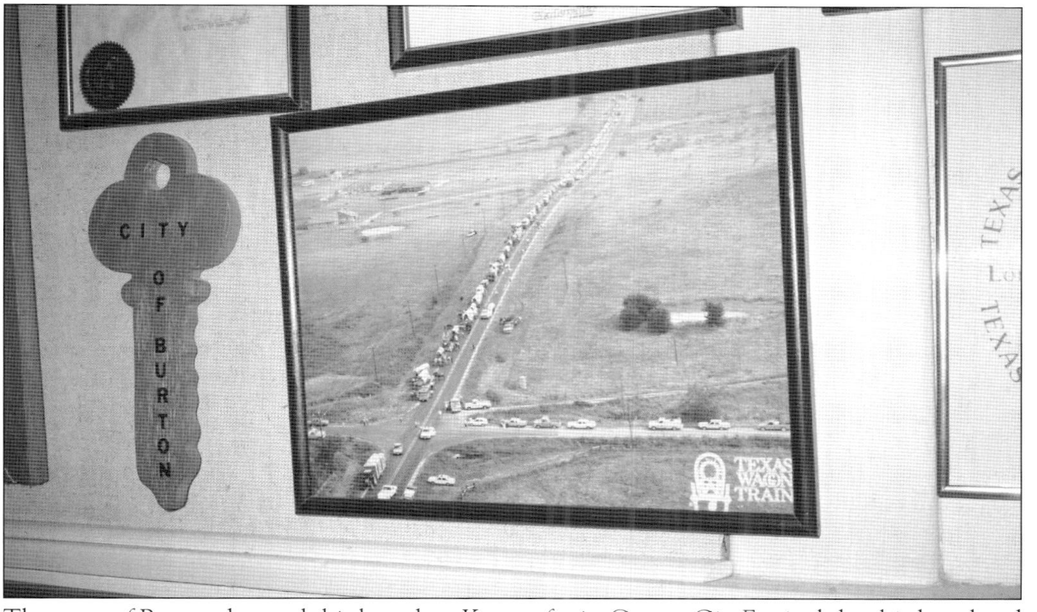

The town of Burton donated this large key. Known for its Cotton Gin Festival the third weekend in April, Burton is home to the Texas Cotton Gin Museum. Note the aerial photograph to the right of Burton's key, in which the wagon train stretches as far as the eye can see. Thousands of Texans and visitors to Texas in 1986 enjoyed seeing the long, slow-moving train.

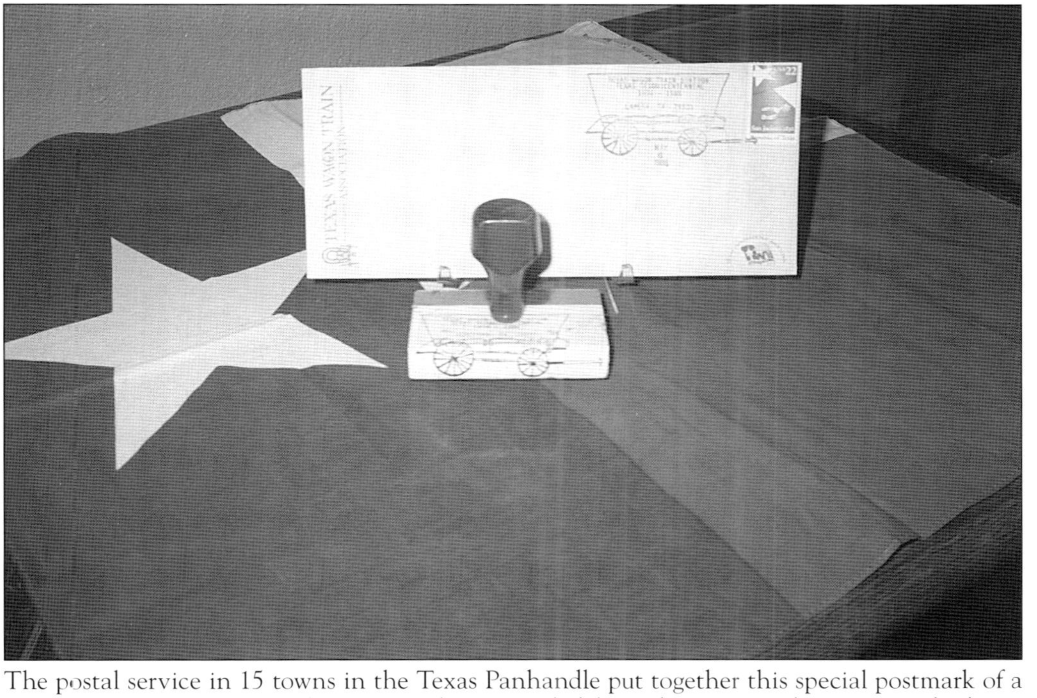

The postal service in 15 towns in the Texas Panhandle put together this special postmark of a wagon. It was used to cancel stamps on letters mailed from those sites. The stamp and a letter placed on a Texas flag with the white Lone Star prominently displayed seem quite appropriate.

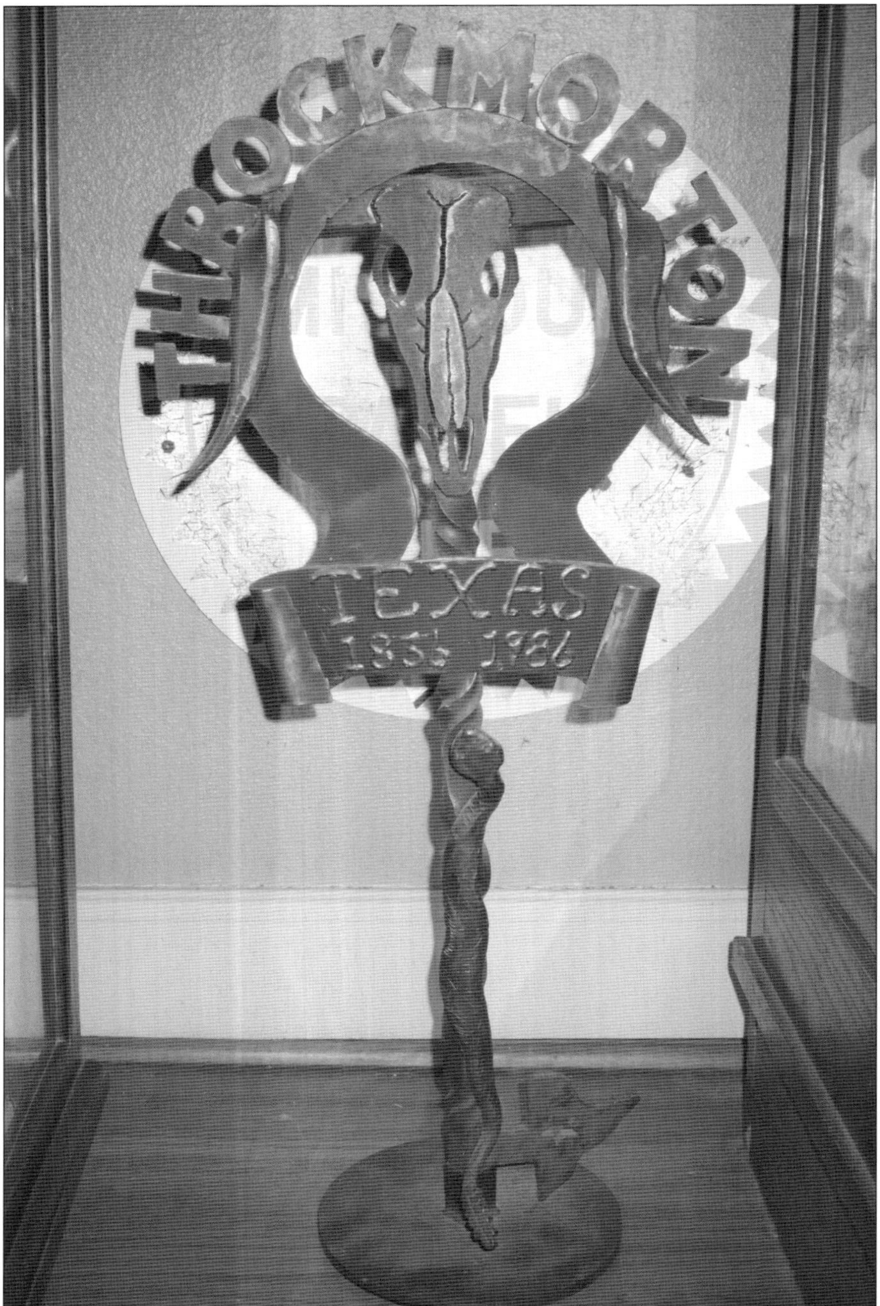

The city of Throckmorton, population 905, donated this large iron sculpture, the largest and heaviest gift that the train received. The Texas Legislature once designated Throckmorton the "Capital of the Cow Country" because of its emphasis on farming and ranching. Oil is another economic boon to the area. Throckmorton, in Throckmorton County, is located about four counties northwest of Fort Worth in North Central Texas.

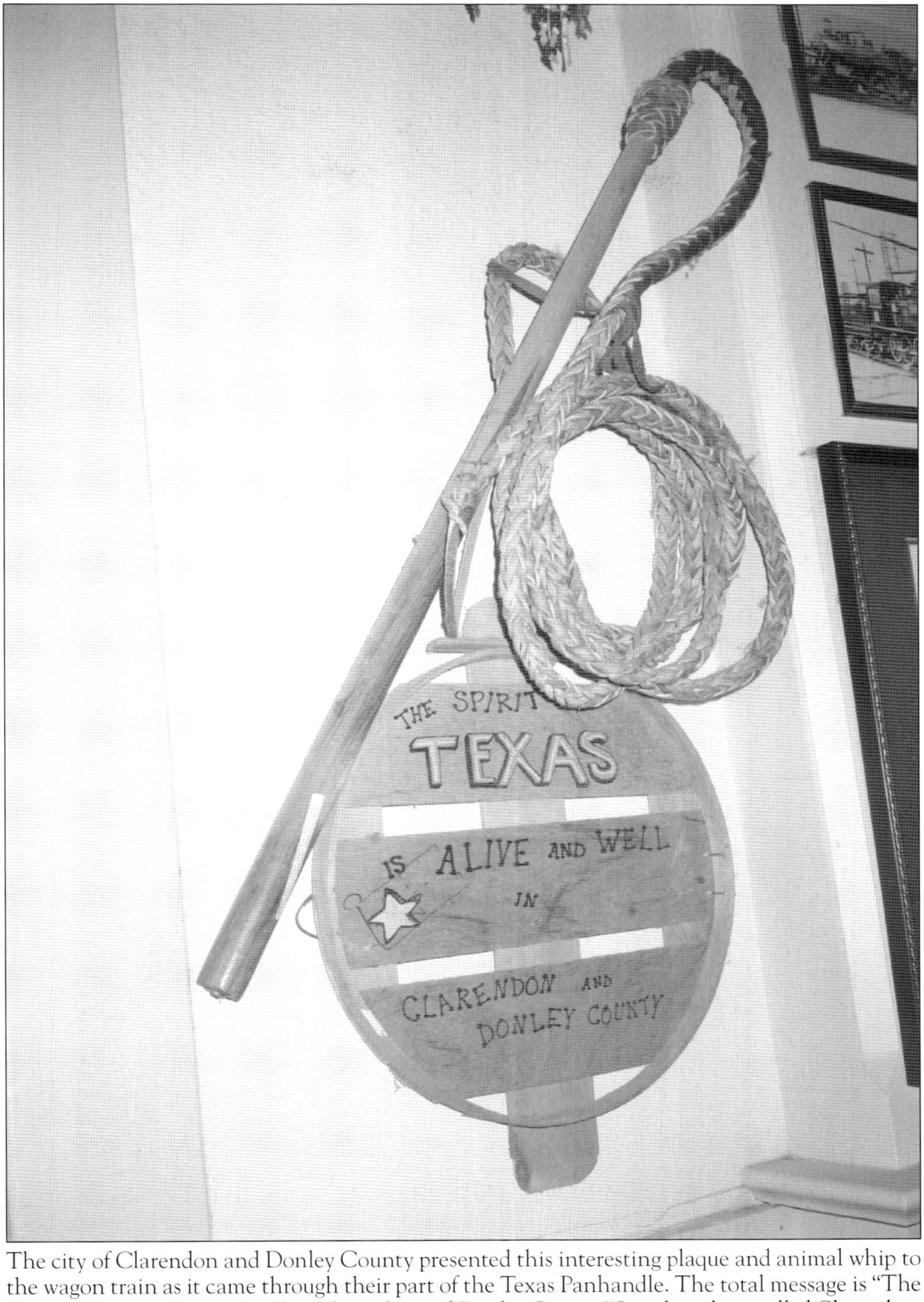

The city of Clarendon and Donley County presented this interesting plaque and animal whip to the wagon train as it came through their part of the Texas Panhandle. The total message is "The Spirit of Texas is alive and well in Clarendon and Donley County." Local cowboys called Clarendon, settled by a Methodist minister in 1878, "Saints Roost" because of his talks of sobriety.

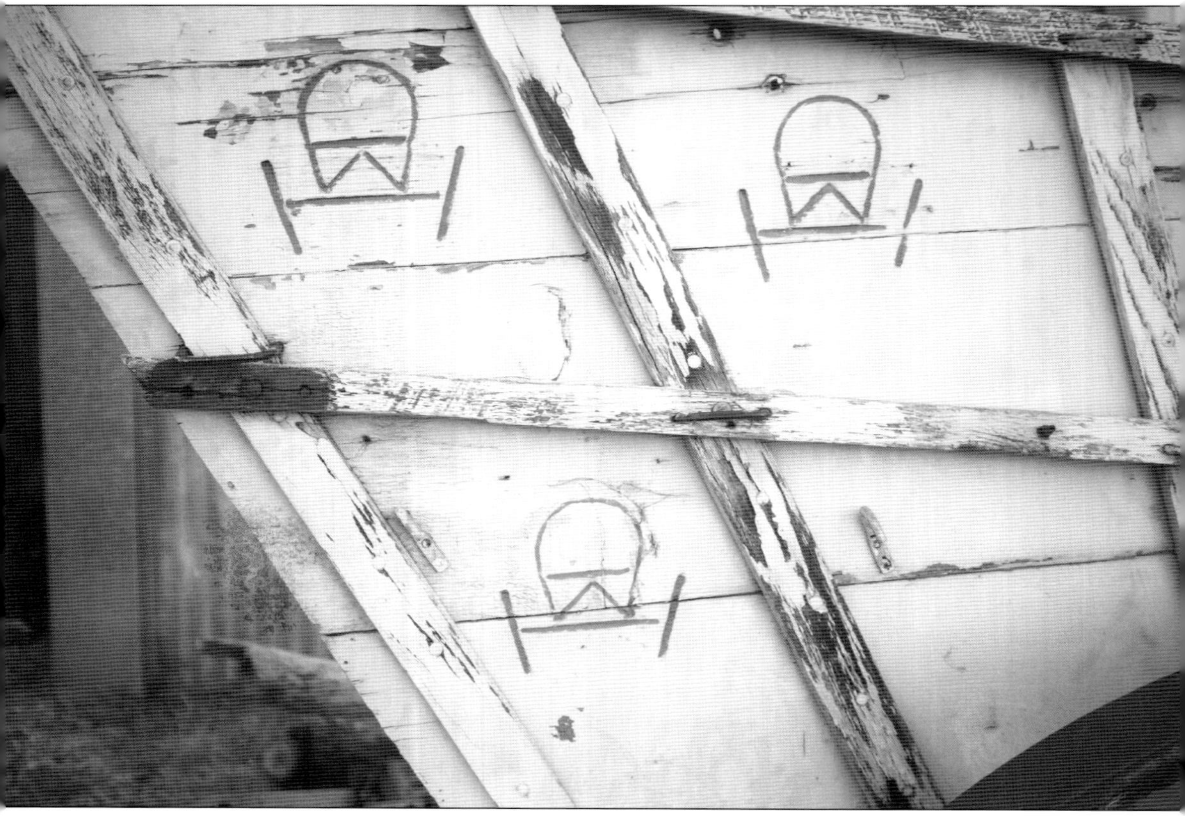

This artifact is not in the stockyards museum. This wagon, which traveled the entire 3,000 miles as evidenced by the three brands of the train logo on the side, currently is located in the Grapevine Historical District. Each wagon logo represents 1,000 miles traveled. Several of the wagons earned the designation. Outriders could get their chaps or other items branded at each 1,000-mile landmark as well.

Four

A Photographic Legacy

Numerous important legacies of the Texas Sesquicentennial Wagon Train remain. Memories may be the most valuable to those who participated in the trip and even those who watched it arrive in their towns or simply heard of it. Any child over the age of eight or 10 who was living in Texas in 1986 and was able to view the train in person or simply see it on television will remember it as will everyone else alive in the state during that special sesquicentennial year. The train and the 150th celebration of Texas independence were significant to all concerned. It reminded them of the strong pioneers who came to Texas amid hardship 150 years earlier.

The artifacts the train acquired that were pictured in chapter three are a lasting legacy as well. This book, however, highlights the photographic legacy that Dominick J. Cirincione left after following the wagon train on several weekends during the half-year trip. At the end of that time, Cirincione developed his pictures, identified where they were taken, and dated them. Then he presented the Heritage Room (the Texas History room in the library of the Northeast Campus of Tarrant County Junior College) with 130 black-and-white, eight-inch-by-ten-inch photographs. Most of the pictures in this chapter were taken at a reception in 1987, in which Cirincione was honored for donating the collection to the Heritage Room. He also gave a set of the pictures to the Hopkins County Museum in Sulphur Springs. The Briscoe Center for American History at the University of Texas at Austin also has benefited from a copy of the set of photographs plus additional items.

If someone were able to collect photographs from newspapers across the state and also request pictures from the many individuals who made their own, a huge number of images of the train would exist. Many photographs have been donated to the North Fort Worth Historical Society Museum. Twenty-five years after the event, Cirincione's photographs, donated to three archival museums and now in book form with this volume, are being published to comprise a permanent photograph legacy of the Texas wagon train.

The authors, great believers in preserving history, suggest that persons with numerous photographs of the wagon train donate them, or copies, to any of the institutions mentioned above to provide a greater record for future generations to enjoy.

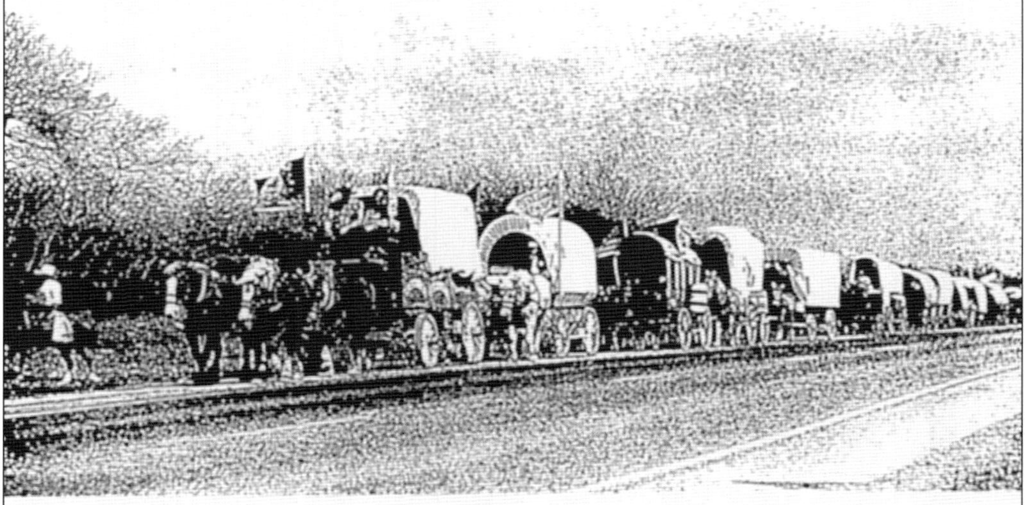

Reception of

Sesquicentennial Wagon Train
Photographic Essay

D.J. (Nick) Cirincione, photographer

Learning Resources Center, Heritage Room
Tarrant County Junior College Northeast Campus
828 Harwood Road
Hurst, Texas

Date: January 29, 1987
Time: 2 p.m.

This was the invitation to the reception held in the Heritage Room of Tarrant County Junior College on January 29, 1987, when the college honored Dominick J. Cirincione for his donation of his student project. The project consisted of 130 photographs he had taken of the Texas Sesquicentennial Wagon Train. A list of guests included then history professor at the college J'Nell Pate, although at the time she had never met Cirincione and did not encounter him again for over two decades. When they did meet later, they both were members of the same history organization called the Westerners, which gets together monthly for dinner and a speech about Western history. Cirincione asked Pate to join him in working on this book. (Courtesy Heritage Room, Tarrant County College, Northeast Campus.)

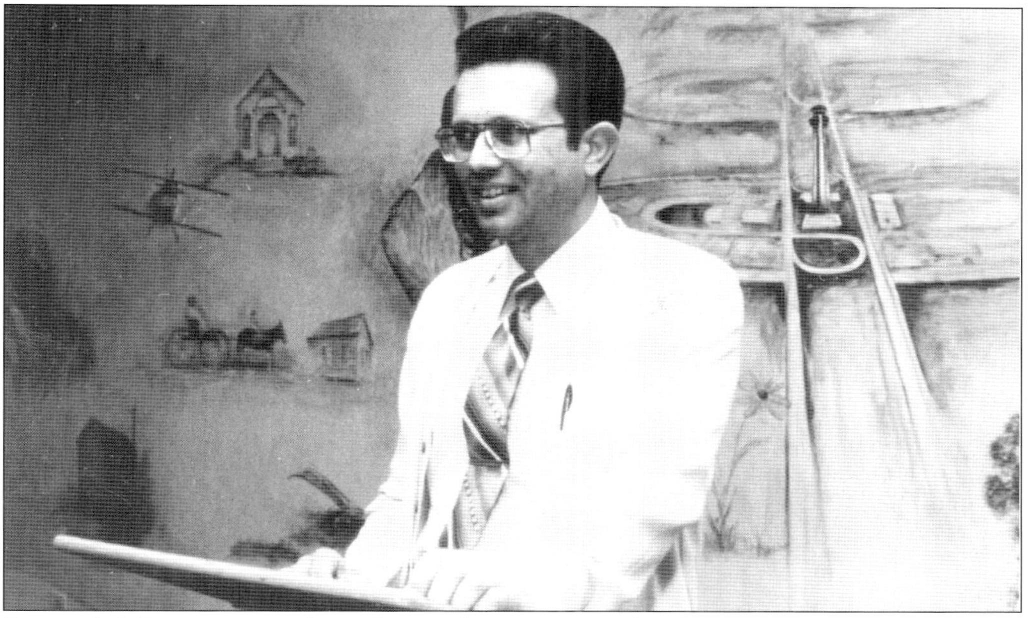

Dominick J. Cirincione is at the podium at the reception in the Heritage Room at Tarrant County Junior College's Northeast Campus library. When he began his student project, he intended to take only 20 or 30 photographs. He changed his mind and decided to select several weekends to catch up with the train and record its travels. (Courtesy Heritage Room, Tarrant County College, Northeast Campus.)

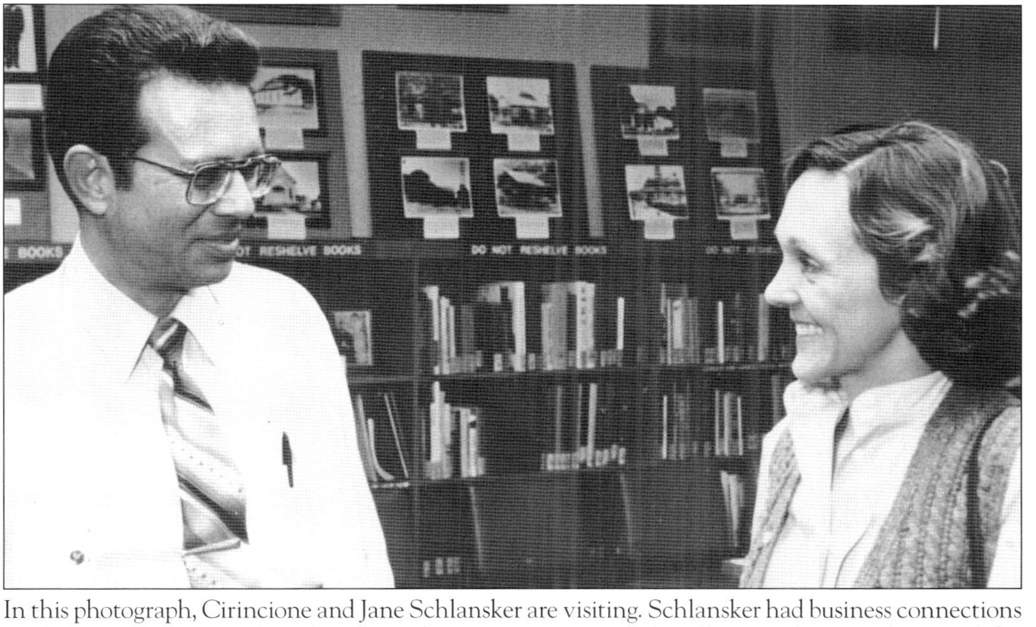

In this photograph, Cirincione and Jane Schlansker are visiting. Schlansker had business connections in the Fort Worth Stockyards, where the wagon train ended. Following the completion of the project, which Schlansker helped make official, she congratulated Cirincione at the reception. She kept a collection of news articles about the train. (Courtesy Heritage Room, Tarrant County College, Northeast Campus.)

FORT WORTH 150 TEXAS SESQUICENTENNIAL

P.O. Box 1206
Fort Worth, Texas 76101
817/927-1986

April 9, 1986

Mr. Nick Cirincione
TCJC Northeast
P.O. Box 363
Hurst, Texas 76053

Dear Mr. Cirincione:

On behalf of the Fort Worth Coordinating Commission for the Sesquicentennial, I am pleased to let you know that the application you submitted for Sesquicentennial sanctioning has been approved. The Wagon Train Photo Album is now an official part of Fort Worth's celebration of our state's 150th anniversary.

As your plans progress from now through the 1986 year, we would like to have an update from time to time so we can include these in our publicity materials and on our planning calendar.

Enclosed you will find reproducible copies of the official local logo and guidelines for their use.

We look forward to having your participation in the 1986 celebration and your help in making this occasion a most memorable event for Fort Worth.

Sincerely,

Jane Schlansker

JS/jrs
enc.

In 1986, Texas will celebrate its 150th anniversary as an independent state. Fort Worth 150 is our city's official celebration of this important occasion, spotlighting the historical, cultural, environmental and social character of Texas' unique past, present and future.

Jane Schlansker, chair of the Fort Worth Coordinating Commission for the Sesquicentennial, notified Nick Cirincione that his photograph project had been approved. His wagon train photograph album would become an official part of Fort Worth's celebration of the Texas sesquicentennial. (Courtesy Heritage Room, Tarrant County College, Northeast Campus.)

The City of Fort Worth presented this certificate to Dominick J. Cirincione to acknowledge his participation in the Fort Worth celebration during the Texas sesquicentennial. His class project at Tarrant County Junior College grew into something much larger than the 20 photographs intended. He called it the "Sesquicentennial Wagon Train Photographic Essay." Cirincione enrolled at TCJC in 1979 and earned an associate's degree in marketing. (Courtesy Heritage Room, Tarrant County College, Northeast Campus.)

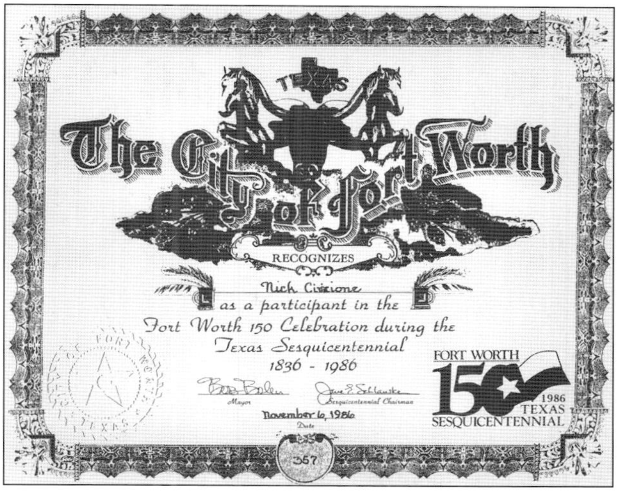
TEXAS

The City of Fort Worth

RECOGNIZES

Nick Cirincione

as a participant in the

Fort Worth 150 Celebration during the Texas Sesquicentennial 1836 - 1986

Mayor

Sesquicentennial Chairman

November 6, 1986

Date

FORT WORTH 150 1986 TEXAS SESQUICENTENNIAL

357

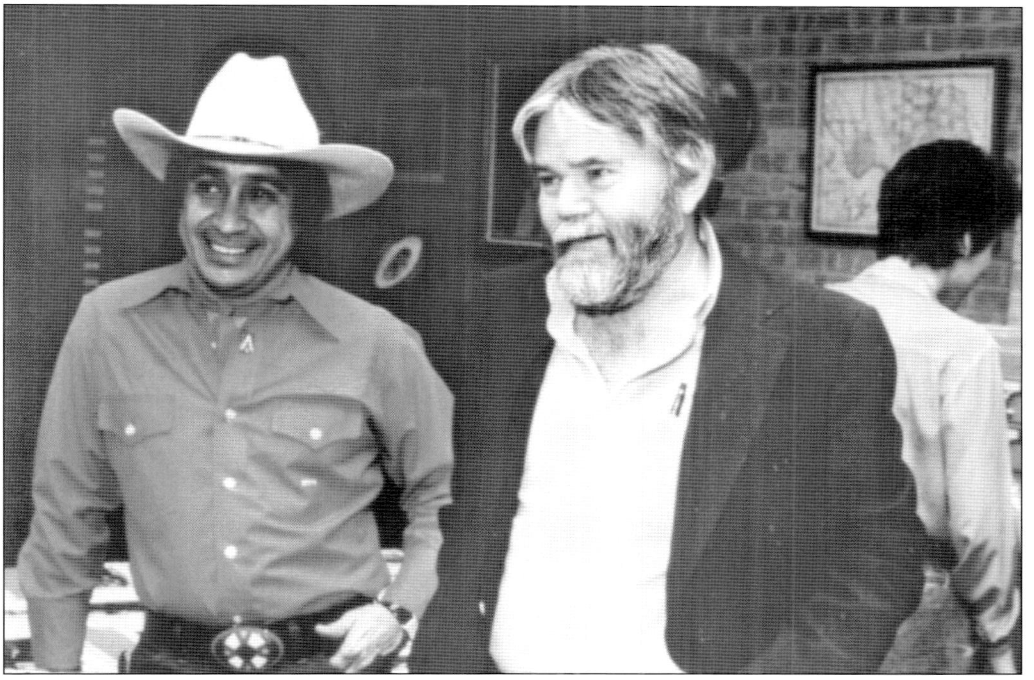

Eddie Sandoval (left) and John McConal socialize at the reception. McConal was a reporter for the *Fort Worth Star-Telegram* at both the time of the wagon train and the reception at the college. He spent much time with the wagon train during the six months and wrote human interest stories about the people on it. Being based in Fort Worth, he also wrote a lot about cattle, the stockyards, and the people who worked with both. (Courtesy Heritage Room, Tarrant County College, Northeast Campus.)

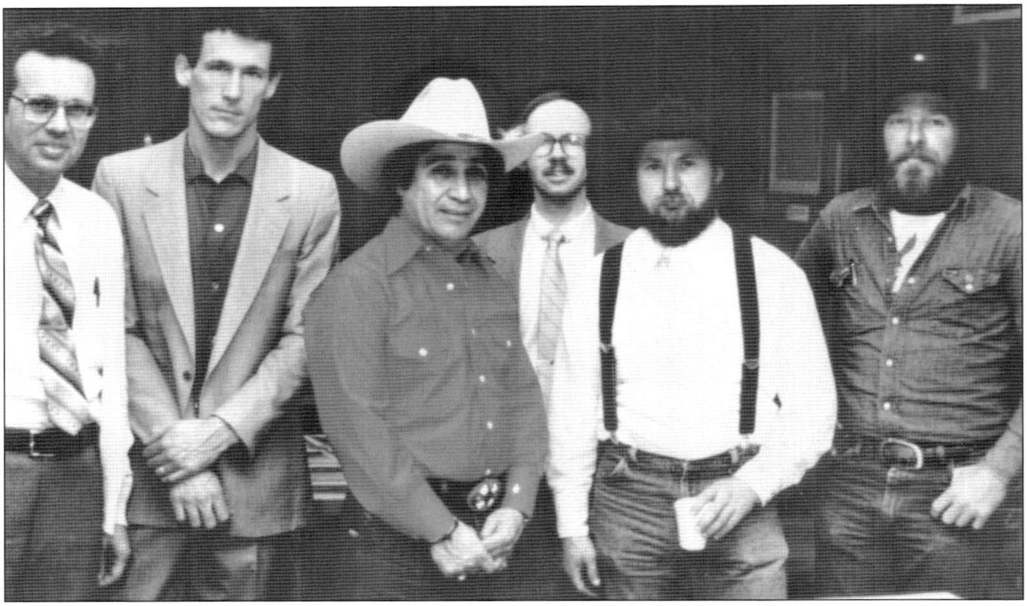

Pictured in 1986 are, from left to right, Dominick J. Cirincione, photographer; Richard Doherty, assistant professor of art at Tarrant County Junior College and Cirincione's mentor for the project; Eddie Sandoval, TCJC counselor; John Paul Davidson, public service librarian at TCJC, who put the project on the Portal to Texas History website; Gotcheye Gaston; and John Chester, assistant camp jack. (Courtesy Heritage Room, Tarrant County College, Northeast Campus.)

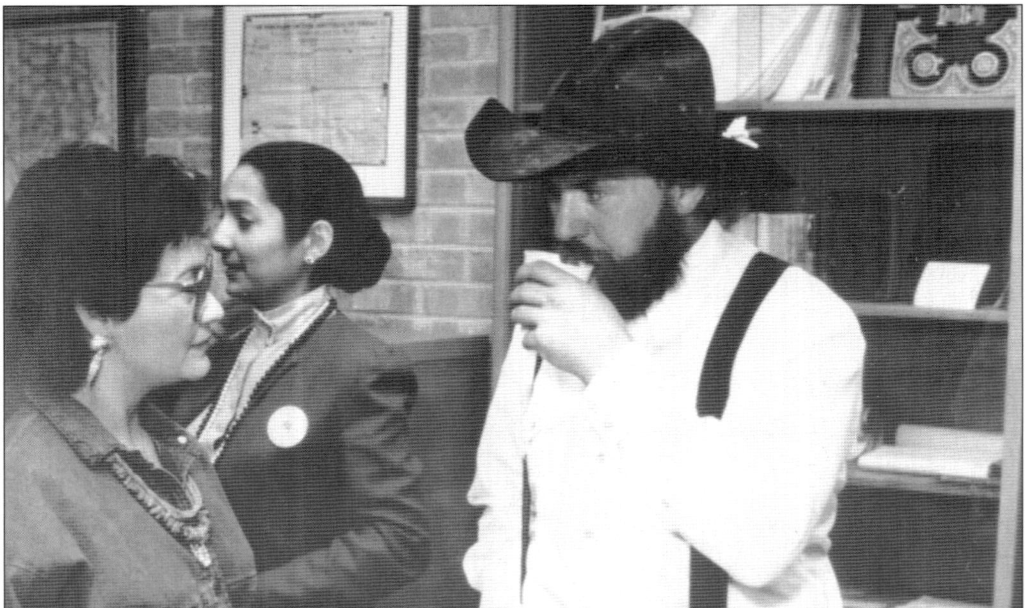

Pictured from left to right at the reception are Mary Ann Sandoval-Greene, an unidentified woman, and Gotcheye Gaston. When Cirincione had to miss the arrival of the wagon train in the Fort Worth stockyards, Greene took photographs and gave him the negatives. (Courtesy Heritage Room, Tarrant County College, Northeast Campus.)

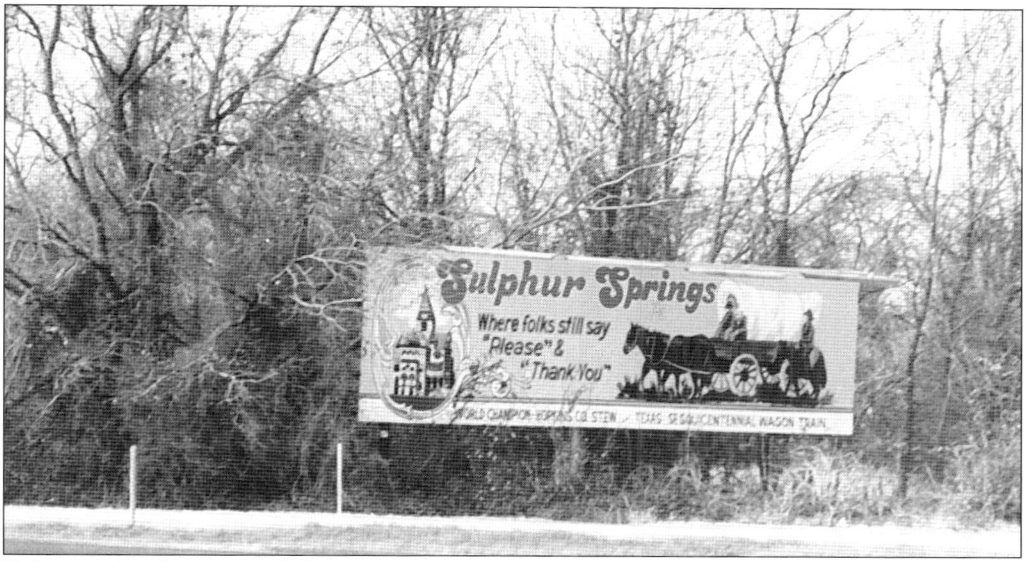

Following his donation of photographs to the Tarrant County Junior College Heritage Room in the library, Cirincione donated copies of the same photographs to the Hopkins County Museum in Sulphur Springs. Even months after the wagon train began its journey from Sulphur Springs, the community still was celebrating its participation with this billboard. (Courtesy John Chester estate.)

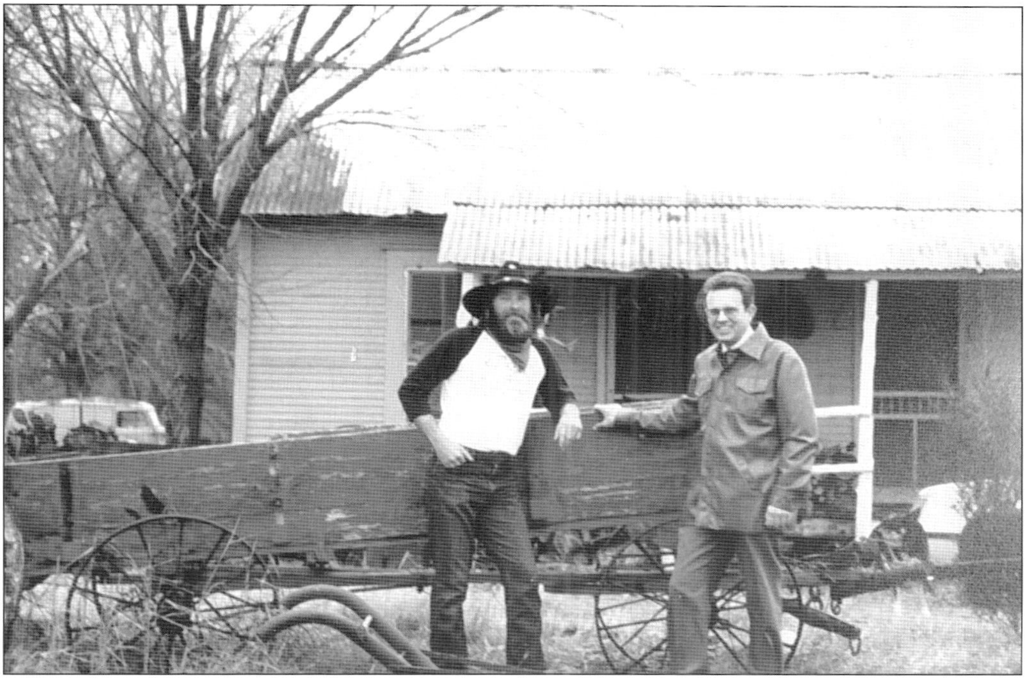

John Chester, assistant camp jack for the wagon train, and Cirincione are pictured in Dike, Texas. Chester persuaded Cirincione to donate a copy of his photograph collection to Sulphur Springs, where the wagon train began its journey. The collection may be found in the Hopkins County Museum there. (Courtesy John Chester estate.)

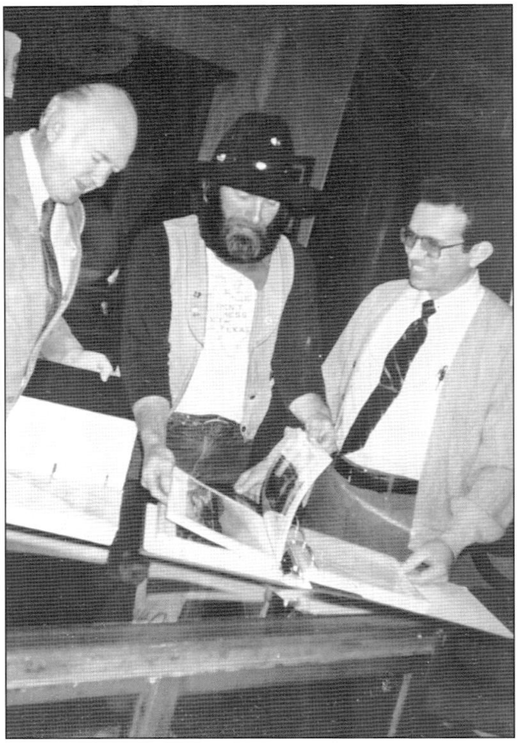

From left to right, Bill Tuck from the Hopkins County Historical Commission, John Chester, assistant camp jack of the wagon train, and Dominick J. Cirincione look over the notebooks of photographs of the wagon train that Cirincione donated to the Hopkins County Museum in Sulphur Springs. Chester helped coordinate the donation. This means that the city where the wagon train began its journey and the city where it concluded (Fort Worth) each have copies of the photographic record of the trip. (Courtesy John Chester estate.)

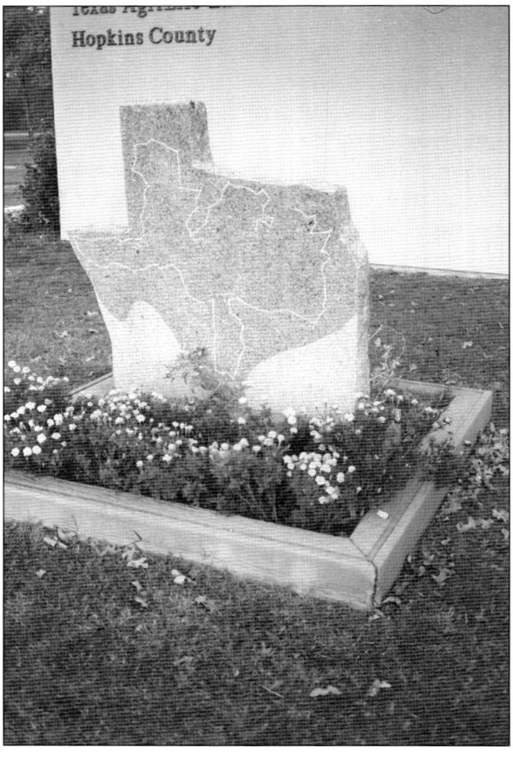

This Sulphur Springs stone marker in the shape of Texas has the route of the Texas wagon train carved into it. Only one other marker like this exists along the route of the train, in Winnsboro, the site of the completion of the actual 3,000th mile. Sulphur Springs celebrates its position as the town where the train began its journey. As a joint project of the Sesquicentennial Committee of Hopkins County (where Sulphur Springs is located) and the Optimist Club of Sulphur Springs, a time capsule was buried under a flat, horizontal stone marker near this Texas-shaped one. The time capsule will be opened in 2036 during the Texas bicentennial celebration. Included in the capsule is a photograph of John Chester, who is from the area.

EPILOGUE

Because Americans appreciate stories of pioneers moving to the West in their covered wagons, they have formed an attachment to reenactment wagon trains as well. In 1936, Texas sponsored a wagon train to celebrate its centennial. The United States, for its bicentennial in 1976, included in its festivities a seven-month wagon train that began in five different states simultaneously and merged to arrive in Valley Forge. This book details the 1986 Texas Sesquicentennial Wagon Train. "Gone to Texas" had a strong meaning in 1836 and the years following. Pioneers were seeking opportunity then, and newcomers to Texas in the 21st century seek the same thing.

There perhaps will be another commemorative Texas wagon train, most likely one in 2036 to celebrate the bicentennial of the Lone Star State. The authors hope that this book and the following resources will assist as reference material in planning for such a future endeavor. The photographs and newspaper articles about it that have been deposited in the Heritage Room at the Northeast Campus of Tarrant County College, the Hopkins County Museum in Sulphur Springs, and the Briscoe Center for American History at the University of Texas at Austin will be of benefit. Additionally, Texas wagon train participant Donna Neal Stepp wrote a book in 1987 called *From Sulphur Springs to Cowtown: The Story of the Sesquicentennial 1986 Texas Wagon Train*. See also "Texas Sesquicentennial Wagon Train" on the Portal to Texas History website, www.texashistory.unt.edu, the North Fort Worth Historical Society Stockyards Museum at 131 East Exchange Avenue in the Fort Worth Stockyards, and the Tarrant County Archives. In the Quentin McGown Collection at the latter is the *Texas Sesquicentennial Wagon Train* magazine, published one time only, which tells its story in full color.